IT'S A METAPHYSICAL WORLD

IT'S A METAPHYSICAL WORLD
Extraordinary Stories from Everyday Life

Marion K. Williams
&
Elena J. Michaels, M.Ed

EDITED BY LYLE J. NICOL

BALBOA
PRESS

A DIVISION OF HAY HOUSE

Balboa Press books may be ordered through booksellers or by contacting:

Balboa Press
A Division of Hay House
1663 Liberty Drive
Bloomington, IN 47403
www.balboapress.com
1-(877) 407-4847

Tagline graphic developed by: L.V. Bruce and Stephanie Bruce.
Cover Artist: S.M. Lee.
Cover Art Photographer: W.D. Lee.

ISBN: 978-1-4525-3411-4 (sc)
ISBN: 978-1-4525-3413-8 (hc)
ISBN: 978-1-4525-3412-1 (e)

Library of Congress Control Number: 2011905911

Printed in the United States of America

Balboa Press rev. date: 7/7/2011

To our family & friends,
without whom there would be
no stories

"He's got the whole world in his hands"
Excerpt from Spiritual
by
Native American, Obie Philpot

Contents

Preface

Dear Reader:

We hope you enjoy our book as much as we enjoyed writing it. In our collection of short stories, we have explored extraordinary events which challenge many of our lifelong beliefs. It has been a fascinating journey which we would like to share with you. First, we should introduce ourselves:

Marion K. Williams:

Marion is a wife, mother and grandmother. She was born in New Zealand, spent her childhood between the United States and New Zealand, and met her Canadian husband in Japan. She has lived and worked in New Zealand, Japan, England, Ireland, and Canada and has travelled the world since she was two. After marriage, Marion relocated to Canada where she and her husband raised their two children. They reside in Ontario, close to their children and grandchildren.

Her career path has been interesting and varied—from flight attendant to television broadcaster, court reporter, paralegal, and assistant in various professions from diplomacy to marketing to law. After taking early retirement, she resumed her studies, and is currently a student of art and philosophy.

Marion has had a lifelong interest in super "natural" phenomena, which began with a childhood fascination with palmistry. She has been actively involved with alternative healing practices for many years. Marion is a certified practitioner of Reiki and Reflexology, as well as a practitioner and teacher of Therapeutic Touch.™ Her studies of various energy disciplines and philosophy prompted her to further explore the field of metaphysics.

Elena J. Michaels, M.Ed:

Elena is a single mother of two young adult children and currently lives in Ontario. She was married for over 20 years and later divorced, which had a significant impact on her life and her interest in spiritual matters. However, in looking back, she now sees that those interests have always been there, and that everything happens for a reason and plays out as it is meant to.

Elena was born in Australia and relocated to Canada in early childhood. Although she was raised Catholic, she has always been intrigued by paranormal phenomena. Growing up, Elena recognized that her mom had premonitions and displayed other psychic abilities. In her teens, Elena was introduced to the work of Edgar Cayce (distance healer) and spent many hours talking to her dad about how reincarnation could even be possible. She set these questions aside during her early adult years while she was going to university, raising children and later working as a senior consultant in the addiction and mental health field, where she spent 30 years. She felt driven to once again explore supernatural/spiritual matters upon meeting someone who had a profound effect on her. She felt that she knew him—but from another time! This set off an insatiable hunger to understand what that could mean.

Her curiosity was further heightened upon reconnecting with her co-author eight years ago and discovering a shared interest in metaphysical matters, which prompted their co-authorship of this book.

The authors are grateful to Dan Lee, Sandra Donnelly and Kathryn Irwin-Seguin for their assistance in reviewing the book.

Introduction

"It's a Metaphysical World" is a collaborative collection of short, extraordinary stories of events experienced in everyday life. The salient facts of each story are true, and either happened to one of us or was told to us by family, friends, or on rare occasions, by acquaintances. Names, locations and/or incidental details have been altered to protect identities.

Every story deals with some aspect of metaphysical phenomena such as intuition, synchronicity, past lives, cell and soul memories, astral travel, time warps, bilocation, healings, hauntings, and sightings. Psychic sightings include everything from angels to ghosts, exhibiting behaviours from helpful and benign, through to evil.

In talking to friends, relatives and co-workers, it seems that most people have experienced metaphysical phenomena to some extent, be it through intuition or sightings, and our belief is that these experiences fall within the norm for our human condition. The only variable is the degree to which we are affected, and that appears to be determined by who we are.

As you will know from our brief biographies, we both experienced early childhood dislocations. Interestingly enough, so did our parents and, in some instances, their parents before them. Dislocations for our parents and grandparents were exacerbated by the impacts of two World Wars which threatened civilization as we know it. We believe that these early stressors set up a pattern of being that conceivably prompts a sixth sense survivor instinct in offspring. If true, then metaphysical abilities may simply be natural human survival responses reflective of life circumstances. Both of our families report psychic experiences back through a number of generations, and each of us has experienced a range of metaphysical events in our own lives.

Sixth sense experiences, or gut instincts, become honed over a lifetime. The more accurate they are, the more they are relied upon and trusted, and rightly so. Our minds are so finely crafted that they operate as super computers.

They recognize, read and analyze both positive and negative situations with super-speed and often provide a gut warning.

How do we do this? Well, consider for a moment that all things living and non-living have energy fields or auras. These fields can be photographed, seen, felt and read, and science does not deny them. We humans are energy beings. This energy does not end at our skin borders. It expands from chakra centres deep within us, to the auric fields beyond our physical bodies, linking us to all that surrounds us. These auras look like full body halos with attendant vibrational colours and sounds. We have included a black and white template of the chakra and auric systems at the conclusion of Part 1. These auras present a holographic template of who we are, and reflect the climate of our being. No two individuals are alike. No two energies are alike. We are all highly individualized yet remain deeply connected to, and impact upon, everyone and everything in an exponential way. In simple terms, we are as one in the intricate mosaic of life.

Just as an onion is multi-layered, so too are human auras. Energy layers repeat in seven-field series around the body, at finer and finer vibrations moving away from the body. They link us to our world (to people, places and things), as well as to other planes of existence, and to other times (past and future).

Most people can be taught to feel the human auric field many meters away, and to see it to some degree or other. We subliminally read it registering a situation as being comfortable or uncomfortable, and safe or unsafe. This triggers a gut response.

When reading auras on a conscious level, the trick is to remember that they are subtle fields of energy. If you have never consciously seen an aura, try looking gently at someone against a plain backdrop. It helps to soften your gaze to see them, and to move gently to feel them. To move otherwise is an invasion of someone's sacred space. Ten centimetres or so beyond their body, you may notice a thin line. This is one of the demarcation lines for one of the auric fields. If you feel that particular area with your hand, you may notice a difference as the energy changes vibration from one field to the next. With time and practice, it is possible to see and feel more fields, and to read their colour. On a subconscious level, we read and process auric fields and innately understand them.

In addition to seeing human auric fields, some of us can see energy emanating from other entities, or other planes of existence. Most of us have experienced fleeting impressions of something irregular, or felt the tingling sensations of danger but it is hard for us to trust what we saw, or thought we saw or felt. We have been taught to be cautious of things we don't understand or that cannot be proven. Nonetheless, most major religions do recognize entities.

Our collection of stories related to sightings and entities is intriguing. It provides us with a large collection of experiences that cover a broad range of entity categories.

First and foremost there are stories of angels. These may be found in "Divine Intervention at Play" and "Out of the Mouths of Babes," amongst others. Angels are heavenly beings who sometimes present with pure white auras and at other times, surprisingly, manifest in human form. They appear unexpectedly to assist, and then disappear leaving you wondering if you imagined them. "Roadside Angel" reports one such encounter. Was this an angel or merely a human inspired by supernatural forces? We will never know for sure.

It is believed that angels never experienced an earthly life per se, unlike spirit guides and ghosts. They are most apparent around the time of sickness and death, and sometimes come in times of stress or danger. They always assist. They may help someone avoid a potentially traumatic experience or they may appear with messages of hope.

There are also stories of transitional beings. At death, the human soul, or soul body, moves from the earthly world to the spiritual plane. The transition period between planes differs with individuals. We have identified six different transition scenarios in our stories, and acknowledge the existence of a seventh one. These scenarios are as follows:

It appears that for some, transition to the spiritual plane is achieved with relative ease. These souls acknowledge that they are dead, and recognize the pathway to the light. They successfully transition to the spiritual plane and remain there until their next incarnation. "Diane's Near-Death Experience" (where she met her deceased son) reports one such situation.

Some souls linger in the earthly sphere for a few days before moving to the spiritual plane. During this period, these entities often retain close ties to the earthly plane, and frequently appear soon after death to reassure loved ones that they are all right. "Afterwards" reports a number of such stories. Often these entities hug and most times they're comforting; occasionally they reprimand.

Others move to the spiritual plane but elect to leave it occasionally to revisit the earthly plane. They usually return to assist loved ones during times of stress. We see these types of entities in "Bedside Visit" and "Twin Love." Returning spirits may present with different appearances ranging from a ball of light to a full spirit body.

Then there are those involved in the near-death-return situations who resume their earthly existence. In near-death experiences, the soul reconnects with the body to return to the earthly plane. In these instances the individuals who have caught a glimpse of the other side return more informed than when they left. Many report that they no longer have a fear of dying because of what they have witnessed. "Samantha's Visits" talk of such an experience.

We believe there are also spirit guides, and that these are beings from the spiritual plane who have lived, died, and returned in spirit to assist humans with their soul purpose. Kirlian photography captured a picture of Marion's spirit guide in "The Psychic."

Although we do not have any stories to support this, we believe that humans who fail to fulfil their soul contract by ending their life prematurely through suicide or other means, must return to the earthly plane. They begin their life again as infants for the purpose of learning those lessons which they were unable to complete.

As popularized by current television shows, other entities, or ghosts, may be seen on the earthly plane. They come in all shapes and sizes, and may have different motivations for staying connected here after death. Some of these may end up with a purgatory-type existence depending upon their vibration level. These entities are not willing, or perhaps able, to proceed to the spiritual plane.

In some of our stories, the ghostly entities wanted to protect and actually saved lives, as in "The House by the Sea" and "The Office on Main Street." Despite their helping ways, these entities were not angels. They did not present as angels or feel angelic. They were, however, good enough to provide a warning of impending danger.

In other stories, the entity or ghost continued an old routine, moving about in familiar territory as if it were alive. This type of ghost may have strong attachments to their former life—to surroundings or people—and these attachments keep them earthbound. Alternatively, they may be trapped by a fear of moving on or not realize that they are dead. While some will be content merely to wander around, others will rearrange things to suit themselves or to be noticed. Occasionally, they want continued interactions with people. Entities like this usually do no harm. We see this type of entity in "At the Hairdresser" and "Snippets ~ The Trouser Tale." In the reverse, humans may tie their deceased loved ones to them and the earthly plane by their deep grief and reluctance to release them.

Even if you do not see entities, you may still recognise some of the many other telltale signs that they exist—a sudden drop in temperature, shadows where there should not be any, noises that don't belong, or things that are out of place with no explanation. Sometimes people experience physical sensations: for example, their hair will stand on end, skin will prickle, or they will develop goose bumps.

It is important to know that while most ghostly entities are harmless, there is one category that is not. These evil entities do not recognize the light as the path to the spiritual plane. They are disruptive and cause grief and unhappiness around them. They have dark auras and sometimes an associated stench. People feel most uncomfortable, frightened, and chilled in their presence. These entities thrive on discord. They disrupt happiness and can deliberately hurt people. Traditional wisdom suggests that these dark entities lived a similar discordant life on the earthly plane where they projected evil and felt no remorse. There are accounts of such an entity in "The Home on the Coast Road" and its sequel, "The Aftermath." We should caution you that you may find these stories disturbing.

To our surprise there is one additional category that turned up in our collection. This group cannot be considered ghosts because they never actually lived. They appear to be small discordant beings. They have been depicted through the ages as disturbingly ugly gargoyle or troll type creatures and although they have been explained another way historically, there is no doubt that people do see them. We believe they inspired the myths and art forms, and not the other way around. These beings attach to people, places or things. Sometimes they're luminescent and sometimes they're noisy. From the stories that we have heard, they are never good company. They are disruptive and continued exposure to them can be harmful. Cassie saw such an entity in "Cassie's Stories" and we saw harm caused in "The Stone House." They appear in other stories as well, but are usually not the central character.

It became clear through our stories that there is a spectrum of entity possibilities and that people perceive psychic events in different ways. For example, some will see an entity in full detail while others see only a blurry mist. There are those who perceive an entity through other senses and those who sense nothing at all. The range of possibility can be confusing, and may cause people to negate their experience as being the product of an overactive imagination. However, it must be remembered that humans exhibit a range of sentient abilities from acutely sensitive to unaware, and that not everyone sees auras and yet these are a scientific fact. Moreover, angels and ghosts vibrate at different frequencies to each other and to humans, and if you are not sensitive to human auras, chances are that you may not be aware of other vibrations either.

While our stories deal with a common theme, each story reports a unique experience. This is hardly surprising when you consider that each individual is unique, as is each entity, and so are their interactions.

It is abundantly clear to us that there is a distinct and recognizable order to our universe. There is an afterlife and there are simultaneous planes of existence, with overlaps between them. There is a synchronicity that is beyond coincidence that supports belief in a master plan. Our stories reinforce the notion of free-will, even in the afterlife.

Other past life stories lend credence to soul purpose and we are relieved to find that we are never truly alone. Help can arrive in the most extraordinary ways, often when we least expect it, regardless of whether or not we believe.

All of the stories presented here are based on true experiences. They lead us to the inescapable conclusion that this magnificence of worlds within worlds (of which we are all a part), is by design. Nothing is random and everything and everyone is connected. It is our belief that all of this is part of a grander scheme by a grand creator, which we cannot possibly comprehend. All we can see are mere glimpses into other planes of existence. Maybe one day we will have the ability and privilege to understand how and why all of the pieces fit together.

Part One
By
Marion K. Williams

The Ouija Board

Insights:

*Entities invited in may be reluctant to leave.
Bad entities are uncomfortable around people
with higher/good vibrations.*

Just before I left New Zealand for an extended overseas trip, I became fascinated with the Ouija Board. In playing it, a couple of my friends had made contact with someone whose existence and life story they had been able to verify. They were intrigued with their ability to reach the other side and communicate. I, too, found this interesting and asked to attend their next séance with them.

I remember rushing home to tell my parents about this otherworldly experience and my father was concerned for me. He warned me not to get involved; that these things could be dangerous and move beyond our control, but I reassured him that my friends were both bona fide scientists and that I would be conducting research with them. However, time was against me, and I left for overseas knowing the theory of Ouija board séances but without having experienced one firsthand.

Once I settled into my new job, I decided to explore the matter for myself. A few friends joined me and we set up our own makeshift board and began. It was early evening, and we all sat around laughing and joking, and accusing each other of moving the glass and spelling out silly answers to equally silly questions. We were all young women, curious about our futures, and for a time, it was fun. After a while, I noticed a subtle energy change in the room. One just knows these things. The atmosphere around us thickened and became more electrical; more charged somehow. Apparently I was not the only one to notice, as a couple of the girls became uncomfortable and decided to call it a night. That left two of us—Joanne and me.

I remember feeling intensely focused as I asked the board questions about me. It was exhilarating to be communicating with spirits. The answers on the board by this time had moved beyond "Yes" and "No" and the entity spelled out whole sentences which we were eagerly transcribing. He stated that he had recently died, but had known me and had lived in my hometown. I was excited by this because it meant that we could verify his existence in life. I asked him who he was but his name meant nothing to me. Then he told me that he used to watch me walk down Penelope Lemans Road.

Something about his response sent shivers down my spine. Firstly, I didn't like his use of the word "watch" and secondly, there was a section of Penelope Lemans that always bothered me and so I avoided walking it alone.

As I reacted to the street name, my friend glanced over at me and said, "Oh, God, there's a man standing behind you." The spirit had manifested. We tried to end the session. We took our hands off the glass but nothing changed. The glass kept whirring around spelling out letters which we stopped transcribing. We watched on in horror. The entity became furious when we stopped writing and literally heaved the glass across the room. First it hit the wall and then shattered on the floor. This entity was not just angry, it was enraged that we had broken off contact, and we were frightened. It is one thing to communicate with spirits through a board and quite another to have an angry one manifest beside you, especially after you have attempted to end the session. This spirit had taken control of the room.

Joanne shoved her chair back from the table and made for the balcony. She wanted to get as far away from the thing as possible. I restrained her from opening the balcony door. We were a few stories up and I didn't want any accidents. She saw my point.

Our flat felt horrid. The atmosphere was thick, angry and seething. It was palpable. I didn't know how to dispel it or get this dreadful thing to leave. Joanne told me the man was wearing black but I refused to look in his direction. I didn't want to acknowledge him further, or know anything more about him. He just simmered and fumed behind me.

There was a knock at our front door. A friend turned up unexpectedly to invite me out for a late supper, but even before he stepped inside, he read the atmosphere and said, "I don't know what you've been doing in here, but I don't want any part of it," and left. His reaction spooked us even more. We hadn't said one word to him about our visitor and yet he knew. This clearly wasn't our imagination. This was real.

I said to Joanne, "I think we need to get someone really good over here." Of all our acquaintances, we only knew one person who fit the bill. I phoned our friend Mike, the man I'm now married to, and begged him to come over to stay with us. I told him we were scared. To give him his due, he never asked why, he simply arrived and, as he walked in, the spirit left. We made Mike stay the night, and his presence dispelled the atmosphere for good.

I put away the Ouija board that night and vowed never to play it again. However, many years later when I was relating this story to friends, they laughed, and I found myself becoming irritated. I told them, "I'm not prepared to do this in my house, but if you want, I don't mind conducting a séance in your home and you can see for yourselves." They took the challenge.

I made another homemade Ouija board and set it up on their dining room table. Shana, Derek, Mike and I all sat around the board. I told them I would summon the entities and then leave the rest to them. They were content with that. I remember watching the curtains blow in, and feeling the atmosphere change as we made contact. I removed my hand from the glass and said, "You're in control now; not me. You'll know whether you're moving the glass or it is." And I sat back. The glass continued to move. They transcribed the message it was giving. The ghost spelled out, "Tell Mike and Derek to leave the room."

That was it—the board was overturned and the game was over.

I recently met up with those friends again. I told Shana I was putting together a collection of ghost stories, and she reminded me of this one. She commented on the strange wind that blew the curtains in, and how spooky the evening felt. In reminiscing about our experience, my husband didn't recall the wind but remembers being appalled by the message, and Derek had nothing at all to say on the subject. We were all there, and all paying attention, yet we all remember different aspects of the event. It was interesting to me that once again a spirit did not want to be in the presence of my husband. I put that down to his vibrations.

Flying High

Insight:

We are capable of multi-tasking with our minds and bodies to a much greater extent than is generally believed possible through astral projection and bilocation.

The idea of astral projection has always unnerved me. Whenever I felt myself spinning out of my body late at night, I desperately clung on trying to stay conscious and waiting for the spinning to stop. I always believed that I had never astral projected; my sister thought otherwise.

Late one night, when I was already in bed in Canada, my sister Rosie phoned from Australia to say that she was sick and taking a day off work. As I hung up the telephone, I thought about sending her a distance healing treatment[1] and then fatigue overwhelmed me and I drifted off to sleep. Sometime later I awoke and thought: I'd better send that treatment, and promptly went off to sleep again. That night I believed that I had failed to treat Rosie.

So, what is distance healing? This is when the practitioner is in one location and the subject is in another. You imagine you have the subject in front of you and sense their auric field in your mind, noting any imbalances. You then mentally adjust and rebalance the field. Believe it or not, distance makes no difference to energy-sensing capabilities or the effectiveness of an energy treatment.

That night I went to sleep with Rosie on my mind, and the next morning she phoned to thank me. She said that I had appeared in her room and she watched me give her a head-to-toe treatment. Well, I do know I was trying hard to visualize her to give her a distance treatment, but I thought I had slept instead. Back then I did not understand that it was possible to appear there. Rosie was insistent that I had, and I was thoroughly perplexed. I shelved the experience in the back of my mind and was grateful that, whichever way it was achieved, Rosie reported that she felt better. The next day she was back at work.

Conventional wisdom on astral projection dictates that when we soul travel, we remain connected to our bodies by a silver cord. My fear has always been that if I leave, something else might step in to replace me. Could that happen? I don't know. Like I said, I have a fear of astral projecting, and if I have done it, it was inadvertent on my part.

An acquaintance of mine, a former policewoman, told me that she quite often astral projects and does so wilfully. She has mastered her flying technique and visits friends and houses that she is interested in seeing. I asked her how she knows that she was actually there and didn't just imagine it. She told me that her previews always match the fact. It's the little details that she notices, the things she couldn't otherwise know, that confirm her travel experiences for her.

Another friend, a university professor, also used to astrally soul-fly. She told me that the difficulty for her was not in taking off, but in returning to her body gently. She complained that she often crash-landed back with a thud and felt crooked until she was able to straighten herself out. I felt her aura on one of these occasions, and she was indeed crooked—literally half in and half out of her body. I repositioned her to the centre of her auric field.

Yet another friend reported that she has occasionally woken to find herself floating through her house. Like me, she has a fear of leaving, so she immediately thinks herself back to her body in bed. Apparently, that is all that is required to return.

My friend, Cate and her husband had some interesting escapades that challenge conventional thinking. Cate's first flight occurred while she was walking outdoors at York University in Ontario, Canada. She suddenly found herself up in the air, looking down on herself as she continued walking along the pathway. As quickly as she was up, she was down again, but she did find the experience interesting. She was obviously wide-awake at the time. Her view from above could not be duplicated from below—but how did she keep walking? What part of her flew and, more importantly, can the body be fully and actively functional without the spirit? This could redefine consciousness as we know it. Her story was so extraordinary that it sent me scurrying for answers. I had never heard of such a thing.

Cate had a friend who was a psychology major, but when she tried to discuss it with him, he didn't want to hear about it. He told her the story made her sound quite mad and if she had any sense she wouldn't repeat it or the experience. She didn't mention it again until now, some thirty years later.

Her second story is even more odd, but has been verified. Some months after she returned from her tour of duty in Germany she found herself dreaming about the place. In her dream, she returned to Lahr and went shopping in the marketplace. She said she met many of her old friends there, and when she awoke, she distinctly remembered talking to them, as well as the texture and smells of the fruits, vegetables and flowers in the market. Her dream was so real that it took her a few minutes to reorient herself to being back in Canada, in her own bed and in her own home.

Some weeks later she received a letter from her friend in Lahr, who had heard from mutual friends that they had seen Cate at the market. She wondered why Cate had not called or visited her when she was in town. Of course, Cate was incredulous. She immediately wrote back stating that she had only dreamed she was there. Her friend replied that if Cate's dreams were such that other people could see her, perhaps the next time she could dream-visit her. Point taken!

Interestingly enough, Cate's husband, Dave also experienced an unusual event. He found the whole thing so alarming that he thought it best not to mention it to anyone, so he didn't, not even to his wife. Dave was a miner. One day while he was busy operating a scoop tram, he saw himself quite clearly standing a little distance away diamond drilling. He could not believe his eyes. He told me that he refused to face himself on the drill and concentrated instead on his driving.

So what is going on here? How was he physically functioning in two selves, in two skilled jobs at the exact same moment? How was I seen in Australia, and Cate in Germany? Were we actually there, or did we think-send one of our many vibrations in lieu? Some belief structures, including religions, hold that we are capable of bilocating or multilocating other selves.

Bilocation is different from astral projection. In bilocation (and multilocation) we appear to split off one or more full body, appropriately attired, holographic versions of ourselves, with each one capable of independent thought and action. In astral projection, we have an out-of-body soul-flying experience and remain connected to our resting physical selves. The operative word is resting.

In the case of Cate she clearly did more than astral project. In the first instance, she separated mind and body, yet remained functioning. She watched herself walking. It was astral projection with a twist. In her second situation, while resting at home, she projected physically to another country where she was seen by others. This leads us to the conclusion that ordinary people are capable of multi-tasking with their minds and bodies to a much greater extent than we generally believe possible.

Dave's situation is again somewhat different. He manifested another fully functional self, working alongside himself. Neither one was resting or simply a spirit version. Was he envisioning himself in the past, or the future? Was there a time overlap or warp? Was this yet another example of bilocation?

I have no recollection of physically projecting to Australia, only of attempting to distance treat my sister. I do not know how to interpret her sighting of me there or the fact that some part of me completed the distance treatment. As there is a close familial connection between us, it could have been achieved by many means—mind-cross, higher self, astral projection or bilocation, or it could quite simply be presumption on her part.

The higher self is a term I use for the alter ego that miracle workers or psychics such as Edgar Cayce tap into. This version of self functions at a higher vibration and in this higher state can perform miracles or other extraordinary feats.

Of the four scenarios, only Cate's distance travel case is clear-cut and provable, yet the other stories lend credence to it. If something extraordinary happens once, we term it miraculous, but if it happens more often, then there must be an explanation for it. Cate remembers being in Lahr and other people saw her there. It appears quite certain that she managed to naturally bilocate, which is an extraordinary feat and one usually reserved to exceptional people or those who have undergone intensive mystic study or training. Some Catholic saints are said to have mastered this technique. For someone to stumble upon this ability is truly amazing. Dave's story is also extraordinary. For anyone to twin himself to operate two distinct pieces of complex equipment simultaneously challenges conventional belief. This is the stuff of Samurai soldiers.

Neither Cate nor her husband knew my story when they told me theirs, and strangely enough, neither had discussed their own experience with the other. I think if people actually start talking about what happens in their lives, even more interesting tales may emerge.

To quote Gregg Braden, from "The Spontaneous Healing of Belief" (12).

> "If the particles that we're made of can be in instantaneous communication with one another, be in two places at once, and even change the past through choices made in the present, then we can as well."[1]

---

1   To contact Gregg Braden, please see his website: www.greggbraden.com

Intuition

Insight:

Intuition is honed with practice and is an invaluable life skill.

I love fortune-tellers. I always have and I always will. I know full well that there are good, bad and indifferent ones but having experienced readings by at least two totally amazing psychics, I continue to be fascinated by the art. How do people know what they know, and how are some of them so uncannily accurate?

Fortune-tellers are often psychic but need not be. Many disciplines inform fortune-telling including: astrology, card reading, I-Ching, mediumship, palmistry, psychometry, and seers and diviners of every type.

When I was about 12, I got a book on palmistry out of the library. I studied hard but showed no aptitude for it at the time. Later, in learning alternative therapies, I studied intuition. Over the years I have attended numerous lectures where I engaged in exercises designed to enhance this innate ability. I believe we fail to develop our God-given gift to its fullest potential.

The first time I tried a cold read at a seminar, I was staggered by the results. The exercise involved me going up to a complete stranger, looking at her, then writing her life story. We had a few minutes to complete the task. We were not allowed to touch our subjects or talk to them prior to the reading. I read a middle-aged woman. I told her that she was involved with children, but had never had any; had been seriously ill, but was on the road to recovery; had a hobby of quilting; and a great interest in something English. I was searching around for what exactly when my time was up. My subject confirmed everything. She was a primary school teacher who had no children of her own. She had been diagnosed with a serious illness which was now in remission. She belonged to a quilting bee, and the something English was that she was in the midst of planting an English country garden. Now some of that might be a lucky guess, but the quilting comment was a bit unusual. It is not an everyday hobby.

Since that time I continue to do cold reads at seminars and continue to be amazed. At one such reading I had to stand behind my subject with my hands on her shoulders and attempt to read her thoughts. I saw fire bolts in the sky. The individual was thinking of fireworks. Close. I find I get a better result when I actually look into the person's eyes. It gives me a clearer emotional read. Of course, there are always individuals that I cannot read.

In discussing intuition with friends one evening, Marie Claire confided to me that she wished she knew more about her birth mother. It was not that she had an unhappy life, she just wanted to know more about herself. She said she often felt like a square peg in a round hole and wondered if there was a reason for this.

My friend had an interesting arrival into this life. She was born in the era where unwed mothers were generally viewed by society as being unfit. She had been put up for adoption at birth. Although the much loved child of her adoptive parents, it had been a somewhat difficult match of personalities. I sometimes felt she understood her mother better as an adult than she ever had as a child. In her younger years, she was critical of her parents, and they were confused by her. Fortunately, when Marie Claire grew up and became a mother herself, she and her mother learned to enjoy each other's company. However, as a youngster, Marie Claire's problems were compounded when she was sent to a strict school. She found herself to be a free thinker in a structured environment. She did not thrive there and today, she dismisses that part of her life as being nonsensical.

Marie Claire's need to know her origins resonated with me. I know mine. I was raised on family stories faithfully related to me by parents, grandmothers and aunts. I sat back in my chair and spoke without thinking, "Well, let's work out what she'd be like; it can't be that difficult. I think she'd have red hair. She's probably Jewish. I imagine that she's fairly left wing, an independent thinker and a bit of a rebel with a great love of books."

My reasons for this conjecture were simple. My friend is a left wing rebel in spite of being brought up in a right wing conservative Catholic household and school. She devoured books, although her parents rarely read. And as for the rest—it was an intuitive guess.

Our imaginings that day gave my friend an image to identify with. To our way of thinking, she was not so different from her family after all.

Years and years later, she phoned me very excited. She had submitted her name to the registry as an adopted person willing to meet her birth parents and there had been a match. Both birth parents were searching for her. The meeting was set for a town out of province. Marie Claire was both thrilled and terrified. It was a nightmare and a dream come true for her. She was anxious that her birth mother might not measure up to her dream mother.

Her husband Peter escorted her to the meeting and they both came over to our house when they returned. "I couldn't believe it," Marie Claire told me. "She was everything we imagined and more. She was a red-haired Jewish woman, with the same politics as me. We share exactly the same views and read exactly the same books, and she hadn't wanted to give me up but was tricked into it. And my dad is like Peter—a history buff."

She then related a sad tale of her mother being a pregnant foreign student in Quebec, and of judgmental people who presumed to act in the best interests of the child. Her mother was coerced into signing her child away and Marie Claire was then whisked out of Quebec to adoptive parents in Ontario where the adoption was rushed through. Although Jewish by birth, she was placed with a Catholic family. Both birth parents and grandparents had been involved in a thirty-year plus search for her. Even though her birth parents never married each other, they had maintained contact, and remained committed to their joint search for their daughter.

Their search deserves its own story but it was intriguing that we were able to picture Marie Claire's mother so finitely. Interestingly enough, her grandparents also pictured their grandchild. They fancied they saw her wearing a specific outfit at Expo 67, and they were right. She was there and they recognized her on sight. There was just that familial indefinable something. Unfortunately they did not trust their instincts and so did not approach her at the time, although her grandmother did have the opportunity to meet her in later years.

My intuition has kicked in at other times in other circumstances. During my career, I have worked for firms the world over, in everything from insurance, to diplomacy, to research, to law. In each of these positions, and in all of these countries, I have relied on my sixth sense.

One day I was working at my desk and a telephone repairman was working alongside me. I was trying hard to concentrate on my work and he was a noisy individual who talked constantly to himself. I found his muttering distracting. Finally I said to him, "What is the problem?" He told me that he had never seen such shoddy telephone work. Something jarred. I asked him to stop working. I then telephoned my boss, who instructed me to call the police.

To make a long story short, after further investigation it appeared that someone had tapped into our office telephone lines and there was a listening post set up in a disused stairwell. When the police officer arrived, he asked if I had noticed anything else that seemed strange. I told him that I felt overcome by fear when I attempted to bring some files to storage in the basement. Instead of completing this task, I ran back upstairs, files still in hand. The officer went downstairs to check it out and found another listening post there, with cigarette butt evidence that the perpetrator had been there recently.

I also told him that earlier that week I had met a suspicious man in the hallway. This individual had been polite and well dressed, but nonetheless seemed "wrong" to me. I felt he was not there for his stated purpose. At that time we worked in a large building with several other tenants, all of whom had clients. There were many corridors in the building, one of which we shared with another firm. As I turned the corner into our shared corridor that day, I saw this individual loitering near our doorway. At the officer's suggestion, a locksmith was called in. He found that someone had chiselled the workings on our lock so that any key could open our door. Our office was all set for a break-in.

Intuition is amazing when we really listen.

I read another situation over the phone. A friend phoned me from overseas complaining that her husband had lost "x" dollars gambling on the Internet. I told her that she had better get to the bank and check the household accounts because I was fairly certain that he had lost ten times that amount. She did and I was right.

My friend had no idea about her husband's addiction or the extent of his gambling, so how could I? I don't know. All I know is, I trust my inner knowing.

Devilish Dealings

I believe in my intuition. If I ignore it, I generally regret it. When I was a child my father wanted to expose me to different lifestyles, so although I was a city girl, at least once a year I was shipped off to learn something about farm life. I loved these times. So, many years later, when a friend approached me to assist with fencing her farm, I naturally agreed to help. It brought back some very happy memories. My husband offered to come with me, and together with a bunch of other people I didn't know, we formed a fencing-bee, and had that fence up in no time.

While I was working my section, I met a striking young woman whom I'll call Marilyn, who was excited about attending a fortune-telling session the following day. I am intrigued by fortune-telling and so I wanted to know all about it. She told me that the psychic was also a healer and had been helpful in treating her back pain. I love to watch healers in action, and my new friend invited me along. The minute I received the invitation, I also received a mental message, "No." I ignored it. I got another message, "Then go in your own car." This one I did not ignore or at least I tried not to.

I thanked Marilyn for her invitation and told her I would make my own way there. She insisted that she would drive me. She pointed out quite reasonably that she had to pass my house to get to the fortune-teller's home, so against my better judgement, I agreed.

The next day Marilyn picked me up at around 4:30 p.m., and we drove the 10 kilometres or so to the next town for the reading. As we entered the psychic's door, she came out to greet us. She hugged Marilyn, and then turned to hug me. For some inexplicable reason I felt like shoving her away from me and was immediately ashamed of myself. I don't generally refuse hugs, and this was a terrible response to a warm welcome. I continued on into the room.

Apparently this healer/fortune-teller did multiple healing sessions on Sunday evenings, and there were a number of people sitting around the room waiting. Marilyn and I were invited to take off our shoes and join the group. I remember thinking that they were an odd looking bunch. No one would look me in the eye or engage in conversation, and they all had a curiously unlit sort of presence. I felt like I had just walked into "gloomsville" but still I was curious, so I settled down in the chair that was offered to me. I then took a few minutes to look around at the décor. It was most unusual. The artwork caught my attention as it was like nothing that I had ever seen before. I have lived in the East and am familiar with dragons and other mystical creatures but this art was strange in its representations. I didn't find it particularly attractive but it seemed to fit the room.

I was interrupted in my thoughts by our hostess who gave a brief introduction and then laid out her plans for the evening's activity. First there was to be a guided meditation, and then those seeking a healing session would be invited to go downstairs one at a time for a private reading. Marilyn had invited me to watch her treatment and, as I am trained in complementary medicine myself, I was interested in observing the healer's technique.

The evening's program got underway. As instructed by the psychic, I got comfortable in my chair, relaxed my body, lightened my mind and prepared to follow instructions. And so she began, "Close your eyes, rest your tongue lightly on the roof of your mouth, relax your body. We are now meditating to the light of Lucifer."

My eyes flew open. The fortune-teller's eyes were firmly fixed on me, boring into me. I broke off eye contact, and scrambled around the floor for my shoes and left. I rushed out that door; I did not wait for Marilyn. I simply ran. I was terrified that the fortune-teller might follow me, and so tried to be unpredictable and ran the opposite direction to my home, and then knocked on a stranger's door and requested to use their phone. Fortunately for me, they let me in, and I was able to reach my husband who came straight out to get me.

When he arrived, he asked me what was wrong. I told him that I had stumbled into a Satanist meeting. Now, I realize that there is nothing illegal about a Satanist meeting. People are entitled to follow the religion of their choice and life is all about choices. It's just not my choice or something that I am comfortable being around. And truthfully, I think that Marilyn should have explained her affiliation to me. She knew mine.

The next day at work, still shaken, I felt the need to wear a cross. I know that sounds superstitious but nonetheless that day I found it both necessary and comforting. I was horrified when Ms. Fortune-teller arrived at my office. She was not a client of our firm; she had no appointment and no reason to be there, yet she had taken the trouble to drive in from a neighbouring town. I had the distinct impression that she was there for me and I did not want her in my space. I took my boss aside and told him of my experience, and he showed her out the door.

Then I became concerned for Marilyn. I phoned to apologize for running out and explained that the reason I left was that I wanted no part of a meditation to Lucifer. She told me not to be ridiculous; that Lucifer was a Greek God. I suggested that she research him further if she believed that to be the case. Our conversation ended with her telling me that I was a very naïve and unworldly person who simply didn't understand these things. I felt I had said all I could. Eventually she moved out of our area, breaking her connection with her healer.

I did meet up with the fortune-teller socially some years later. Although she was still involved in healing work, she no longer had an unlit presence. Presumably her source had changed, and she had moved on from her devilish leanings, but to tell you the truth I was not much interested in discussing the matter further with her.

This was a big wake up call for me to listen to my intuition. Healers can tap into many sources for their skill and this one chose a source that was unacceptable to me.

Mind-Cross

Insight:

Our minds are capable of "computing" much more than we realize—analyzing voice tones, expressions, and body language, etc., to calculate a balance of probability.

From my 20s I have been able to mind-cross. It is not something I can will to happen or control. Sometimes when I ask, answers come; sometimes the information comes without a request. It doesn't happen often but when it does, it's about something important. I never doubt the information because it has never been wrong.

It happens to me at work, at home, and in my personal relationships. It's not always a comfortable thing for me because when I know something, I feel I must act on it. This usually attracts a backlash for me of some duration—shorter, longer or permanent—but I feel that I am told for a reason and therefore some action is required on my part. Otherwise what would be the point? Unfortunately, this ability can make me sound like a know-it-all, but I do feel compelled to speak up nonetheless.

Occasionally, very occasionally, people mind-cross with me, but that appears to be a different ball game.

Rosie

One such incident involved my sister, Rosie. She and I generally talk every night—that is, my night and her day as we live 16,000 kilometres apart. She is nine years younger than me but we have always been close. She accompanied me on many of my dates when I was a teenager and has always been an integral part of my life; my keeper of secrets. She was my parents' idea of a chaperone.

When I married, I relocated to Canada. When Rosie married, she relocated to Australia, but distance has never hindered our relationship.

One day I had the strong urge to call Rosie now; right this minute. I did and I reached her as she was walking up the path to her front door. She had just taken the children to school. She asked me why I was phoning so early and I said I didn't know, I just thought I should. She opened her front door and said, "Oh, someone's left the chest of drawers open and everything's falling onto the floor." I said, "Rosie, get out of the house now; hang up the phone and call the police. You're interrupting a burglary and they're still inside." Fortunately, she followed my suggestion without argument.

I then spent a nervous time worrying about what was happening in Australia, and whether I should call the police myself or leave everything in her hands. I followed my instincts and left it to her.

She told me later that as the police ran in her front door, the criminals ran out the back. Rosie's house has a large yard that backs onto a laneway. They simply ran through her yard, hopped the fence and made their getaway... but not for long. The police eventually caught up with them. The officers told Rosie that this was a violent crew, and she was lucky she did not interrupt them.

In talking with Rosie, I had one further insight. I told her that I believed it was somewhat of an inside job and not a random hit. She argued with me. However, the police investigation later revealed that her boarder had worn some attractive jewellery to college, which made her the envy and target of another not-so-nice classmate. The classmate put her name out to some unsavoury friends.

Baby-Cross

While it was not really a surprise that I could mind-cross with my sister, I learned that it is possible to mind-cross with newborn babies as well. This one took me completely by surprise.

My friend Jessie married in her late 20s. She was a successful and elegant professional. She had a degree in Fine Arts, was a whiz on computers, and worked as an assistant television producer prior to settling down. Jessie asked me to look after her newborn for a few hours while she and her husband bid on a house at auction. Of course, I immediately agreed. For one thing, Jess had not seemed herself since the birth and I felt she might need some time out. She appeared strangely disconnected to everyone and everything. I had mentioned my concerns to her husband but he said, "Oh, give her a break. She's just a new mum." So, I backed off but I was worried. Usually new mums get into a routine after a few days and that didn't seem to be happening. Her reactions seemed odd. She was always pleasant enough, but just strangely inept and this was the girl who used to be a model of efficiency.

When I arrived at her house that day, Jessie told me that she had just fed her son, and she left me with the usual set of instructions. After she left, I sat down in a comfortable chair in the living room, turned on the music, and cuddled the baby. He was resting quietly at the time so I could have put him in his bed to sleep but for some reason I just wanted to hold him.

As I looked down into his tiny face, I noticed that he did not gaze back at me as newborns do. He looked "shuttered" somehow and had an expression that I had never before seen on a baby's face. Something was wrong. As I rocked him in my arms I asked out loud, "What's wrong with you little baby? Talk to me." I was stunned when he did.

He told me in my mind, in words not pictures, that he had a very sore bottom and finger, and that he was hungry. I told him out loud that I would take care of that, and I did.

I took him to the change table and took off his clothes. He had a diaper rash, and his bottom was so red and raw that he could have given a baboon a run for its money. I took him to the bathroom sink, rinsed him off, and then coated his rear with lots of soothing cream. Next I inspected his hands, and sure enough, he had what we used to call a whitlow—an infection that requires antibiotics to clear. It can be a serious condition for babies. There was nothing I could do about that except acknowledge his pain and promise to get help, and I told him that. I then went to the cupboard and mixed him a bottle. He drank the whole thing. He almost inhaled it. And then he slept—a sad little sleep—with little silent sobs that shook his body. He broke my heart.

I was troubled. I phoned Jessie's mother and discussed the situation with her. I said I thought Jess was struggling and needed help and while she did not disagree, she was at a loss as to what she could do. She reminded me that Jessie was under a top specialist who had noticed nothing untoward. She wanted to be certain that we weren't overreacting. She told me that she did not want to interfere because it could undermine her daughter's confidence, and complicate their relationship. She said that she would try to check on her daughter more often, which was of some consolation. I felt that Jessie's husband would be of no assistance because he seemed quite unaware there was a problem, and so in the end I called Jessie's physician and asked that she intervene. The doctor told me she would not discuss the situation with me. I told her she didn't have to; she just had to listen, and then act in the best interests of the child.

She phoned Jessie that afternoon and invited her for a visit the following morning. She told Jess that she wanted to see her new baby and just catch up on things. I dropped by Jessie's home prior to her appointment to make sure that she actually got there. That day, Jessie didn't manage to get suitably dressed and went out in gardening clothes—which was not her style at all. She was definitely not herself. And the baby didn't fare any better. He wore a one-piece outfit and was wrapped in a blanket but he lacked the usual bonnet and mitts so essential in winter months. Although I accompanied Jessie to her appointment, I did not assist her beyond ordering a taxi to get us there. I wanted the doctor to understand the full impact of the problem.

The doctor was wonderful with her. She greeted her with open arms and spent a great deal of time admiring the baby and congratulating Jess. She then stripped the baby down, ostensibly to weigh him, but noted the state of his bottom and his finger, and told Jessie that he needed medication.

The doctor then turned her attention to Jessie and questioned her closely on how much sleep she was getting. She suggested that new babies are sometimes hard to get on a schedule and that their mothers become too exhausted to cope. She offered her help, but in such a subtle way that Jessie found herself agreeing to it without really making a decision. In the end, both mother and child received nursing assistance. Jess was diagnosed with postnatal depression and the baby with failure to thrive. Fortunately, both made a full recovery.

I thought Jessie might never forgive me for interfering, and I know her husband was annoyed with me. It was too sensitive a topic for me to discuss with either of them for a few years, but then much, much later Jessie told me that she felt she was drowning and that no one was noticing.

Labour Problems

Some of my mind-crosses took place at work.

As a young woman I worked for a senior executive. He was well seasoned in his role and had lived all over the world. He had held his current post for five years whereas I was a newcomer, and had only been in my position for about five months. One day while I was transcribing a report, I noticed an unusually intense conversation amongst our local staff some 12 metres away from me. I could not see everyone involved because I had a partially obstructed view, and I could not hear what they were saying but my interest was piqued. I wondered what had prompted such a serious discussion. I got the message back in my mind that they were unhappy with their salaries and intended to strike.

I tried to warn my boss but he told me that he knew his staff very well and assured me that I had misread the situation. The next day the local staff went on strike. My boss called me in. He wanted to know what I knew and how I knew it. My answers were not what he expected. I told him I had sensed the situation from the staff's body language, and while I knew nothing for a fact, my strong feeling was that he should deal with X, whom I believed to be the leader.

At the time our office operated with two salary grids. Those posted overseas received additional compensation, whereas local staff did not. While this is standard practice the world over, our local staff did not understand and felt they were being treated as second-class citizens in their own country. My boss did follow my suggestion and was able to bring the strike to a fast resolution.

People Skills

While I am fairly good at recognising a liar, in the course of my career, some of my bosses had no such skill. One, in particular, did not know people. If something sounded good, he went with it and this caused us all sorts of problems.

One year he decided to upgrade all of our computer equipment and programs, and in due course introduced us to his new computer contact. At the first opportunity I suggested that he not deal with this individual, however, my boss was convinced that he had made a good deal and pressed on with his expensive purchase.

We all wanted new equipment as ours was outdated and slow, but the new programs never seemed to function as they should. Weeks went by and, despite my willingness to learn, I found I was still experiencing programming problems which were slowing me down. One day I simply could not get the formatting to work on an important document. I decided to call the programming company directly. My boss joined me on my call. I was not surprised to learn that I was trying to operate a defective pirated program, and my boss was appalled to find that every program in the office was the same. In addition to programming deficiencies, there were installation errors, and problems with the hard drives. My boss had spent thousands of dollars in office upgrades, which he was unable to recoup as he found himself at the end of a long list of creditors bilked by this con artist.

Court Antics

Another time I attended court with my boss. Opposing counsel was not well known to me as he was not local. That morning I asked him in my mind what on earth he was up to, and he answered—or someone did. I was told that he would instruct his client to take matters into his own hands, and plead such and such a defence.

I did not know the sections of law by heart but that day I heard them chapter and verse in my head. I told my boss. He said that counsel was an officer of the court and would never act in such a way. I said, "Well, if he does, this is his defence."

My boss phoned me at home that night telling me that I had foreseen counsel's actions correctly. Our knowledge of their defence was a tremendous help the next day.

Mike

I have had several mind-crosses with my husband and this one stands out in my memory. In this instance he was the "reader" and I was the "projector" and he was able to read my fears.

I had a friend whom I regarded as emotionally fragile. She was bright and gifted, but given to frequent bouts of unexplained tears. I didn't understand her nervousness but figured she had always been that way. Similarly, I never gave much thought to the fact that she always wore long sleeves and long pants even during the hot summer months. She was elegantly dressed and that was all I noticed. In retrospect, I really wasn't thinking. We were friends and I enjoyed her company. We were both busy young mothers who got together for a chat every now and then.

She was married to a handsome executive and she had four children. The older two were from a previous marriage. One evening, her husband dropped by unexpectedly while my husband was at work. I was surprised to see him, but welcomed him in.

As he entered our home, however, the whole atmosphere changed and the room dimmed around him. The change was immediate and marked. I took a closer look at him. He had a very dark aura and a black entity with him. I asked him outright who it was. He didn't deny it. He just said, "Oh, so you can see him too, can you?"

He walked on into our living room and sat down. I too sat down. I could not talk to him; I was too frightened. I just kept praying over and over for help. I realized I was in the presence of evil and now clearly understood why my friend was in the state she was. I don't know why that man continued to sit there, unless it was to torment me. I did not talk to him. I did not offer him a drink or any hospitality. I simply sat and so did he. The time ticked by.

Then the door burst open and my husband came in. He asked if there was something wrong. I said, "Yes. Him." Mike didn't hesitate; he didn't ask questions; he just threw him out the door. Mike was actually at work when he got the overwhelming sense that I needed him. He rushed home because he had a gut feeling he should.

Later I told my friend what had happened. I asked her why she had never told me what she was living with, or why she had not asked for help, and she said quite simply, "Would you have believed me?"

That day we sat down and planned her escape, which she eventually carried out with all four children in tow.

Conversationally Speaking…

There is one other mind-cross that occasionally happens. That is when I think something and someone hears my thoughts and answers me. The first time this happened to me I was at a dinner party being introduced for the first time to my sister's circle of friends. There was an attractive young man sitting across the table from me and I wondered what his background was. He looked at me as if I had posed the question out loud, which I had not, and said, "Very similar to yours actually. My father was a diplomat and I spent my childhood in England. The only real difference is that I was an only child." Others at the table looked a little confused at his comments, which appeared to be a complete non sequitur and all I could think was, "Oh, my God, he can hear my thoughts."

A similar situation happened to me in England. I was working in market research at the time and shared my office with a marketing executive from America. We both had solitary jobs, and rarely chatted about personal matters.

One day she looked at me and said, "Don't worry about your flat. Close it up and you can stay at our place until your flight leaves." I was surprised. I had been sitting there mulling over the logistics of leaving the country but had not mentioned these out loud to anyone. She looked at my stupefied expression and said, "Oh, did I forget to mention?…sometimes I read minds." While grateful for her offer, I was not comfortable with her disclosure and spent the next few minutes wondering what other thoughts of mine she might have eavesdropped on.

I was telling my friend about this situation years later. She said something similar happened to her at a doctor's office. She wondered about the gentleman sitting opposite her, and he had answered her thoughts. She was quite embarrassed at the time. One doesn't always like to have one's thoughts read.

But regardless of embarrassments and other difficult moments, intuition and mind-cross are very much part of my life. I couldn't operate without them. How do they work? I'm not sure. I think our minds are like advanced computers and if we load the right insights in, we get the right answers back. We probably note a million clues in a day, and our little observances can eventually paint a picture of probability which is more or less accurate depending on our skills and abilities. But in the final analysis, if it's garbage in, it will almost certainly be garbage out. And some instances just defy all rational explanation.

Cate's Mind-Cross

Insight:

Love connections can be so close that one feels another's pain.

For years my husband and I have had a weekly night out. It's our date night. In earlier years we used to go to the Tuesday night movies. In more recent times we have joined a bunch of friends for Friday night suppers. Our suppers are lively affairs that last for hours. We dine on exotic food, and topics of conversation range from religion to politics to books and personal stories, and we all sit glued to our chairs until the staff start hovering and we realize that we really cannot stay a moment longer.

One evening my friend Cate regaled us with stories of her younger years in Germany. In her early 20s Cate was stationed at the Canadian Army Base in Lahr, and it was there that she fell in love with Tim, a Canadian broadcaster. He was her sunrise and sunset, and she was in love with love.

It was during her time with Tim that she learned that she could mind-cross. She rarely does it now but back then, she was on exactly the same mind frequency as her young man.

The first time this happened was when Tim's mother became ill, and he had to leave Germany suddenly. Apparently, his mother had a heart attack and her survival was in doubt. Tim hopped the first plane out of Germany and landed first in England, and from there flew on to Montreal. Cate was upset. She felt his concern and worry about his mother as if it were her own. He was very much on her mind and she found it hard to concentrate on her duties.

Around 4 o'clock on the day he left, she doubled over at her desk. She had a knot of fear in her stomach, and felt like vomiting with fright. Her dread was real and tangible and she had no clue why. It lasted a short while, and then disappeared. It literally faded away. Over the next week or so she was lonely for Tim, but not physically upset by his absence.

In due course Tim's mother came out of crisis and he returned to duty on the base. Cate asked him if something had happened to him at approximately 4 p.m. on the day that he left. He thought about it for a moment and then said, "Yes. How did you know? We lost an engine over the English Channel. I was glad to land in one piece." Cate's terror was actually Tim's.

This was the first time, but not the last, that Cate picked up on Tim's feelings. Cate worked in Administration on the base. Her job was not difficult but it was time sensitive, and it kept her on her toes. She worked directly for Sgt. Hirogi, a Japanese-Canadian. One morning as she was doing the routine filing, she suddenly felt sick with apprehension. Sgt. Hirogi noticed her discomfort and asked her what was wrong. She told him that she had the worst feeling about Tim and she didn't know why. He told her to call Tim right away. He said that his wife had premonitions like hers and they were always right.

No sooner were the words out of his mouth than the telephone rang and it was the hospital emergency unit. In preparing his Jeep for a trip to town, Tim had released the radiator cap and steam had badly scorched his arm. He was calling for Cate. Of course, she rushed to his side, and over the next few days she helped nurse him through his recovery. She had a special rapport with that young man and registered his physical pain as her own.

I wish I could tell you that they lived happily ever after, but as is often the case with these close mind connections, they cannot last. Relationships as intense as these can only flame out. In due course both Cate and Tim moved on in different directions.

Remote Viewing

Insight:

Seeing is believing.

Remote Viewing is something I began to experience for the first time in my 20s and it has occurred intermittently since. I am not sure what triggers it but I have no reason to doubt its accuracy.

The first time it happened to me I was lying in hospital recovering from meningitis. The crisis was over and I had just been moved out of isolation. I was 20 years old. I had given everyone quite a scare—my mother in particular, as her older sister had died from this—but I was now on the mend, and had been assured that I would soon fully recover.

As I settled into my new bed, my thoughts were on other things. My life was extremely busy at that time. I worked full time as a flight attendant; part time for Drake's Office Overload; attended night classes in Japanese and shorthand, and had a whirlwind social life.

I was mulling things over when I saw this television-type drama switch on in my head, and I found myself watching the most extraordinary scene play out in front of me. I saw my boyfriend at his home, standing in the front hallway next to the phone. A friend of ours was with him. He was clearly upset, and she leaned in to kiss and hold him. He returned her kiss. I had no reason to doubt what I was seeing—and what I saw proved true.

In fairness to my friend, we were not engaged and he was free to kiss whomever he wished, but it was interesting to me that I could "tune in."

The next time my vision kicked into gear was in Japan. I was returning from work and received the feeling that I must rush home now. As I raced along the hot dusty roadway in the overwhelming heat, I asked the questions in my mind—why? What's the urgency? I received a mental image of a friend waiting for me. I saw him in full living colour sitting at my kitchen table, and was able to eavesdrop on his conversation. My friends were giving him a difficult time as they felt he was too old for me.

I relaxed and slowed my rush down to a more genteel walk. I felt quite confident that he was more than capable of fielding their questions. When I arrived home some time later, he was sitting exactly where I'd envisioned him, and was wearing the clothes I had pictured him in, and my friends were being less than charming to him.

What blew me away with this pictorial image was the accuracy of the detail. You see, I didn't know anything about his clothing options. I had only met him a short time earlier and American men dress with a different sense of style from New Zealanders. He was wearing an olive green shirt and matching trousers. Our men during those years were much more conservative dressers.

There is another type of remote viewing that I have been exposed to. This is when someone else sees through my eyes. One year my husband and I took a family holiday in Queensland and while there, explored some new homes in the region. I fell in love with a vintage design home which the builder called a Queenslander. I found it to be the perfect family home, and the house of my dreams.

When I returned to Canada one of my friends joined me for coffee. She told me that she dreamed of me while I was away. She said she saw me walking through a house of a very distinctive design. It was a bungalow with a central hallway, and a large wrap-around porch. She said she saw me admiring each and every room, and felt my happiness. I was smiling and laughing in her dream. From her description, it appears that she went on my home tour with me. She saw what I saw, and saw what I felt. She had remotely viewed me with great accuracy from over 15,000 kilometres away.

She has dream-viewed me on other occasions as well, and it is interesting to note that each instance involved another heartfelt emotion—joy, love, happiness, grief or sadness.

Snippets

Insight:

Ghosts may be attached to people and/or places. Their spirits mirror their life personalities, and death does not make them omniscient. Sometimes they need things explained to them.

Ghost stories are not a popular topic of conversation in our family as they can promote discord and none of us likes that, but there have been times when we have sat down to a real ghost-fest. These occurred at a couple of family get-togethers in New Zealand and at our parents' home in Singapore. Here are some of the stories that I recall.

The Trouser Tale

My brother Sam has been surrounded all his life by friends and family who see ghosts. He was always interested in our stories, and on this occasion had one of his own to tell.

When he and his wife were first married, they moved into a quiet residential neighbourhood in another city, far away from family and friends. Over time, they made new friends, and became close with their neighbours Naomi and Pat, who were mother and daughter. These two eventually became the surrogate grandmother and aunt to his two small daughters.

Pat was about my brother's age, a bit of an eccentric and a gifted potter. She looked and behaved like an overage hippie and, in fact, grew some of "her own" in her back garden. She lived life in a very mellow state. Naomi was a widow, long retired. I am not sure whether she had been a nurse or a teacher—in any event, she was a kind woman who was good with young children, and made a wonderful grandma to Sam's kids. She was not one to criticize her daughter's idiosyncrasies and the two lived a fairly harmonious existence.

Sam never actually met Naomi's husband. He had been dead for some years by the time my brother and his young family moved into the neighbourhood. However, Pat and Naomi fondly remembered him, and by all accounts he kept a close watch on them from the other side. He frequently joined them on their evenings at home. As they sat chatting or playing cards, he would announce his presence by turning on the gramophone and playing records. By this time records were actually quite passé and the player was just an ornamental oddity, but Fred managed to turn it on with some regularity. He even had favourite tracks on favourite records and was precise in his selections. Pat and Naomi were content with this practice when there were just the two of them, as they found it comforting to know that he was still around. However, Pat was less impressed when she brought a date home and her father chose to make his presence known. His visits cut her dates short and, over the years, had curtailed her social life. She had the impression that her father did not approve of her boyfriends, who apparently never measured up to his exacting standards.

One Sunday morning Pat joined my brother and his family for brunch and told them the following story.

She had just met someone new and exciting, and after a wonderful evening out, the two of them returned very late to Pat's home. Rather than send her young man away in the wee hours of the morning, Pat invited her new friend to sleep over on the couch. She provided him with a pillow and blankets and retired to bed but she forgot to mention her ever-vigilant father. He had been strict with her in life and he was not about to lower his standards now. He waited until the young man was comfortable on the living room couch—minus shoes, socks and trousers—then pulled his famous appearing trick, and when he had the poor fellow's full attention, he ordered him out.

When she heard the commotion in the next room, Pat thought, "Oh, no!" She leapt to her feet and fought her way into her dressing gown, but she wasn't quick enough. She heard "Out!" and then the back door slam. She raced to the back porch but her young man had hightailed it out of there. Pat told Sam that she found the poor fellow's trousers still folded neatly over the arm of the couch. He ran through the city streets without them.

Janna's Monk

Janna and her husband, Vince, had taken a six-month sabbatical from teaching in order to take an extended European trip. They viewed it as their second honeymoon. They were both seasoned travellers and in their single years, had travelled alone. They now looked forward to exploring Europe together, each acting as a guide for the other. But Janna knew that her husband would have a bitter-sweet return to his old stamping grounds because this time his close friend would not be there to greet him. She had met an untimely death some years earlier.

Vince loved France and especially Normandy. He booked them into a 14th century farmhouse in Mont Saint Michel—a town renowned for its religious history, and boasting some of the more popular historical sites in France.

The farmhouse was comfortably set up as a Bed & Breakfast operated by a retired teacher and her daughter. Janna said it was a beautiful old stone building with antique furnishings and wonderful scatter rugs across the worn stone floors. It was, in her words, sparsely elegant. That evening they were shown into a pleasant suite on the third floor. It was a spacious room with huge floor to ceiling windows. The outer doors were locked and guests were expected to be in their rooms by 10:00 p.m.

Janna and Vince were both tired from traipsing round Europe and retired to bed early. Jana generally takes a while to get to sleep and this night was no different. As her husband slept, she lay quietly in the dark, lost in thought, and watching the moonlight play across the walls.

She was just beginning to doze off when she felt the bed depress beside her. She said that she initially thought that Vince had woken, so she rolled over to talk to him, and then, in the moonlight, she clearly saw a monk sitting on the end of their bed. She knew he was a monk by his garb, but she did not recognise his order. He wore a white hooded tunic. The only monks she knew wore brown.

The monk was staring intently at her husband who was still sound asleep. At first she was too startled to say or do anything. The monk showed absolutely no interest in her—didn't even look at her. Instead he seemed fixated on her husband.

Janna finally found her voice, and called out, "Vince, Vince" and tried to prod him awake, but he was tired and not easily roused. She did, however, disturb the monk in his reverie, and he was not pleased. His tender attitude evaporated. He rose from his position at the end of the bed and went and stood directly behind Janna. She said she felt pure terror. His annoyance was apparent. She prayed for help, and he dematerialized. Her husband never woke during the whole ordeal.

Eventually Janna fell asleep, and the next morning she and Vince attended the dining room for breakfast. As there were few guests overnighting, and none in the dining room, Janna felt comfortable in asking a few questions. She wanted to know whether the farmhouse had ever been a monastery but was assured it had not been. She told her hosts that she found that surprising as a monk had visited their room the previous night. Her comment raised no eyebrows; her hosts were not fazed. It was not the first time they had heard it. They told her that sightings were common in the area.

Later, at the historical site of the old Mont Saint Michel Benedictine Abby, she saw a plaster model of a Benedictine monk and recognized his robe immediately. It was what her ghost-monk wore.

This was Janna's first "visitation" and it made a huge impression on her. She rarely sees ghosts.

Deb's Entity

"What did you think of that house in London?" my sister, Debra, asked. I told her that my room was nice, but I was glad that I didn't have to sleep in hers. Mum was a little miffed. She had spared no expense in doing up the London home from scratch, literally from the floorboards up, and any criticism of her masterpiece was not going to go over well.

Debra reassured her, "Not the house mum; the feel of the house." "Well, what was wrong with your bedroom?" my mother wanted to know.

"Let me guess," I said. "An unwelcome male ghost; a nasty, creepy sort of individual who lurked about." My mother wasn't going to have it. "That was just the residual feeling from the previous owner," she said. "Walls pick up impressions and he was a bit strange."

Debra disagreed. "No, mum. This was definitely a ghost. I've no doubt the owner was a creep, but this was an entity. He wasn't overly scary but he came into my room every night and sat down on my bed. I saw and felt the mattress depress."

My parents were shocked into silence, but I was more interested in Deb's coping strategy. "What on earth did you do?" "I told him to get out," she told me. "They usually do when you put it like that."

Had that been me I would have immediately sought a religious remedy. Deb didn't bother. "Get out!" from her was all it took. She's a take-charge, no-nonsense sort of girl and there isn't too much that she can't cope with.

Looking back, it is interesting that I knew that room was haunted and I avoided it. I wouldn't even enter it to change the sheets on the bed, but I never discussed it with my sister or my parents. In those years we had this strange sort of logic that if we didn't talk about something, then it wasn't happening. In retrospect, I realize what a horrible position I had placed Deb in. When we don't acknowledge things, we leave people isolated and alone in monstrous situations. In our family we have those who readily admit to seeing ghosts; those who admit there are ghosts but don't see them; and those who think that the topic is the recreation of mad people. I have found that people who have firm convictions will rarely change them, so I don't bother to argue with them. They're entitled to believe what they want, but now that I'm older, I try not to leave people to deal with these things alone. I call it as I see it, and it's their choice what they do with the information. Needless to say, my insights are not always welcome.

At the Farm

I remember discussing one other haunting story. My friend Julie and her husband had bought a nice piece of farmland, which they hoped to work together. Then, unexpectedly, things went wrong. Her husband became terminally ill, and she was forced to put the farm up for sale. One day, in despair, she complained to a neighbour that nothing had gone right in their lives since they bought the property. Her neighbour said, "Well, what do you expect? You bought an old burial ground." This was news to Julie.

A group of us were out for lunch when she told us the story. "Do you think it's true?" she asked. "How do I even go about finding out the history of the place?" I said to her, "Well, first of all, what sorts of things have gone wrong? Are they routine or out of the ordinary?" She reeled off a litany of incidents and accidents and bad luck stories. She'd been ill; the kids had been ill; her husband was dying; the animals had one thing after the other. There had been a number of strange accidents and now she couldn't even attract an interested viewer, let alone a buyer, and with her husband no longer earning, she desperately needed to sell the place. I said, "Well, there must be something you can do about this. Even if it is sacred land, it's not as if you deliberately did anything wrong. Ask an elder what he suggests."

Julie didn't know any elders but our friend Mary did, and she volunteered to help. When he heard the story, the elder felt an appeasing ceremony would be appropriate, and he provided Mary with instructions on how to proceed.

As instructed, Julie walked the perimeter of the property, and made a tobacco offering at each corner. As she completed the final offering, a small whirlwind encircled her and then died down. Julie was assured that her offering had been accepted and within a week the farmhouse sold. Fact is often stranger than fiction.

Visiting an Old Friend

Insight:

Close ties continue to bind between planes.

I am very loath to let go of friends and that includes old boyfriends. Usually I keep them in my circle, with the friendship moving to a different level. I choose my friends carefully. My husband feels the same way. We have each maintained friendships that go back to our pre-marriage days.

On one of our many visits to the South Pacific to catch up with family, we received two other invitations. My husband's old girlfriend invited us to stay with her family, and an old boyfriend of mine invited our family there. As luck would have it, our friends lived close to each other although neither knew the other. Because of time constraints we decided that my husband and our son would visit his friend, Sylvie, and that our daughter and I would visit my friend, Tom.

Both families met us at the airport. Mike and I, each with a child in tow, set off in different directions. I was interested to meet Tom's wife and children. It had been 12 years since Tom and I had last seen each other, and I had heard lovely things about his wife, Krista.

The first night we caught up on all the family news and Tom couldn't wait to tell me that something I had said to him years before had proven true. At the time it had been the cause of a huge fight between us, but everything changes with time.

I first met Tom at the Magestic Ball when I was 19 and he was 24. Over the ensuing years, he spent countless hours at our home with my family, but only once did I ever visit his family home, and the strained atmosphere struck me. Ours was a touchy-feely, big boisterous family. My parents were always kissing and hugging each other and us. Tom did not have that same closeness at all. After our first visit to his home, I didn't care if we ever went back, and in the time we dated, we never did. But although he seemed to have almost no relationship with his father, he often spoke to me of his mother. She died when he was 15 and he told me that he felt cut adrift after her death. Over the years, in his mind, she became the perfect mother. He had two older brothers but they had already left home by the time his mother died, and so Tom had been a bereft and lonely teenager.

In trying to make sense of his mother's life and death, he realized that there was a period of time which was a complete mystery to him. No one knew where she lived or what she did from the time she left home at 19 until she married in her late 20's. Neither his immediate family nor her friends could or would shed any light on the matter. He told me about this mystery period when we were dating. Back then, I often spoke without thinking and I said, "Oh, that's no mystery at all. She had a baby and hid out for a time until she could provide a good home for it." Tom was furious with me. He felt I had cast aspersions on his mother's character, which was not my intent at all. We simply viewed illegitimacy in different terms. At our home, we frequently had unwed mothers helping out and that personalized the situation for me.

After his father died, Tom received a phone call from a woman named Bernadette, who claimed to be his half sister. He remembered meeting her years before when she visited their home. He hadn't paid her much attention at the time as she was much older than him. Bernadette confirmed my off the cuff remark and told Tom that she had respected his parents' wishes during their lifetimes, and had not disclosed the relationship.

We chatted long into the night, and eventually decided it was time for bed. Tom's sons volunteered their bedrooms for us; Kaitlin, my daughter, was in one and I was to have the other. Kaitlin by this time was long asleep upstairs. As I undressed and slipped into my bed, things felt wrong to me. Despite Tom and Krista's warm welcome, I had the strong sense that I should not be in this room. I tried putting my head under the covers to block everything out, but it didn't work. I was too terrified to close my eyes. There was quite definitely something in the room with me, and that something did not want me there. I fought with my feelings for an hour or two, and then slipped out of bed, crept down the darkened hallway, and climbed into bed with my daughter. There, finally, I could sleep.

The next morning I felt embarrassed. Krista and Tom's young children had gone to my room to bring me a cup of tea in bed. They found me instead in

Kaitlin's room, but now I had explanations to make, and how does one make them without giving offence?

Krista asked me if there was something wrong. I tried to put her off by saying I just needed to be near my daughter, but she pressed me and eventually I told her that, "It may sound silly, but sometimes I see ghosts." I saw Krista exchange a glance with Tom, and they both said together "mother."

Tom told me then that after they moved into their new home, they discovered they had an unexpected visitor. At first they dismissed the usual telltale signs—things moved about; a sensation of another person in the house; then one night there was no ignoring it. They awoke to someone playing the piano and Tom recognized the music and his mother's touch. Krista said to me, "She must have seen you as a threat to our family and so tried to scare you off. It's not the first time. Don't worry, I'll have a word with her and she won't bother you tonight." And she didn't.

However, it has since occurred to me that Tom may not have been the only one offended by my careless comment about his mother's missing years. Did she overhear our earlier conversation?

The Death Mask

Insight:

Entities can attach to things as well as people and places, and those invited in may prefer to stay.

Since I was a little girl, masks have always intrigued me. My fascination was prompted by an interesting conversation I overheard between my father and some other individual whose name escapes me, about extraordinary things they had seen in other cultures. My father, like many of his friends, spent a minimum of three months a year overseas. There were not too many places in the world he hadn't been, and not too many cultures he hadn't seen. As he had the curious mind of an intellectual, he was like a walking encyclopaedia.

At the time, he and his friend were talking about shrunken heads and various death masks. I can't remember where I was when this was going on but I suspect that I was sitting on the stairs out of sight of the adults. They would never deliberately have held such a conversation in front of the children, and I was very young at the time.

Sometime later, my father brought home some pottery masks, and I snaffled one right away for my room. When he discovered it proudly nailed up on my bedroom wall, he removed it and told me that such things often attract unpleasant elements and I should not have it in my room. I don't know where it eventually disappeared to, but I was not permitted to display it. And that, for me, ended all discussion about masks and other such paraphernalia for the next 30 years.

Fast forward to adulthood... My friend phoned me one day. She said she needed my opinion on something, but that I would need to come over to her house first.

I love a mystery so as soon as I could, I drove there. My friend Therese is a level-headed woman, older and more settled than me. She grew up in a northern town and married a man from another northern town. They both enjoyed fulfilling careers and raised three responsible children. Their youngest, Jodi, was in her first year of University, and working part-time. I was interested to learn what had upset Therese's very ordered life.

I arrived at her home and, as was our habit, sat down on her comfortable kitchen chair and awaited my coffee. Therese made excellent coffee and I used to love to chat with her over a cup or two. This day I was dying of curiosity.

She told me that Jodi had run terrified into their bedroom the previous night. It had given both Therese and her husband a terrible start as they had awoken from a sound sleep to bloodcurdling screams. At first, they thought that Jodi was in the throes of a nightmare but it was a strange one because she was awake and coherent, yet insistent that there were things in her room. It took a long time for them to calm her down, but cups of tea and much talking later, they finally did. She slept in another room for the remainder of the night. Therese said her husband was inclined to pass the whole episode off as just a bad dream, but she was not so sure. She called me for a second opinion.

She told me that when she went into her daughter's bedroom that morning, the light in the room was odd, and there was a strange "thick" atmosphere. She found the situation alarming.

I have known Therese for years. I am familiar with her house and her daughter's bedroom and so I asked to see the room. As we walked up the stairs, she explained to me that Jodi was developing her own style, and so her furnishings were a little unusual. Therese said her daughter had found most of her knickknacks and artefacts at second-hand stores and curio shops. I understood exactly what she was trying to tell me when we opened the door and stepped inside. I am not really sure where her collection came from but she had a variety of objets d'art which were odd, if not downright bizarre.

In particular, there were three wood carvings of small beings, each standing about a half metre high, which Jodi had placed in different corners of her room. These beings were the style and type that one sees in primitive art except for their eyes, which were almost alive. I could feel them watching me. It was eerie. It was more a curious than menacing watchfulness. These little creatures seemed to be standing alert and on guard in the room, and I felt that Therese and I had been placed under keen observation.

I knew what my impressions were and I was interested to hear Therese's. I asked her what disturbed her, and she indicated these same three carvings. I told her that I too, found them unsettling. I suggested that we bless the room. I said I didn't think there was anything bad present, but maybe we could just ask whatever entities were there to go, and maybe they would. So together, she and I blessed the room with a crucifix. We suggested out loud that there was no need for any visitors to stay.

The room felt immediately different to both of us. The atmosphere brightened and it seemed less "watchful" in there—at least we thought so, but of course we had every reason to hope this was the case.

We went back to the kitchen for another cup of coffee. Therese asked me not to mention the incident to her husband or her daughter. She did not want to incur the criticism of either. She knew her husband would think her silly, and she didn't want her daughter to view our visit to her room as an invasion of privacy, or a betrayal of confidence.

The next morning Therese called me bright and early. She told me that when her daughter arrived home from school the previous day, she went straight to her room to study. She then marched right back downstairs and said to her mother, "What have you done to my room? It feels different in there." Therese finally told her that she had blessed the room, and although initially her daughter was annoyed with her, she did become reconciled to the new atmosphere, which was much more peaceful and serene. Interestingly enough, Jodi herself displayed a calmer disposition, perhaps because she was not so sleep-deprived.

Therese, meanwhile, was intrigued. She went to the curio shop to enquire about the history of the three affected pieces. She wanted to know whether the vendor believed these items could be haunted. He showed no surprise at her question. He told her that while he would never knowingly sell a haunted piece, nonetheless, items had been returned to him that allegedly were.

Jodi's interest with other-worldly things did not stop with objets d'art. Her next foray into the unknown led her to explore Ouija boards, and she and another science-major friend of hers set up their own séance sessions in a downstairs bedroom in Therese's home. The sessions were interesting in and of themselves, but what happened afterwards left them completely leery of further explorations into the unknown. Some of the entities they casually invited in were not too inclined to leave afterwards.

Neither Jodi nor her mother was initially aware of this, and they discovered it when Jodi's friend Beth stayed over one night. When Beth was getting ready for bed, she heard heavy breathing behind her, which tickled the back of her neck. She initially thought it was Jodi being silly as she is known to be a bit of a prankster, and told her to stop fooling around. She was stunned when Jodi answered her from the bathroom further down the hall, and when she turned to look behind her, there was no one there.

That night the girls were too terrified to turn off the lights and they slept badly. The next morning they told Therese what had happened, and she was annoyed. She told Jodi that she had attracted these unpleasant entities into the house with her dangerous activities and strange purchases, and she asked her daughter to cut it out.

She then went downstairs and cleared the room with holy water² and blessings, and she has never had any trouble down there since. But the day the entity breathed is still etched in both girls' minds. They discussed it again last Christmas, ten or so years after the fact.

Around about the same time as the breathing incident, Therese found it necessary to cleanse her own bedroom. Apparently, Jodi's entities were quite comfortable in moving around her home. They did not confine themselves to the séance room.

Therese told me that she was lying in bed reading a book when she thought she felt the cat leap on the bed. She reached out to pat it… no cat! She looked under the bed, in the closet, around the room… no cat! Her bedroom door was closed, so whatever animal was in there never left. She had a nasty suspicion about what may have leapt on her bed, and she swept her room of spirits at the first opportunity.

There was one other interesting occurrence. Sometime earlier Jodi brought the dearest little Alsatian puppy home and, for a time he was the much adored family pet. Then the dog became unrecognizable. He eventually had to be put down after he lunged at Jodi's throat with fangs bared. Did the dog's slide into savagery have anything to do with the entities in the home? I do have to wonder.

My Friend's Stories

Insight:

Not believing in entities is no protection against them. Once your eyes are open to another plane, you will see more.

We were sitting around the fire with our friends one Christmas and chatting over a few glasses of wine when my friend Jenny told this story.

Jenny grew up in a remote northern town, situated at the apex of two rivers. It is noted for its wild thunderstorms and evergreen beauty. Jenny found the smallness of the town too stifling, so she moved to the city the minute she left school, but her younger sister and brother remained put. Her brother died of cancer in his early 30s, and her sister, Pat married and moved a few blocks away from her childhood home. There she and her husband, Bill settled in to raise their two daughters.

Pat and Bill bought an older home in an established area of town. Pat's mother had initially expressed reservations about their intended purchase as she believed the street to be haunted. Apparently, when she was just a child herself, a young man had committed suicide in the house next door to the one her daughter was looking at. She told Pat and Bill that over the intervening years, she had heard stories from people who had seen the entity strolling through his old neighbourhood. Pat's mother was then in her 70s, so that is 60 plus years of ghost-wandering. While her mother never personally saw the ghost, she knew many people who had, and found them credible. Unfortunately, the young man's story has been lost to time. Anyone who knew the whys and wherefores of his life and death is now long gone.

Pat and Bill were stoic individuals. They were not at all superstitious and they paid no heed to the warnings. The house was suitable and the price was affordable. That's all they knew and all they cared to know. Neither of them had ever seen a ghost, and nor did they expect to. Bill was a woodsman and Pat was a nurse. They were both down-to-earth and practical people.

But everything did not go as planned when they moved in. It was little things at first. An early indicator was that they could never persuade the family dog to join them in the recreation room. This was an animal that loved people, and loved nothing better than to be in the midst of the family, frolicking with the children, or lying peacefully at their feet. He simply would not go down the basement stairs. He refused. He would sit back on his haunches and whine and wail if they tried to drag him down. Then they noticed that children and visitors complained of cold drafts and chills. Even the fireplace could not warm them for long.

So although Pat and Bill had a beautifully finished recreation room, they rarely used it for its intended purpose. Pat ironed there, and sometimes she and Bill escaped downstairs for a bit of privacy away from the kids.

On this particular day, she was ironing and because she had the house to herself, she sang along to her old records at the top of her lungs. I have heard her sing. She doesn't have a great voice, but it isn't off key either. She told her sister that suddenly the room grew chilly, and it was more than a draft. The hair on her head prickled and she knew she was no longer alone. She thought it might be her brother visiting as he had recently died, and so she called out to him, "Guy, if that's you. Cut it out! You're scaring me!" The entity did not respond. Then the pictures on the tables were slowly and deliberately turned over. These were happy family pictures, and they were clearly offensive to someone. She ran up the stairs.

When her husband returned from work, he was matter of fact. He calmed her fears, re-set all the pictures on the tables, and pointed out that they could have fallen for any number of reasons. Heavy vehicular bus or truck traffic can cause an older home to shake. While Pat didn't really buy his explanation, it beat the alternative, so she was prepared to go along with it. She joined him downstairs later that evening.

They settled in on the couch to watch old movies together. The children were fast asleep upstairs. The fireplace was on and for a time they were cozy. Then it started again. The room chilled and the pictures were slowly turned over one by one. It was a very deliberate action. They sat transfixed in silence as an apparition cast a moving shadow on the wall. It was going upstairs…

Jenny tells me that they sold the house shortly afterwards.

But the entity was not quite finished with them. When she was packing up to leave, Pat made her way down the hallway towards her bedroom. As she crossed the centre hallway, a large light fixture above her head smashed to the ground beside her, narrowly missing her. When Bill investigated the incident later, he told his wife that there was absolutely no reason for the fixture to fall.

The entity was simply furious with their decision to leave, and his anger was such that he did not mind injuring someone to prove his point.

So who was the entity and why was he in their house? I do not believe for a moment it was Guy. I knew him. He was a kind man—a social worker. He so adored his sisters in life that I am very sure he would not torment them in death. And I am not convinced it was the ghost of the young man next door, as he did not have the reputation of being difficult. He simply walked his old neighbourhood. Perhaps they were seeing the entity that persuaded the young man to take his life in the first place.

This apparition did not like children, happy family pictures, singing, music or dogs. Whoever he was, he was nasty, and Pat and Bill elected not to share their living quarters with him.

That was the first time that Jenny's sister and brother-in-law saw a ghost but not the last. The next one targeted Bill.

Bill has not only spent most of his career in the woods, but also his childhood summers. As an only child, he appreciated being included in his friend's larger family circle, and regarded their camp as his second home.

He was also fond of his friend's mother, who treated him like another son. She was one of those strong and independent northern women whom one admires. She pulled no punches; she could do everything and do it well. The camp for many years bore a bullet hole through the porch window—a silent reminder of the time she took care of a nuisance bear that was breaking in while her family was inside. She loved that porch and spent many of her evenings out there in her rocking chair. It was where she wound down after a summer's day.

After she died, and over the course of time, Bill and his friend went their separate ways. Then, one year, Bill's work brought him close to the old camp, and out of curiosity, he took a detour to see it. It had fallen into disrepair. He told Pat that it broke his heart to see it in such a tumbledown state.

He found himself spending time at the end of his workday tidying the grounds, repairing boards and restoring the place to some of its former glory. Of course, he phoned his childhood friend to let him know what he was doing.

He worked on the place over the summer months and the camp responded. It was looking clean and cared for. One September afternoon as he stood back to admire his work, he looked up at the old veranda, and there in the clear light of day he saw the rocking chair in motion. Rock, squeak, rock… It was not moving in the wind. It was clearly occupied. He told his wife that he has never before packed his tools so quickly. He scuttled out of there as fast as he could go.

Again, what is the explanation? Who knows? It was probably his friend's mother overseeing his work but Bill couldn't be sure. When the entity came, he left, and he hasn't been back! Entities aren't his favourite thing.

That Tribal Connection

Love binds on all levels with mental, emotional and physical ties.

Our family was always close. Growing up we were one of those rare families that actually liked each other. I credit my mother for that as she was always fun to be around and created a joyful household. My father was overseas a lot, so for months at a time, all family responsibility fell to my mother and she took this on with ease.

In addition to our rather large family, there were additional unrelated children who moved in to live with us from time to time. During the years I was home, there were two extras, and as my parents never turned a child away, that number varied. Everyone was treated the same. If they lived with us, they were one of us. My father picked up the bill for all of them. He was always good about that sort of thing.

I think one of the reasons that my mother was so laid back and happy was that she never actually had to wonder where we were or what we were up to as she had the ability to hone in on us at will—kind of a distance watcher. She knew people very, very well.

When I was in my teens, it used to annoy me that she could provide a warning based on a simple introduction. I would be told: "Don't waste your time on this one. He'll be petty / a womanizer / dishonest," etc. And the annoying thing was that she was invariably right. My father said he trusted her people skills implicitly, and she certainly managed to steer him through some tricky situations in his highly competitive field. I was relieved that she approved of Mike when I brought him through the door. It would have unnerved me if she had not. And once again, she approved him on sight. There was no need for her to get to know him. It was just another case of instant verdict.

When I was about 15, I went to boarding school. Our house was under construction at the time and I was trying to study for the state exams. The combination of workers hammering and a household of active children made this impossible. I loved boarding school. For the first time in my life, I had my own secluded space and was responsible for no one but myself. It was a novel experience for me.

However, one morning I woke up with a feeling of dread. I sneaked away into a downstairs office and placed a call home. My sister answered and said mum was busy—which she would be. It was not an unexpected response but I still could not shake the feeling in the pit of my stomach. At 8:00 a.m. I met the boarding school mistress with my bags packed and told her that my mother was ill and I was returning home. I did not ask her permission, and I did not wait to receive it. I went straight home. I found my mother in the kitchen, and her complexion was ashen. That was the first time that I realized that her pain was my pain.

Our closeness remained throughout the years and despite great distances. Every family argument I had in Canada prompted a telephone call from my mother from whichever country she was living in at the time. My pain was her pain.

My grandmother eventually passed away in her 90s. By this stage, most of us had grown up and several of us were overseas. My grandmother had been manageably ill for years, and then suddenly contracted pneumonia and died. Within an hour of nana's death and before my parents could inform us, those of us who were overseas had phoned home from various points around the globe. My mother was astonished by the coincidence but I think of it as a familial bush telegraph; an unspoken form of communication of feelings. The Australian Aborigines have something similar, and I'm sure that all families do, but may not have fully developed it. In our family, distance was no obstacle.

When I was hospitalized, our family messaging activated again. At that time my parents were in different parts of the United Kingdom. They both rushed back to London, each thinking the other was in trouble, and then Mike phoned them about me.

Another night, unexpectedly, I experienced crushing chest pains and checked into emergency. The doctor could find nothing wrong with me and I was embarrassed. In talking to my sister the next day, I learned that she too had checked into the hospital with chest pains, and there was nothing wrong with her either. The coincidence struck us both as being too unusual and we phoned home. Dad was in hospital with heart problems. His pain had become our pain.

In later years I would occasionally end up with strange pains and I would know to phone home. I found that the only way to be fully private was to mentally shut down the connections. That leads me to wonder, is that what society teaches us to do?

The House by the Sea

Insight:

Ghosts mirror the same personalities they had in life. If they were helpful before, they will likely continue to be so.

For as long as I can remember my parents' homes have been haunted, everywhere, the world over. I knew that. Some of my siblings knew, and some didn't and they and my parents steadfastly denied the fact. When I was a child, and too terrified to close my eyes, my parents called me high-strung. In my younger years, my grandmother stayed in my room with me until I felt safe enough to sleep.

Our family travelled the world. My first trip was at age two, and I have travelled ever since. I met my husband on one such overseas trip, and moved with him to Canada, but my family roots were strong, and I joined them wherever they were, whenever possible.

When my children were young, my husband and I decided to take a family holiday at my parents' new home on the bay. "It's a perfect location," my mother said. "We have the sea at our doorstep."

At first view, the home was older, but had been tastefully modernized. It was a wooden structure built into the side of a mountain. It stood atop three garages, and boasted balconies, balustrades, marble patios and glorious sea and mountain views. My mother fell in love with the views, and the fact that the structure contained two self-contained units with ample room for visiting children and their families.

The renovations had taken a long time to complete. My father was a thorough man, and had consulted experts in the field. Pictures of the home now adorn placemats and calendar pages in souvenir shops. I bought some for myself the last time I was back.

That year, we had an uneventful flight, and upon arrival, my mother showed us into the bottom suite that was to be ours for the duration of our visit. It comprised two bedrooms, a living room, kitchen and bathroom, and garden doors out to a patio reminiscent of Italy, with comfortable stuffed wicker chairs and large waist height pots of flowering shrubs. Our patio was above street level so that we could look down upon life unfolding on the street and beach below us. We gratefully settled in.

Any niggling feeling of discomfort was shrugged off as I joined my parents. We are a close family and, like all my siblings, I loved being in my parents' orbit and never tired of it. My parents were highly social. They hosted the best parties, had the most interesting friends, were generous to a fault, and were great raconteurs. My mother was a very light person—one of those people whom everyone is drawn to because of their joie de vivre. My father, a more scholarly type, quite simply adored her.

As I settled the children in that first night, they were restless. Strange beds, strange house, and strange country—it didn't surprise me. And by the time they finally settled down, I found that I, too, was ready for sleep.

Mike and I shared the bedroom at the back of the house, and the children's bedroom adjoined ours and faced the street. Our room, like theirs, was set up with twin beds. I climbed into the bed positioned on the interior wall. The other bed was closer to the window. Beside it was a steel door that opened onto a private path fenced off from a public pathway that ran parallel to it, and up the mountain. Despite the fence, that room did not feel private to me. I closed the curtains but still had that creepy feeling of being watched and on display.

Mike remained upstairs with my parents while I settled the children, but I was most uncomfortable without him and although I was extremely tired, I could not relax. I remember getting up a couple of times to check the outside doors. There were three to our flat—one in our bedroom, the front door, and the patio door. It was my parents' habit to leave all doors open and unlocked, and usually that does not bother me, but this night it did. I felt the need to close and lock all doors.

I had just drifted off to sleep when I was rudely awoken. A face thrust itself close to mine and said, "Get out." It was not pretty. I sat up to see an old woman backing away from me. She looked like a crone—old, wrinkled and angry. "Get out," she repeated.

I leapt out of bed, ran into the children's room and pulled them out of bed. Somehow, I pushed and cajoled both sleepy children up the stairs and burst into the living room with both of them in tow. My mother was playing patience, and my husband and father had a crib game going. "What on earth are you doing and why aren't the children in bed?" my mother asked. "There's a ghost," I said.

My parents looked at me in disbelief. "You can't be serious. Go back to bed." "I am serious and I can't go back there and neither can the kids," I said. Mike just shook his head at me.

When it became clear that I was not returning to our room, my mother settled us into the spare bedroom upstairs, and there the children and I slept three to a bed. My husband didn't believe in ghosts in those years and he refused to give up the comfort of the guest suite, so he remained downstairs for the night.

Things were a bit awkward the next morning. I was annoyed with Mike and he was dismissive of me. The kids were ratty at being crowded into one bed. I was embarrassed at creating a scene, but I was also fearful of going back to sleep in that room. However, after spending a lovely day relaxing in the sunshine, the question again arose about our sleeping arrangements for the night. The children elected to sleep in their own room and Mike was quite clear that he would remain in our room, and that I could go where I liked. I said I would try to stay with him. I had hoped that we would all remain together.

As we settled into our rooms that second night, I had just drifted off to sleep when, again, that hideous old hag woke me and said, "Get out!" I was terrified. Mike had seen and heard nothing and thought me mad. I wasn't prepared to argue with him. I took the kids and left.

We didn't have our best holiday that year. Our sleeping arrangements were the elephant in the room that no one talked about. My parents never mentioned that I was upstairs with the children, and that my husband was downstairs alone. The children never asked to return to their room, and after a time we all got used to our crowded bedtime existence.

Towards the end of our holiday, my mother informed me that she would be selling the house. She told me that they had bought it so that the family would always have a place to stay. I was deeply embarrassed. I begged her not to sell on my account. I knew my parents loved this home and, besides, I did not want to ruin it for my brothers and sisters who would appreciate the use of the self-contained flat. It was then that my mother told me that I was the third of her children to complain. All of us had described the same apparition. I asked her why she had not said something sooner. She shrugged and said she didn't believe in ghosts and that we were all suggestible. We are closer than most families so that explanation was possible. She explained that if three of us were uncomfortable, then no one would want to stay, and that would defeat the purpose of having two houses in one. It would be better to start over somewhere else.

Naturally, I wanted to know who else had seen the old woman, but my mother was not forthcoming. She did not want to get into it. She did tell me that Mark and Debra had both complained of a ghost. Later I learned that the apparition had woken my brother from sleep, just as she had me, and that both Debra and her fiancé had been made well aware of its presence while they were overseeing the renovations. Debra said that although she could never make out the entity's face, she was quite familiar with its confrontational vibration.

Eventually, we returned to Canada and my father sold the home. He received a good price for it and my mother and he were delighted with their new purchase in the foothills over the other side of the bay. For the next number of months we received updates on renovations to their new home, and I felt that all was forgiven.

Then one day we received another type of call from my mother.

The new owner of the old house had called, requesting copies of the engineering report. He had installed a home office, with office suites downstairs, and his home above. He told my mother that the flooring in his office (where my bed used to be) had given way and everything had fallen through to the garage level below. Apparently, the support beams had eroded and the engineers had missed the structural weakness. He told mum that he had been lucky to escape injury—and so was I. The old hag had actually tried to protect us.

The Home on the Coast Road

Caution—This story may upset and frighten some readers.

Looking back, I suppose there were many clues, but sometimes you just don't see the forest for the trees. I was dead smack in the middle of trouble before I realized the danger. But let me go back to the beginning.

It was on one of my yearly family get-togethers that things went awry. When I stepped off the airplane in Australia, I had no idea that anything was afoot.

Money was tight for us that year, so I had flown back alone leaving the children with my husband in Canada. As usual, I couldn't wait to see my sisters and as the plane taxied down the runway, I felt the fatigue slip from my shoulders and excitement start to build.

My sister, Rosie was meeting me at the airport and Janna was to join us soon afterwards. The minute I was through customs and immigration, I rushed into Rosie's arms and in no time, we were making our way over the bridge to her new home. This was Rosie and Jack's first home which, she was delighted to tell me, was located a block from the sea.

Her excitement was contagious, and as we drove onto her wide tree-lined street, I was impressed by the look of her solid all-wood home complete with brick path, artistically surrounded by established trees and garden in bloom. It was a most presentable vintage home.

I remember shivering as I entered the house through the beautiful stained glass door. In spite of the heat of the day, the corridor was cold. My first impressions of the place were probably impaired as Rosie was chattering on happily beside me pointing out all the features that they loved. There was a functioning fireplace in every room.

The home was a turn of the century standard bungalow, designed somewhat like an old-fashioned railway carriage. All rooms were positioned one behind the other off the main corridor, which led to a large eat-in kitchen and finally a new family room at the back of the house. The corridor appeared long, drab and unlit. In contrast, the rooms opening off it were airy and pleasant with 4-metre high ceilings and deep windows with wide and comfortable sit-on sills.

As I oo'ed and ah'ed my way through the house, Rosie led me through the kitchen to her pride and joy—the new addition. This was a large 5x6 metre family room with floor to ceiling windows on three sides, all of which looked out onto a delightful walled-in garden in full riotous colour.

I had heard all about this new addition. My mother told me that neither she nor my father could stand the smelly old porch that had previously stood there. They told Jack it would have to go. Now, in its place, stood an impressive room with an enchanting garden view. Rosie informed me that the old porch wasn't that bad, but that the new addition was a definite improvement.

She returned to the kitchen and put on the kettle for tea. I didn't get around to unpacking. Instead, I settled in on the couch and relaxed until my sister, Janna joined us with all nephews in tow.

I remember so clearly the bliss I felt in the company of my sisters. I settled down on the couch, with a blanket over my knees, and a cup of tea in my hand. The children played happily on the floor beside me—or at least two of them did. The oldest of the three appeared to become more and more agitated and upset, and eventually he was simply out of control. My sister decided to send him home for a nap and called his father to pick him up. As he left, Janna noted that for some reason "he just goes nuts in this place." She assured me that he didn't usually behave that way.

I put it all down to "kids will be kids" and the excitement of too many aunts and too much going on. I never gave it another thought, until later.

We caught up on family news—there was lots—and then Janna commented that a school friend had been arrested for abuse. I was surprised because this individual had been one of the more popular boys, and the charge seemed out of character with the person we once knew.

As the coolness of night crept into the room, I shuddered and snuggled deeper into the blanket trying to warm myself. I distinctly remember that the thought flashed across my mind that perhaps we should find a happier topic of conversation.

I glanced at my sister Rosie and was startled by her appearance. In the fading evening light, her features had coarsened and I thought, "What a pity. She's become quite masculine." I was intrigued by her coarseness. Her brows seemed darker and more angular. Her cheekbones were chiselled. Her big blue eyes had deepened, and held a different expression. It was like looking at someone else entirely. But as I watched her, the coarseness faded and once again, I was looking at my sister's soft and pretty face. I realized that I had been up for over 40 hours and decided that it was time to call it a night.

I folded up the blanket, and slipped my shoes back on my feet, but before I could leave for the bedroom assigned to me, Rosie pointed towards me, saying, "I see your aura." By reflex, I turned to look behind me. It was quite clearly not my aura—it could not be—but I did see a spectre walking outside the window. It walked slowly and deliberately the length of the new addition, turned the corner, and faded from view. I recognized that this was a young, masculine presence. I spun back to face Rosie and said, "Who was that?" She avoided my gaze, and said, "Oh, that's just headlights hitting the washing on the line." I knew that simply was not the case. Headlights do not penetrate the length of a house, pass through two rooms, enter a walled in garden, and then turn corners. I argued with her, but she was evasive and remote, and continued to deny that she had seen anything. Janna looked from one to the other of us in confusion. From her vantage point, she had seen nothing out of the ordinary and it must have seemed to her to be much ado about nothing.

By now I was agitated. I knew full well that I had seen a ghost, so had my sister, and that she was lying about it. I couldn't understand her. I also now understood that my sister's face had actually morphed in front of me and I didn't know what that meant. I was spooked and I wanted out. I looked at Rosie and said, "You can choose to live this way but I won't." I got up and invited myself to Janna's home for the night.

This was awkward. Janna didn't have a spare bedroom, but I didn't care. I was adamant that I would not stay a moment longer in this house. Rosie's face was stricken and I knew she was hurt.

As we walked down the central hallway, I felt a shudder pass through me, and I looked back over my shoulder to see three entities following me. I hoped they would stay behind, but, no, they followed me out into the street. I felt the hair rise on my head. I started to run but they kept up with me. As I ran faster and faster with Janna puffing alongside me, she asked me what was going on. I told her, "We're been followed."

I don't know what possessed me to think I could outrun ghosts. You can't. All I can say is that I was terrified, and any action on my part seemed preferable to standing still. As we ran the laneway shortcuts, down her driveway and up to Janna's front door, I distinctly heard a voice say, "You're safe now." I didn't know where the voice came from. It was a reassuring and firm voice—I knew it didn't belong to the entities chasing me—and on one level I trusted it, although another part of me was screaming that now I was hearing voices! And I didn't know what was happening all around me.

Janna and I didn't talk much that night. I was too shocked and she had gone unusually quiet. She made up a bed for me on the floor and urged me to rest. I found that I could not until I had positioned my head into the corner of the room, so I could see whatever might approach me. It was light outside before I finally drifted off, and when I did, I slept fitfully and guiltily.

When I awoke later that morning, I felt compelled to go outside to the place where I heard the voice, and there at the corner of the house was a tile with a saint's picture. I don't know which saint, but occasionally ethnic builders will dedicate their work, and Jana's home reflected this religious symbol.

Rosie's place had no protection. I was feeling very guilty that I had fled and left my sister and her family with such dreadful spirits. I told Janna that I had to go back and talk to Rosie. Janna looked at me steadily and said, "There's something I have to tell you first. Sit down." She drew up a chair alongside me. "There's something you don't know about that house; Rosie doesn't know it either. Years ago someone committed suicide there. Jack didn't find out until well after he had bought the place and a neighbour told him. He didn't think it would be a problem because it happened so long ago—a generation or so back." I asked what had happened. She said she thought the young man hung himself.

I felt no surprise. It was an "ah-ha" moment. I recognized the truth. He was the entity that had strolled behind me. That was why the hall was murky, but who were the other two? I said to Janna, "Well, that explains one spirit but what about the rest?" She shrugged. Ghosts are not her thing.

My mind was racing. What could we do? Whatever it was, it would have to start with Rosie. Together we made our way back there. This time I felt stronger and ready.

Rosie opened the door warily but did not want to hear me out. She preferred to tell me that I was jet-lagged and mistaken. I persisted. "You have children here. You're the mum and you have to protect them. You can't raise them in a place like this." She looked shattered but resolved. "You're wrong. There's nothing wrong here." I stood my ground.

Finally, she broke down. She admitted she knew about the ghost and that it appeared in every mirror she looked into. She was scared to let her children out of her sight and she worried about losing her mind. I reassured her that she was not, and that I was not. She said that regardless of what we thought, her husband would never believe her. I said that he would have to. There were two of us now, not just one, who had seen it.

Janna was quiet during our heated exchange. She invited us both to sit down and discuss the matter in a more civilized fashion. I have a tendency to be authoritative and bossy. Janna is quieter, and more reasoned. She reminded Rosie of the series of incidents that had occurred at the house—people being locked in bathrooms; children being poisoned and scalded. She spoke of lights that flickered during dinner parties, and of contractors who panicked for no reason. Janna listed these items off. She did not go into detail—she just listed them, calmly and endlessly. I asked Rosie, "How could you ignore this? How could Jack ignore it?"

Janna left. She had said all she was prepared to say, and had things to do. I stayed put at Rosie's and she and I talked more. After our argument, she was pale and drawn. Rosie is a peace-loving person and discord makes her ill. Nonetheless I said to her, "You have to deal with this, you know. Someone is going to get hurt. This is not a benign haunting."

Rosie slumped down into a chair and said, "So you really do see it; it's not just me? You do know it's here? You're not just saying that?" I confirmed that I absolutely knew it was there. And, yes, I had seen it. In fact it had chased me to Janna's place—even worse, three entities had. She nodded; she knew. She said, "I thought I was going mad." I said, "What's going on?" She started to talk.

"It started soon after we bought the place. When we looked at the home, it was beautiful. The sun was shining, the rooms were bright, the yard was large, and we could not believe our luck at the price. When we moved in, however, I became aware of things being not quite right. First, there was this awful smell in the bathroom. We had to call in the plumber and he told us that our plumbing was only half done. It was as if the original plumber had left mid-contract. The sewerage pipes were to code, but other piping was incomplete, and although we liked our plumber to begin with, he became more and more agitated and bad tempered as time went on. The bathroom door kept slamming shut on him and locking him in. At first I thought it was a combination of an old rickety lock, a drafty home, and a very cross man. Then mum and dad came over and said the porch smelled and it didn't. Dad insisted we rip it down, which we couldn't really afford to do. And when the contractor came to build the addition, he became more and more impossible. He fell off his ladder and insisted that someone pushed him, and that someone had given him an electric shock. None of it made sense; he wasn't even working with electricity at the time. He demanded to know what was going on and we couldn't tell him. And after he left, the ladder, which was hung up, flew off the wall and hit the baby, and we had to take him to emergency. His little foot was cut and all black and blue. If it had landed on his head, it could have killed him."

I was appalled but I did not interrupt. Rosie had finally started to talk and I let her go.

"There were mists that would enter the house even when it was sunny outside... Grey, heavy, thick mists, but they were electrical somehow, and they would shroud me, and I couldn't think. My head felt like it would explode. And I was terrified for the children and so I would just hold them—sit on the couch and hold them—and pray that it would leave, and it would, but I was scared. And the worst day was the day of the baptism. There were these awful blowflies that kept swarming around me and buzzing my head; big black flies. And then when I was trying to prepare the readings for the baby's baptism, the Bible wouldn't stay put. All the loose-leaf stuff flew out of it and kept flying around the room, and the pages kept turning and turning. And there was this strange wind inside and none at all outside. It was all so difficult and scary."

I was speechless. This was far worse than anything I could have imagined. She continued. "There was no place safe for me to go. The house was infested. There were these horrible obscene little creatures that laughed and leered and scratched themselves. I didn't even know if I was me any more. I kept seeing a man in the mirror instead of me." I nodded. This was the morphing I had seen. "And at night his ghost-mother would wake me, 'Are you all right, dear? Do you like it here? It's a nice home isn't it?' She wouldn't understand that I didn't want to see her or talk to her."

I told Rosie that it was time to get help; that she had to get rid of these things—especially the evil one. The minute the words were out of my mouth I received a strong electric jolt. The source was not a household circuit. I have never been hit with a cattle prod but I'm sure it feels similar. The thing attacked me. And so started a reign of terror for me every time I visited... If I entered a room, doors slammed and locked around me. I found myself either locked in rooms or locked out of rooms. If I leaned over to clean a bathtub, cold water rained on my head. I was lucky as hot water poured onto my sister, and onto her child. I was aware of leering eyes and lurking entities—that creepy crawly feeling that someone was watching. The bathroom was really affected. I always made sure that someone stood outside the door so I could get out of there. Like the plumber, I found myself locked in. Then there were horrible little creatures on the wardrobe in Rosie's bedroom—I tried not to look at them or acknowledge their existence but out of the corner of my eye, I saw them jump up and down trying to catch my attention.

I recalled some things my mother had told me. She said that my sister had peculiar neighbours; that she felt watched and had the feeling that people were peering in the windows. Well, she was right, but it wasn't the neighbours! She also told me that Rosie's home was old and smelly. It might have been old but it wasn't smelly. I later learned that my mother had picked up the psychic smell of evil. I wasn't attuned to that and neither were my sisters.

Acknowledging a haunting is one thing. Getting rid of spirits is easier said than done. I tried to visit with Rosie as much as I could over the next few days. At one point she handed me the baby and walked over to fold the washing. As I looked down into his beautiful eyes, another more sinister face glided over his baby features, leered up at me, then left. I felt sickened. Nothing was safe from this thing, not even a child. I held the baby tight. I could not tell his mother what I had seen. She had been through enough.

I didn't know about morphing. It was just a word to me. I was terrified for Rosie and her children. My mind was spinning… who could we call to help?

We waited for Jack to come home. Rosie tried to tell him about the situation but he remained unconvinced, and then became annoyed. He ridiculed our story and he was furious with me. He saw me as the instigator and told me over and over that I was stupid or mad, or both. I finally lost my cool and told him that he was ignorant. I challenged him to research his own religion, which is rife with such stories. He slammed out of the room and into his bedroom, and I left the house and made plans without him.

Janna and I sat up late into the night working out how best to deal with the situation. I believed that, at the very least, we needed to get the house blessed. I only knew one priest in the whole of Australia but had lost touch with him many years before. I just didn't know how to go about finding him. Janna then surprised me. "I have his address," she coolly informed me. "He wrote to me six months ago and told me I may need to get in touch some day." I asked why. She didn't know. They had never been close.

Janna found the number and the next morning I called him on the phone from Rosie's house and invited him over to bless her home. He was instantly alert. "Bless?" he enquired. "Well, whatever you want to call it," I said. "There are children here and I think the house needs some attention." "Why?" he asked. I told him I didn't really know; I just knew we needed him. I don't know why I was so guarded. All I know is that it didn't feel safe to say some things out loud. He told me that the invitation would have to come from Rosie. By this time Rosie was in her bedroom, and I called out to her to take the phone. The hall door slammed shut between us. I tried but I could not open it. She could not open it. She was trapped on her side with me on the other. I called through the door, "Fr. John wants an invitation to dinner." She yelled back, "Invite him." I did, and the door unlocked.

Fr. John must have heard our exchange and the fuss about the door, and he probably read between the lines but we did not discuss it. "I'll be there at 5:00 o'clock," he said. He then told me he was leaving for New Zealand the following morning, and that I had been lucky to catch him in. He doesn't know the half of it.

That was at 10:00 that morning. At 1:00 there was a knock on the door, Rosie answered, and an old woman came in. Rosie defiantly stated that the woman was a psychic. I was alarmed. "You don't want to give these things a voice," I argued, but she informed me that, yes, she did. She wanted to know what was in her home and what they wanted.

As I looked into this woman's eyes, I calmed down. My instinct told me that she was a good soul and my panic receded. She walked the length of the house. She pointed out how the home used to look, and referred to the hanging. "But this was not the only death here," she said. "There was an earlier one, a murder. I sense a really bad entity that drove the young man to suicide; and a female spirit, a mother. She's kind and I think she's related to the young man. She's here trying to protect you and your children. There is also something out in the garden."

As she pointed out the features of the earlier homestead, I recognized the truth of her statements. In my mind's eye, I could see the home as she described it then. She told us about a carriageway alongside the house. She showed us where the hanging took place, which was actually in the old blocked-in doorway to the new addition where the smelly porch once stood. The murder, a shooting, happened in the bathroom, which was once a pantry. She said, "You will not be able to rid this house. Some places are just too evil and too haunted. The evil in this case extends beyond the confines of this home and takes in a much larger area."

Rosie seemed to understand that. "The woman next door has disappeared and no one knows where she is. The house over the road burst into flames one night. There was a murder in the house behind us and we were told that there's a carriage buried in our garden…" I was flabbergasted by her information.

The psychic, who was English, told us she had seen this sort of thing before. She told us about another home that was similarly haunted in England. It was built on an old gibbet site and although it was a brand new home, no one could live in it. In desperation, the builder had offered it free to anyone who would stay there. No one could, although many tried.

She explained that sometimes these hauntings are attached to the site, and sometimes to a person. She felt that the entities in Rosie's house were attached to the site and that one was evil, one was unhappy, and a third was trying to mitigate the damage caused by the other two. She said there could still be other lesser entity-personalities. She felt that the evil one would not be inclined to leave, while the others might be persuaded.

At 4:30 p.m. Jack arrived. He was still angry and not at all pleased to see me. I don't think he knew about the psychic. Rosie was not forthcoming, and I certainly wasn't about to tell him.

At 5:00 p.m. Fr. John arrived. Rosie greeted him at the front door and led him through to the kitchen where he joined the rest of us. Once there, he looked directly at Rosie. "You are not imagining this," he reassured her. "I met an entity in the hallway and see what you're seeing." Up to this point we had told him nothing. He asked us what had happened in the home, what we had been doing when the entity appeared, and what we saw.

Rosie started to tell him about the incidents and then I mentioned the morphing. I had not told Rosie about this before. Father asked me what the face looked like. I told him a masculine presence, a horsier-faced version of Rosie, blonde but with more definite colouring. Rosie nodded in recognition, and Father said that he had met him.

He then told us, "These things cannot exist around happiness. They rush in at any momentary discord or sadness and try to make things worse." He instructed us to go into the next room and think only happy thoughts. He said, "Leave me with the house."

Jack was stupefied. It was one thing for his wife and sister-in-law to make wild claims and another for a Catholic priest of some standing to agree with them.

Fr. John did bless the house that night. We were not invited to attend the cleansing ceremony as he preferred to deal with the house on his own. He then blessed us.

Months later Jack told me that the temperature in the affected rooms became markedly warmer. He said the new addition had always been cold but since the cleansing, it had warmed up by a couple of degrees. And, for a time, doors stopped slamming and faces stopped morphing. It seemed that everything was better... but only for a time.

Then one day Rosie awoke to the sound of a carriage travelling through her home. She could hear the wooden wheels rumbling over cobblestones. She tried ignoring the sound. She put a pillow over her head. Nothing worked. She couldn't ignore it and it wouldn't stop. It seemed that the whole place was overrun with carriages.

There was a knock at the door, and the retired police detective from next door came in. "What on earth's going on?" he asked. "The noise woke us up." Rosie looked stricken. She was white and obviously in shock. He glimpsed someone running through the house and took off in pursuit. As he reached out to apprehend the man, his hand passed through. "Now you understand," she said. "The ghost has returned."

The psychic and Fr. John agreed on one thing. Such apparitions are not comfortable in happy spaces. The trouble is, how do entities define "happy"? In life, babies cry, and kids fall over. We listen to the news, sad music and cry over books and movies. Conversely, we love; enjoy our families and friends; party, play and laugh. We experience a wide emotional range. We have emotional depth. Apparitions such as these do not. They exist in a murky grey world with one emotion—negativity. Janna's sorry tale about a criminal act gave the apparition a backdrop of horror that was comfortable for it. Yet, we were all happy that day. We experienced momentary sadness about someone we once knew, but it was a fleeting emotion. We were merely catching up on news—some good and some not so good. Had we engaged in more uplifting conversation, perhaps I would never have seen the entity. In retrospect, it was a good thing I did, because I was able to verify what Rosie was dealing with.

Why the entity chose to return after the cleansing, I have no idea. Perhaps, as the psychic suggested, it is so attached to the area, that it will never leave.

Today Rosie and her husband are happily married, and their children have grown into fine young men. This was a real test of their love as it involved a clash of fundamental beliefs. This situation could happen to any one of us. No one is perfectly happy in life. Most of us will have melancholy moments or unguarded speech from time to time. Much as we would like it, we do not live our lives in a state of bliss.

In that particular house, some emotions and conversations were dangerous but then so were a lot of things. The entity did not like children, family, friends, fun, or laughter. He didn't appreciate the home being altered. More than one person was hurt; more than one dinner party was sabotaged, and more than one construction person was interfered with. This entity was a bully who existed at the worst end of the entity spectrum.

Fr. John felt that the evil entity had a mission to cause unhappiness all around it. It probably drove the young man to suicide.

Rosie has since told me that she regards her survival as a miracle. She said that before I felt the need to take a holiday I could ill afford and visit her in Australia, that she had walked the beaches, and in her words, she stormed the heavens for help; she simply couldn't take it any more. She told me that on one occasion she screamed out loud and shocked some poor man who was walking on the beach at the same time, but that she no longer cared. She was beyond embarrassment. She was at her wit's end.

She told me that the entity had become stronger and stronger and bolder and bolder. It was one thing to be terrified in your home, but she couldn't get away from it. It followed her outside. It followed her into her car and wrestled for control of the wheel. If it couldn't destroy her mentally, then it would do it physically. I knew it was capable of anything. It had also physically attacked me, the builder, and the baby.

Soon after that incident, Rosie and Jack sold the house and have never been back. She tells me that the house is put back on the market every 18 months or so. No one is comfortable there for long.

From time to time Rosie still hears gossip from the old neighbourhood. The stories go on and on and by and large they are not happy tales. Houses the length of the street have been affected to varying degrees: some with spectres, and others with smells which engineers can't trace. The evil entity appears to despise children. Rosie's neighbour tracked incidents of foul odour and found that these always coincided with visits from children or grandchildren.

By contrast, Rosie's new house is peaceful and happy. It even has stone angels in the garden, which is a good thing.

Many years after the fact I asked Rosie for more detail about what happened to her back on the Coast Road but she was reluctant to go into it. She said talking about it might give the entity an invitation to come back and she couldn't live through that twice. I completely understood.

I also tried to verify some information with Betty, a former neighbour of Rosie's, whose home was also affected. Betty is now a woman in her 80's, but she said to me, "You must understand. I live here by myself. I just don't want to talk about these things." She did mention one curious fact, though. When she was in her 20s, she moved into the home next to Rosie's. She said that the two properties to the left of hers were once owned by the same family and at one time had been a double lot. The young man who committed suicide lived in the far left property with his wife and two children; and his parents and sister lived in the home right next door to Betty, which is the property that Rosie eventually bought. When his wife left him, the young man hanged himself in his parents' home and was later discovered by his sister. She was an old woman by the time Betty moved in, but despite the disparity in their ages, they became good friends. Although the old woman often talked about her brother's suicide, she never mentioned a murder in the home. Betty felt certain that she would have heard about it if there had been one... or if one had ever been discovered. As the young man's sister is the one who raised his two children, I can't help but wonder where his wife disappeared to. Was the psychic right about the murder or mistaken? We will never know for sure.

I have tried to look up the history of this place myself but have not been successful. I know that there were originally five cottages on this street, but what existed before remains a mystery.

In later discussions with clergy I have learned that this haunting had most of the hallmarks of evil. There is verification for these happenings, and no way that anyone imagined them, or that it was simply a family hysteria thing. Rosie and I saw it, as did the psychic, the police officer and Fr. John. The contractor, the baby and I were attacked by it. Rosie heard it, the police officer ran through it, and mum and dad smelled it. Additionally, many others were locked in by it. It made itself very well known through four of the five ordinary senses, with a sixth sense confirmation. This was real, and it was evil. And Rosie's house was not the only home affected by it. I don't know the details of the other hauntings, but I am aware that another neighbour phoned Betty while I was there to complain about a haunting in her home, and even today, decades later, I can feel the strange atmosphere the length of that street.

Australia has had a brutal history. Stories abound of whipping posts and hangings and tales of man's cruelty to man. Some areas just become so imbued with horror that the imprint of evil is forever there. Whatever happened on that hillside must have been major.

I am still impressed at the synchronicity of events that allowed us to assist Rosie. Despite the fact that money was tight, I extended my visit to New Zealand to include a side trip to Australia. Once there, I was able to verify the haunting.

Unexpectedly, Fr. John left his address with Janna. Why? What would have prompted him to contact my sister? When I phoned him, I caught him just before he left the country. Talk about luck—or was it? My sister believes that Heaven heard her cry and sent her help. I'm inclined to believe it.

The Aftermath

Insight:

Ghosts range from capricious to downright evil.

Caution—This story may upset and frighten some readers.

After my visit to the "Home on the Coast Road" and the horrible haunting in Australia, I flew over to New Zealand to spend time with my parents before returning to Canada.

My parents greeted me with some apprehension. By this time they had heard all about the stories of the haunting at Rosie's house and, as it was beyond anything that any of us had ever been exposed to, they were not sure how to react.

I have two brothers who are lawyers. My brother Rick felt that I was playing a dangerous game by repeating such a horrendous tale. His fear was that my brother-in-law would have legal grounds to take his children and seek full custody on the basis that his wife and her family were clearly mad. He had a point. That is how it could be perceived. I knew that; Rosie knew that. That was the reason she had denied the haunting in the first place.

My brother, Sam, took a different approach. He wanted to know what other psychic experiences Rosie and I'd had over the years, when they started, and how they could be verified. His attitude was more like: "anything's possible, I suppose." It was not a ringing endorsement, but not a dismissal either.

My parents were uneasy as to how the incident would play out. No one was sure whether Rosie's marriage could survive the trauma, even Rosie. So, on the one hand, my parents had my version with all its unbelievable elements, and on the other, sage legal advice from Rick. It was a fraught time for all of us.

While my mother didn't actually come right out and say that she disbelieved the situation, she greeted me with, "Oh, you must be tired. You'll get a good rest at our place." The ambiguity of her greeting upset me because I felt her message was that I must be jetlagged and therefore not quite myself.

You might wonder why that matters. Well, in a close family, it does. None of us enjoyed being out of sync with our parents or siblings and this situation had the potential of blowing the whole family apart. Sometimes I felt it was Rosie and me against the world because although Janna had supported us throughout the incident and strategized with me, she had only circumstantial evidence of the haunting. She had never seen the ghosts. Because of the strong connection between Rosie and me, others might view the event as hysteria.

So there we have it, another elephant in the kitchen. As they were always the consummate hosts, my parents in typical fashion shelved the topic, made me welcome, and we didn't discuss it further.

My first week or so at my parents' home was uneventful. My mother and I went for walks, shopping trips, drank endless cups of tea, and relaxed. I slept in my usual bedroom at one end of the house, and my parents slept in their room at the other end, several rooms away from me.

My room was quiet and lovely. It looked out to the east and I always woke to the most beautiful sunrises. There was a calm ambiance, and gentle artwork of rural scenes on the walls. That is why it was a surprise to me to be rudely awoken one night and find myself being hauled out of bed by my feet. I usually sleep on my side in a tuck position, knees to chest. My legs were pulled straight, and I was literally dragged down to the end of the bed and I couldn't seem to kick myself free.

The next thing I knew my mother was at my side, rosary in hand, and she thrust it at me and said, "Wear this!" I did. The room calmed down. My mother went back to her bed and eventually I went back to sleep.

We never talked about the incident in the morning, but by some sort of mutual agreement we headed into town to a jewellery store and mum and I selected a pretty cross and chain, which I wore for many, many years.

I know that I did not yell out that night. Everything happened too fast. What I don't understand is how my mother knew I was in trouble the minute it happened, and knew precisely what to do about it. She just arrived, remedy in hand, and the situation resolved itself. Whether or not she ever discussed it with my father, I have no idea. She certainly didn't discuss it with me. It was one of those, "If we don't acknowledge it, it didn't happen" situations.

I was fairly sure that this was the malevolent entity from Rosie's house that had tracked me down, and that confused me. Up to this point, I believed that the ghost was attached to Rosie's neighbourhood, and I was floored that it had followed me to another country. I really didn't want to think about it as it might mean that the thing had actually attached itself to me.

Sometime later, after I returned to Canada, I told Janna about my fears one night on the phone, but she reassured me. She told me that I was not the only one that the thing had come after, and she told me this story.

Approximately one week after I flew to New Zealand, Janna and her husband were out on their yacht for a day's sailing. It was a substantial yacht and it was their habit to take a leisurely sail around the harbour and then pull into a little marina restaurant for brunch. Prior to leaving their slip that morning, her husband performed his ritual walk-about to ensure that the yacht was sea-worthy, and that they had all their safety equipment on board. It was his standard operating procedure.

Janna told me it was a comfortable boating day—sunny and warm with a moderate breeze and calmer seas. She is not the best sailor, so is always grateful for a tranquil passage around the harbour. At times it can be unbelievably rough. She remembers sunning herself on the deck and her son, who was about five, spent the morning beside her with his sketchpad and crayons. Janna told me that that day he was fixated on crosses. Earlier that morning, he had tried to construct one out of two pieces of wood and when she asked him what he was doing, and why, he said something to the effect that crosses keep you safe. She found his comment odd.

Anyway, the family pulled into their favourite marina around 11:00 a.m., and because it was such a gorgeous day, they elected to sit outside at a dockside table. Their yacht was moored close by in full view. They enjoyed a pleasant and relaxed meal, and then crossed the wharf. It was then that Vince noticed that the steel railing around their boat deck was completely smashed in. It had not been that way when they left for brunch and their yacht had been right in front of them the whole time. They knew that nothing had even come close to hitting it; and besides it would have to have been a significant crash to cause that sort of damage. Even stranger, there was no impact visible on the hull. So what could be strong enough to cave in a steel railing, and yet not impact the rest of the yacht? They were flummoxed, and later, the boat repair people couldn't shed any light on the matter either. There was no apparent structural weakness and it just made no sense.

It was not until later that Janna wondered whether the entity got even with her for helping to rid it from Rosie's house. She wondered too, if her son's crosses that day saved them from an on-board encounter. I think that's entirely possible, given what happened to me, and the fact that my mother cleared it from my room with rosary beads.

Thankfully, these two incidents closed the chapter on this entity for us.

Mel's Ghost

Insight:

Sometimes ghosts have such strong attachments to their homes and surroundings, that they become shortsighted and don't see the light.

Over the years, I caused my parents lots of consternation with my claims of weird sightings and unusual happenings. First there was my childhood insistence about screams in the closet, then the incident at their "House by the Sea" and finally the Australian affair. My stories were getting pretty fantastic. Yet there appeared to be confirmation of sorts in each instance. My father was uncertain what to believe and decided to ask around. That was unusual for him. Our family was very private. What happened in the family stayed in the family and a family member would never, ever put another family member at risk of ridicule. So it surprised me when he raised the topic of psychic phenomena with a friend. I guess his curiosity got the better of him.

Our friend was a few years older than me, but we knew each other for most of our lives. Our parents were friends and, as a child, I was routinely sent off to her parents' farm in the Hawke's Bay to see how the other half lived. Similarly, when she was a teenager at boarding school, she would spend some of her days off at our home.

At this time she was working as a nursing sister. In these years, New Zealand based its nursing structure on the English format. The hierarchy went from student nurse, to nurse, staff nurse, sister, with the head nurse being the matron. Melanie was a nursing sister, or 2-IC, in the hospital. She had a speciality in Nephrology. In this role she oversaw things for my father when he went into kidney failure, and they had become close.

In later years she was promoted to the position of District Manager for a large territory in New Zealand. My father respected her judgement and loved her down to earth common sense.

Dad tried the direct approach. "So, tell me, Mel, have you ever seen a ghost or is it just a load of malarkey, do you think?" She surprised him with her response. "Actually, Tom, I've had to deal with one myself."

My ears perked up, and dad sat up a little straighter in his chair. "Tell me more," he said. Mel settled in with her cup of tea in one hand and scone in the other, to tell us her story. I sat quietly in my chair. Vindication!

She reminded us that shortly after her divorce she moved up country with her two small children and bought a residence on the outskirts of town. At the time, she had absolutely no idea that the previous owner, a woman, had died in the place. She told us that she was exhausted from her divorce and subsequent move, but finally it was over, and she had a place to call her own.

That first night she awoke to the sounds of cupboard doors slamming in the kitchen. She got up to close them and found herself standing in frigid cold temperatures. It didn't make any sense to her. She didn't know where the cold draft was coming from. The nightly slamming and freezing went on for weeks and a nasty suspicion was forming in the back of her mind.

Finally, she had enough. She talked to a psychic friend who told her that the previous owner had not wanted to leave her home and world, and so her spirit kept returning to the familiar. Mel was advised to sprinkle holy water around the outside corners of her home and inside the kitchen cupboards, which she did. It was further suggested that she bless the spirit of the previous owner. She was to address the ghost directly and tell her that it was all right for her to move on to the spirit world because Mel would love her home and care for it as she had once done.

Mel said she felt ridiculous but she did it anyway, and it worked. The cupboards stopped banging and the house never felt so bone-shatteringly cold again. Dad asked her if she ever actually saw the ghost. She said she had not, but she had absolutely no doubt there was one. And I thought, "So there!"

The Tudor Brick House

Insight:

Some people can raise the vibration of any place and others are incapable of doing so. It can be overwhelming for those who see entities but cannot clear them.

My parents' last home was two blocks from each of their parental homes. They returned to their old neighbourhood to die. It was a beautiful Tudor style three-bedroom brick home, with wrought iron gates and an impressive rose garden. At one point a movie producer approached my parents to shoot a film there. It was an attractive, eye-catching property.

My parents loved this place. It had doors everywhere. I counted six doors to the outside leading to side patios, side gardens, and onto a private deck on top of the garage. Downstairs there was a large living room, dining room, family room, bathroom, kitchen, and former maid's room cum pantry, all with leaded windows and an old-fashioned bell-pull system, which was used in olden times to summon servants. There was a wide and comfortable staircase to the second floor. The master bedroom had a dressing room and sunroom attached. When I visited, I stayed in the large guest bedroom, which was complete with a fireplace.

During the war, the home became a hospice for battle-fatigued soldiers, and I think a few of them must have died there. I was always conscious that a few spirits lurked around in the hallways, and whenever I stayed, I was not inclined to leave my room at night. Some rooms were more affected than others. The dining room felt occupied as did the upstairs hallway. That being said, during my parents' time, the home was a happy one, and the house generally rang with pleasant sounds—music and laughter, parties and people.

By the time they moved in, my father was already an ill man. My parents knew that this would be their last home and they set about making it as comfortable as they could for their remaining years. The garden was their pride and joy and used to attract all sorts of attention. It was not the usual rose garden that one sees. This was more like an English country garden—a riot of colour, with benches set artfully around to catch the sun at different times of the day. You would often see my parents outdoors, deadheading roses or basking in the sun's rays, book in hand.

My parents died within three months of each other. My father passed away in hospital, but my mother, ever resolute, died in her own bed at home. She steadfastly refused to move in with any of us, and until the very end, cancelled plans we made for staff to assist her. It was her preference that we each visit her in turn, at her invitation. She would tell us when to come and when to leave. In this way, we each had a special time with her and she remained in control of her life.

I had not long returned to Canada from my visit with her when my brother phoned to tell me that her death was imminent and I made plans to leave immediately. I spoke to my mother by phone before she died. She told me that she would probably be gone by the time I got there and I told her that I was coming anyway. I also said, "Do what you have to do. If you want to go, go." She had cancer and I did not want her to suffer.

My mother did die before I arrived and I was the last of her children to fly in. My flight connections were problematic and I barely made it home in time for the prayer service.

As my mother was already dead, I did not rush immediately to see her. Instead, I sat down at the kitchen table and talked to my family. They were all in deep grief and it seemed more appropriate for me to be with them, but eventually, I did make my way upstairs to my mother's room where she was laid out. The funeral home had performed the usual duties, but my sisters undertook the final touches to prepare my mother for viewing and attended to her hair, nails and makeup.

My sisters told me that every time they worked on a specific area—for example, my mother's nails—a strange light lit the area for them. They didn't know the source of this light. It was not from an electrical fixture either inside or outside. It just mysteriously appeared and spotlit areas as required.

When I saw her, mum looked beautiful and very much at peace, and her room was hushed in a way I have never known it to be. It was as if the trees and wind held their breath. There was a deep stillness and a deep silence, one that you feel sometimes in old churches.

As I entered the room I saw a white whisper of energy rise and leave. It did not rush. It rose gracefully into the atmosphere, and I understood that, in her own way, mum had waited for me. She wanted me to see her leave.

Eventually I made my way back downstairs and we all moved into high gear. My mother had standards and would want them met. Her funeral mirrored the one she had planned for my father, but there were other details that had to be sorted out and these we did.

Then came the problem of what to do with the house. Following mum's death, my youngest sister and I remained in the home, and the rest of the family stayed at various boarding houses and hotels in the neighbourhood. It was during this period that my sister and I became concerned about the entities in the house. The ghosts were hovering everywhere. They choked the corridors. We talked it over with my other sisters and it came as no surprise to them. They, too, were aware of the situation. We all felt sure that these entities were poor lost souls who came back in, or out, during a time of abject grief. I felt they probably dated back to the war. They were not scary or menacing, but were nonetheless grey and heavy, and the house felt weighted by their presence. I didn't know what to do. The atmosphere inside had become maudlin. My sisters and I see ghosts, however, only one of my brothers does, so we did not involve them in our discussions.

I called the local parish office and enquired whether there was a ceremony to restore the joy. At first, they didn't know what I was talking about, but I explained that there had been two recent deaths in the family, and that we wanted to celebrate my parents' lives rather than wallow in grief. I did not get into the ghost-thing. I find it is often better to not be quite so direct. The secretary said she would have someone call me back. I had a sneaking suspicion that she thought me mad.

However, the next day the parish priest dropped by to bless the house, and if he thought my request odd, he gave no indication of it. We didn't invite our brothers to the ceremony as we didn't think they'd be interested. However, they were, and two joined in while the third one watched from the doorways of the various rooms.

It was the most extraordinary service that I have ever seen. My mother died in June and so there was a chill winter sun outside with shortened rays which barely reached into the rooms, yet as Father moved from room to room praying, each brightened with a brilliant light and the drab grey atmosphere literally melted away before our eyes.

Although some will say this is simply a case of mind over matter, this situation was extraordinary. These rooms burst into light in the blink of an eye. The light was brighter than I have ever seen in that house, and each room lit up in turn immediately the prayers finished. That house had umpteen rooms and the same pattern followed true for each room. That is too much of a coincidence. It surprised all of us. It was not what we expected.

There is no doubt in my mind that Father helped a few lost souls into the light that day, and that night my sister and I slept in the house in peace.

Addendum ~

There is one additional item of interest concerning this home. Before they became too ill to travel, my parents used to fly over each year to join me in Canada. One year my father decided to rent the house out while they were away. Their home was quite close to the parliament buildings and the downtown core, and so it was an attractive rental proposition. However, his first foray into home rental ended abruptly. Their tenants were a pleasant young couple, but apparently in the brief time they were there, the wife had a terrible breakdown. The neighbours allegedly heard her screams and when help arrived, she was trying to stab at things with a carving knife. I can only imagine what she thought she was trying to kill.

When my mother was alive, the atmosphere around her was light and happy, but my sisters and I were conscious that when she left, a gloomy mist crept back in. That poor young tenant was probably too sensitive to her surroundings, and without anyone light to clear the atmosphere, she was quickly overwhelmed. I don't know what happened to her afterwards. I hope that she is all right.

Afterwards

Insight:

Our viewpoints on life depend on our viewing-points along life's track, and no one on this plane can see it all.

Sometimes it's hard to know where to draw the line between angels and ghosts. I believe that angels are heavenly beings, whereas ghosts are earthbound spirits. There is a category of spirits in transition between the earthly and afterlife planes, and a further phylum of sub-spirits that I believe are created from negative energy and/or negative thoughts. I believe that these thoughts can take on a persona or life of their own.

Ghosts, like people, come with a range of personalities from good to evil. Some are friendly and helpful, some are playful, and others are their mirror opposites. If at all possible, I think that ghostly beings should be encouraged to move on towards the light. However, I am also cognizant that if they are truly evil, they will be incapable of coping with light.

Communications with angels and transitional beings are one thing, but I am a bit cautious about communicating with ghosts, especially certain ghosts. However, there are many experts around—for example, church ministers—who have the skill and training to do this.

In the years before my mother died, I seemed to see endless ghosts. This was not my favourite experience, and truth be told I was beginning to be very upset with the nature and frequency of the visits. They were not ghosts attached to me, or to my home, and I was always being involved in other people's dramas and I was sick of it. So, before mum died, I said, "Please don't visit me when you're gone." She laughed and promised she wouldn't. I did see her leave her body but other than that, she has been true to her word. She has never visited me and neither has dad. I still think of them often, and I can hear dad's advice in my head, but I don't actually see them and I like it that way. However, that is not true for everyone.

The evening after my mother's funeral, I was sitting in my parents' living room with one of my brothers and my sisters. We were grief stricken, and, in the cool winter's night sat huddled around the heater, reminiscing. There were happy recollections and sad ones, and I can't recall now exactly what dreadful thing my brother said, just that it was chilling. I remember looking at him and thinking, "What an appalling thing to say." There was a sudden coolness, and then my brother received an audible slap across his face, which caused him to reel back and sideways. None of us slapped him but someone certainly did. We all heard it; we all saw it and we all thought it was mum. In retrospect that was extraordinary because she never slapped people—it was not her way, but nonetheless that is the impression we were left with. And afterwards my brother said, "Well, I guess I won't say that again."

My mother also visited my sister the same hour that she died. By the time my brother phoned my sister to advise her of mum's death, she already knew. Rosie told me that she saw mum happy in the afterlife. She heard a party going on in the background, and recognised my father's and grandmother's voices. They were calling my mother over to join them. She said it sounded just like one of the old family parties with lots of music and laughter. Mum called to them to wait up, and then paused to tell my sister not to grieve her passing because she was exactly where she wanted to be.

That message resonated with me as mum had told me something similar before she died. She said, "In my life I've done everything I wanted to do and seen everything I wanted to see. Now I want to join your father." They were joined at the hip those two. Neither wished to live without the other. In reaching out to my sister, she helped to ease her grief and mine.

My father's death occurred three months prior. I was not there, but I was in touch with my mother through it all. He actually died twice in the hospital. The first time he passed away, my mother could not bring herself to sign a do-not-resuscitate order, so dad found himself shocked back into life. She phoned me guilt stricken. I told her to let dad go, that it was his time, and we should not hold onto him. I didn't need to worry about convincing her because when dad regained consciousness, he quite firmly told her that he had been happy where he was, and requested that she not attempt to bring him back again.

This was an important conversation for my mother. She needed to know that these were his clear instructions. Prior to this event, my father had always fought hard to live. He had come through so many serious operations over the years that we called him the bionic man. With this death-return, he put her mind at rest not only in regard to his death, but also her own, because by this stage she was terminally ill.

My friend Celia had a different experience, but also had her fears put to rest at her husband's deathbed. He succumbed to cancer after a lengthy illness. She was tireless through the ups and downs of his dying, the failed treatments, and shared hopes and disappointments. She was a devoted wife. She roomed in with him at the hospital. He was never left alone from the time he was deemed terminal until the end. He didn't want to die alone, and she promised him that he would not. He was in the most upbeat palliative care room I have ever visited, complete with his favourite artwork on the walls. This was a man at peace with his life and his death. When I visited him a week or so before he died, I felt that I was in a saintly presence.

After he died, my friend told me that her husband's spirit left his body, hugged her, and then passed on. She said the hug was extraordinary, and left her feeling calm. It was a: 'don't worry about me; I'm OK' sort of hug. She said it set her free, and it certainly seemed to lessen her grief over the following months.

Her sister-in-law was present when she told me this story, and she had one of her own to relate. She is one of four sisters, and all were present when their father died in the hospital. She said that they were thoroughly immersed in grief as he passed, and sat sobbing at his bedside. They no sooner realized that he was gone, than a sensation simultaneously passed through all of their bodies. She told me it wasn't so much a hug as an amelioration of grief and a sense of joy—almost bliss. The pain of grief was temporarily set aside for each of them, and all four sisters spontaneously burst into laughter and sat there giggling. To an outsider it would have been a highly inappropriate scene for all four daughters to be laughing at their father's deathbed, but that's apparently what he wanted. His message was simple: don't grieve for me.

Another close friend, Samantha experienced a return visit. Growing up, she was close to her maternal grandmother. In many ways she was more in simpatico with her than her own mother. Grandma was her confidante and her fount of wisdom. Sam was devastated when she passed away.

Some months after her grandmother's death, Sam was still restless. She woke in the middle of the night and could not get back to sleep. So rather than disturb her new husband, she crept out to the living room and sat down in her favourite chair. She didn't turn on the lights. She simply sat there hugging herself in a grieving little ball. As her eyes adjusted, she looked across the room and saw her grandmother as clear as day sitting on her sofa. Her grandmother smiled at her with a: don't fret, I'm still around message, and was gone. Sam said her grief eased and she felt immediately at peace. She went back to bed and slept undisturbed until morning.

Many of my friends have had their loved ones drop by afterwards. I have a friend whose husband turns up and opens books at pages he wants her to read. These books migrate from the bookshelf to the coffee table, and are left open for her review. She is the only person in the house, and she did not put them there. The chosen pages relate to family-specific things with messages for her or her daughter.

He also turns up in the car and at her daughter's home. She is not alone in seeing him. He is not shy in his appearances. He continues to be around his family, to the chagrin of her daughter's big, brave Alsatian dog, which hides under the nearest chair, but his visits are not without purpose. He shows up when his wife is upset about one thing or another—like when her daughter was in a serious car accident—and he leaves messages of hope for her. He is there to support her through life's crises.

Another of my friends comes from an Italian family. Although there are only two daughters and two grandchildren in the direct line, family events tend to be rather large affairs as the extended family are always included.

I was there the night that Lyn introduced her husband's family to her mother. Lyn married a man from Central America, and his parents and three sisters flew in to meet their new Canadian connection. Lyn and Jorge made the introductions. His family were all gracious, but one sister, Francesca, looked a little puzzled. She said something to Lynn and Jorge in Spanish, which clearly startled them. My friend asked what was wrong. Jorge explained that his sister had asked about the gentleman standing next to the tapestry chair. Of course, there was no one there, but my friend did not seem surprised. Jorge asked Francesca to describe the person that she was seeing. She did, and my friend showed her a photograph, which Francesca recognised. It seems that my friend's father also wanted to meet the new extended family and had arrived to join the celebration. He was always a highly social man, and nothing had changed now that he had crossed over. He doesn't turn up for every event, just the special ones.

When his own wife died many years prior, he'd known instantly. My friend arrived to give her father the bad news, but he told her that he already knew as her mother had visited him. She had dropped by, he said, to let him know she was fine.

Many cultures expect their loved ones to return to say goodbye. While I did not want this for myself, I do see the importance of it. It reassures people that there is an afterlife. It can also short-circuit grief as you appreciate that your loved one is happy, sentient, and still around, albeit in a different space. Their soul energy didn't get absorbed into the nearest tree, for example.

I believe that it's important not to tie our loved ones to us. Some cultures will not allow a dead person's name to be uttered or their belongings to be kept. There is a wisdom in this. It is my belief that if we grieve too much or for too long, it is not only unhealthy for us but it also ties our loved ones to us and to our world. It's better for everyone for them to move on. Like the song says, "To everything there is a season…"[3]

My parents moved on. They died in their time and I am content with that. However, there was one time when I did appreciate a visitation… from a very small angel. I'd had a miscarriage sometime earlier and was not handling it well. I thought that if I kept busy everything would be fine and my grief would fade. So I worked all day at an exacting job, and half the night on busywork—non-essential and time-consuming tasks. I was trying not to think.

One day as I was preparing a transcript, the door to my office slammed hard behind me. I found that odd as our house is not drafty and doors do not usually slam of their own accord. I continued with my work. Then my whole transcript was dumped on the floor. This was a nuisance because even though the pages were numbered, the document was lengthy. I re-organized the transcript. The whole package was again dumped on the floor. As I bent down to get it, I saw the smallest angel standing in the doorway. She stamped her foot and said, "Enough." I knew immediately what she was telling me and put my work away.

I always thought that angels would be sweet beings, but this little one was forceful, and I knew that she was right. It was time to stop running, and the smallest angel came to tell me that.

My experience is not unique. I have met other women with similar stories. One special woman, who is now in her 70s, regularly sees angels. She was formerly a nurse, and now specializes in hospice work. She tells me that the rooms literally fill with angels before someone passes and that no one ever dies alone, no matter how isolated or even criminal they may have been in life. Sometimes these angels have her relay messages to the person who is passing, and these messages are always something that the dying person needs to hear. It eases them. When you see this woman, the most striking thing about her is her sense of serenity and her pure white aura. She is the only person I have known to have one. There is something reassuring about meeting a woman like this.

My sister Rosie has always seen angels. When she was a youngster my mother took her to say goodbye to a dear friend who was dying, and was surprised when she referred to the others present in the room. Mum started to correct her, but our dying friend, a doctor, was also psychic and he confirmed the angelic presences to my mother. He cautioned mum that Rosie was special and had a gift, which was to be valued and not dismissed. Mum respected him enough to listen.

So what are these psychic abilities and what do they mean? I think that some of us are firmly rooted in this existence and others of us have a foot on both planes. Nothing is ever absolute. There are infinite shades of grey and infinite experiences. So no one is right or wrong; everyone has a different perspective. Think of it this way: imagine life as a pathway up a mountain. Now imagine people positioned at different stages on that path. Their view would be entirely dependent upon where they were standing. I believe that we only achieve a full overview when we pass over.

Rosie's Reprieve

Insight:

Life is full of everyday miracles.

During mum's lifetime and afterwards, clergy would often say to me, "Your mother is a saint." I always dismissed the notion. I thought: no, she's not. She's too much fun. To me it was implausible that saints would be happy. I thought of them as tortured people. Now I'm not so sure.

My mother's death was extraordinary in so many ways. Her funeral was unforgettable, as was the graveside service. The priest who officiated told me he has never been to one like it. It was the stuff that movies are made of. I don't believe I can do the whole thing justice so I will leave that story for another day, but there were some interesting events after my mother's death.

Most of us had to fly in for the funeral. There was work to be done, and we divvied it up between us. Rosie arrived in a few days ahead of her husband, and so, initially, she and I shared a room. When I met up with her, I noticed that she was upset, but then so was everyone. It was to be expected. It wasn't until later that evening that she finally told me what was going on.

Following the fraught times with the ghost some two years earlier, Rosie had not felt well. The terror of living with that thing had taken its toll. There had been too many sleepless nights and too many exhausting days. She was completely drained of energy and exhausted on every level, and she had two small babies to look after. When she first told us how she was feeling, my mother and I suggested that she get some home help. She did, but despite her diminished workload, she had not regained her strength. Finally, she went to her doctor for a check up, and found herself referred to a specialist. There was a very inauspicious lump on her breast. She was scheduled for surgery on the morning of our mother's funeral; however, she had not disclosed this fact to any of us.

That night she told me about her situation. She said her doctor was furious with her. He was adamant that, despite the funeral, her operation must proceed as scheduled. However, Rosie couldn't do it. She refused to miss mum's funeral. She cancelled her surgery and flew over to join us. Had she told any one of us, we would have insisted that she listen to her surgeon.

When Rosie told me her news, I was worried. I pleaded with her to reschedule her surgery as soon as possible and she said she would. We both recognized that her prognosis was iffy. I could not imagine life without Rosie.

Following the funeral, Rosie returned to Australia, and I returned to Canada. She rebooked with her surgeon, but her operation never took place. New x-rays revealed that her lump had vanished. Her surgeon was astonished, but Rosie and I thought, "Mum."

The Bridge

One year as my husband and I sat captive in our seats on yet another long trans-Pacific flight, I became fascinated as I listened in to his conversation with the man sitting next to him. He told us he was going skiing in Canada. He and his wife had planned this trip together, and now that she was dead, he just knew that he had to complete their dream trip alone in memory of her.

I found this heartbreaking to listen to. He was a nice man, middle aged and fit, and obviously still in deep mourning. I leaned over and asked him how she died, and the story he began to relate was so interesting that I swapped seats with my husband and drew closer to hear and absorb every detail.

His wife and he were skilled trampers.[4] It was a hobby of theirs, and they had been doing it for years. They knew the ins and outs of rugged climbing and spring run-offs. They had planned to walk one of the more remote tracks in the South Island of New Zealand. It's one that only experienced bush-hikers would attempt, and it takes days to complete.

Some months prior to their trip, his wife seemed to develop an attack of conscience. Her husband noted that she was mending fences with anyone and everyone with whom she had ever fallen out, going right back to her schooldays. No argument was left hanging. She seemed to be on a personal and very driven make-it-right campaign. He noted this without paying too much attention. It was after all her personal business, and she was resolving things in her own way. However, he did find it curious. She had suddenly become forgiving and prepared to take her share of the blame where she had not been so inclined in the past.

Eventually it was time to go. They donned their packs and set off. From what I remember, they were into about their second day on the trail when they found themselves at the edge of a shallow, but wide, mountain stream. It was a typical New Zealand stream with a stony bottom. Their plan was to cross the river and pick up the track on the other side.

He said that there were others on the trail that day, not travelling with them, but not too far away and certainly within hailing distance. So that effectively they were in their own private world, but with the comfort of knowing they were not alone in this remote and wildly beautiful region.

His wife started across the stream first and he was some distance behind her. As she stepped further into the waterway, there was a sudden and unexpected surge of water which, in his words, turned the small riverbed stones into marbles under their feet—rolling and churning and making it impossible to stand. They were both thrown off their feet. It was a spring surge of run-off waters from the mountains. These occur without warning and they're deadly.

He regained his balance and immediately backtracked to shore. His wife did what you're supposed to do, and what she was trained to do. She lifted her feet off the ground and rolled towards what she thought was the water's edge, except that she was disoriented and so rolled the wrong way and into the centre of the tumultuous waters. He watched in horror as she was swept downriver in a surge of water. He ran down the bank screaming and trying to grab at her, as did others along her path, but she was moving too fast and was too far off shore. No one could reach her, and she was gone.

The police were called. There was probably a radiophone at a rest-shack and someone called out the search team. They apparently hunted for her for days, but she did not turn up. There was a waterfall further downstream, and it was presumed that she went over it. The team searched the depths at the base of the waterfall but she was nowhere to be found.

Of course, there was a police investigation. It always looks a bit suspicious when the wife of a husband and wife tramping team ends up dead, and especially one with her training and experience, but as luck would have it, her accident had been witnessed by a number of people, and so thankfully, the investigation was short, and her husband could return home to mourn her death.

When he arrived back, he was met by his daughter. She was inconsolable. She was not only grieving, but also guilt-ridden. Prior to the trek, his daughter dreamed that both her parents would leave but only one would return. Her dream didn't show her which one would survive, and at the time, she didn't know what to do with the information. She was uncertain whether to warn her parents or to ignore her dream. In the end, she decided not to say anything, as her dreams were not usually prophetic, and there was no reason to believe that this one would be any different. However, since the accident she had been overwhelmed with feelings of "could have; should have."

Her father reassured her. He told her he would have done the same thing. Anyone would. Nightmares are usually just that, and even if she had told them, it is likely they would have shrugged off the information.

After returning home, the husband was traumatised and grieving. He could not work. He was distraught that he had not given his wife a proper burial, and thoughts of her water-tossed and battered body haunted him.

Then one night, approximately a week after his return, he had a dream. He saw the stream where she had fallen. He saw the waterfall. He saw the river tributaries, and then he saw his wife. She showed him exactly where to find her, and he trusted his dream. He immediately phoned the police, and returned to the South Island. At first, the police were sceptical but they were persuaded to accompany him. They re-hiked the trail and followed the pathways he had dreamed about.

They found her face up in the water, peacefully floating in a little backwater pool. The water surge had taken her kilometres downstream on an unexpected watercourse. Incredibly, her face was not traumatised. It was beatific and smiling. This is not the way that bodies normally appear after a lengthy time in the water. The search team were so affected by the sight of her that one year later, they returned to the site where she fell in and hand built a bridge in her honour. They felt there was something miraculous about this whole thing. And so there is.

When he met us, the husband was still grieving, but he had an agenda. He told me that he was going to complete all the plans that he and his wife had made together. He had to; he felt driven. He didn't know why, he just knew this was something that she wanted him to do. So, he never returned to his job; instead, he followed his heart.

I never saw him again, and this many years later, I don't even recall his name, but neither my husband nor I have ever forgotten his story.

The Stone House

Insight:

Exposure to negativity is destructive at best,
and life threatening at worst.

Some years ago my husband and I went on our first Mediterranean cruise. We found ourselves seated at a table with six delightful dinner companions. One couple, Lindsay and John, we continue to cruise with and now count amongst our close friends.

When we first met, our friends had just relocated to Southern Ontario from the Maritimes. In those years we used to visit back and forth, and I quite vividly remember our first stay at their stone house.

This was a magnificent home built on a high plateau with wonderful city views, but despite its architectural glory, Lindsay had some serious reservations about the place. She told me that she felt watched every time she went into the family room downstairs. This confused her, as their home was newly built with no apparent history. Her husband was not affected, although he respected his wife's opinions and concerns.

Lindsay's children did not adapt well to their new home. There were three children—one son and two daughters. Of these, two children were affected. Her son, in particular, seemed to undergo a personality change, becoming both tense and difficult when they moved in, and although he remains a much-loved son, his relationship with his parents became quite fraught. Lindsay was able to preserve a better relationship with her daughters. The older of the two, like her mother, had reservations about the house, whereas the youngest appeared unfazed.

The difference between the children and their reactions I believe, lies in their natures. The son is a sensitive introvert. The oldest daughter is also sensitive, but is more extroverted and comfortable in discussing off-the-wall subjects. She never attempted to tough things out alone. The youngest child—well, some people are simply not attuned to spirit vibrations.

In due course, Lindsay's concerns brought her to a psychic who told her that her family would never be happy in this house. She indicated it was bad space. Sometime after this, Lindsay's husband, John, developed a life-threatening illness, and sometime after that, she did as well.

When she told me this story, I was curious. I told her that entities could be attached to land as well as houses, and that I would be interested to walk in the space and see what I noticed. A few months later we drove down for our first visit.

I felt nothing untoward as I entered through the main door of the residence and walked into the foyer. There was nothing special in the kitchen or other rooms on the main floor; however, upstairs one of the smaller bedrooms felt claustrophobic and occupied. This was her son's bedroom. And then, as we proceeded to the basement, half the area had an oppressive and watchful atmosphere.

I noticed something lurking at the far end of the recreation room. It was a small, malevolent presence—very intense. I detected another entity in her husband's office. It was a dark, unlit entity. I told Lindsay what I felt. Her impressions of the recreation room matched my own. My comments about the office and bedroom surprised her.

She asked me what I would do in her situation. I said that I would get the place blessed. I felt that the impact upon the family was already serious. She asked me if I would do it, but in these circumstances I thought it better to call in the professionals, and so we did.

We contacted a friend, a clergyman, and requested that he bless the home. I understand that he did conduct a full sweep of the house, and liberally sprinkled holy water about. Afterwards everything settled down, and in due course the children grew up and moved out of the Province.

Lindsay and John stayed put. However, Lindsay was never able to completely shake her fears about entities lurking in corners, or forget the trouble they had caused, so some years later, they too moved out west. Today Lindsay and John are managing their health, and the whole family dynamic is slowly and steadily improving. Let's hope it continues.

These entities caused this family to be under stress, and while I am not for a moment suggesting that they caused my friends' illnesses, it is a fact that when people are under stress for a period of time, their immune systems weaken, and opportunistic illnesses can then take hold. The same is true of the impact on children. A few sleepless nights and you have a tense child. A few tense months or years, then things intensify, and interpersonal relationships suffer.

These were not the usual type of ghosts that one encounters. These were members of the ugly phylum that I have referred to in other stories—the gargoyle type creatures of negative energy. They are not pleasant and they cause havoc in people's lives.

Martha's Jump

Insight:

Can we will ourselves out of harm's way or does God intervene to help?

I met Martha and her husband John for lunch. Both were hospice workers until their retirement, and they had driven into town for the day. I have known Martha for about 15 years. We met at a conference through our mutual interest in energy work. Like me, Martha is a teacher but she has a different repertoire and is a practitioner of Craniosacral therapy and Reiki, and an instructor in Tai Chi and Therapeutic Touch.™

Martha had been involved in a health recovery process. Many years earlier she had a serious car accident, which left her semi-paralysed. Through grit and determination, she taught herself to walk and talk again, and to regain control of censored speech. Her accident affected the right frontal lobe area of her brain, and this initially left her with an inability to control her speech. She could not mask her feelings or the truth, or refrain from speaking it. She would blurt things out. While she never regained all of her former skills—for example, she was once an ace in mathematics—she has regained most of them, together with a few new ones.

Over lunch, our conversation got around to near-death experiences, and it was then that Martha told me hers. She said that she did not hear or feel the accident happen. When she realized that impact was inevitable, she called out to God to be with her. She was then "jumped" out of her body prior to the crash. She immediately entered another dimension. There she was faced with a wide and steep staircase. She heard a voice from above the stairs instructing her to come up. She knew that she could not and said so. The voice said, "Yes, you can." She believed it but never did climb the staircase because the minute she thought of ascending it, she found herself at the top. She was immediately surrounded by (in her words) a "lovely, comfortable, brilliant, white light." The voice was now beside her. It told her to lie down but she saw nothing to lie on. Again, she indicated that she could not, and again she was told she could. She then floated in a horizontal position, face up. There was a presence behind her head. She sensed arms moving down both sides of her, although they did not physically touch her. The voice said, "You will be healed." This experience was more special than she can describe. She said she was exposed to pure love. She has no recollection of descending the staircase. She came to in her hospital bed, but not in her body. She was resting alongside it in her soul-body.[5] She told me that she did not reintegrate back until much later.

I asked Martha whether she met an angel or God. She said it was the "Source." Martha is not a Christian and has her own terminology. She said that the one thing that kept her going through years and years of therapy was the assurance that she would recover. She had no doubt. She believed her Source. Her near-death description is different from others that I have heard. There was no tunnel, and there were no family members on hand to greet her. Yet the experience left her serene and happy. She had a one-on-one relationship with her Source and felt loved.

This is not the first time I have heard about people being "jumped out" of accidents. Last year I attended a conference where the presenter (Eldon Taylor)[6] spoke about his motor vehicle/train accident. He and his girlfriend were out for a drive when his vehicle stalled on the tracks. A train was speeding towards them. He never felt the impact. His car was flattened but he was bodily removed to a nearby hill.

From the safety of the hillside, he saw the wreckage on the tracks. By the time he made his way back down to the site to check on his girlfriend, the police were already on the scene. Initially they prevented him from approaching because they were still combing the wreckage for the driver (him). Miraculously, his girlfriend was still alive, although injured. The police were incredulous when they learned that he was the driver. His girlfriend confirmed that he had been sitting beside her when the train hit.

The speaker has addressed this extraordinary event in his book.[7] For her part, Martha believes that God/Source came to her assistance when she called. These jumps differ from each other in that one was a soul leap, and the other a body and soul leap, however, both individuals describe these events as life changing for them. It is reassuring that it is possible to be jumped out of harm's way.

Diane's Near-Death Experience

We met Diane and her husband Pierre a few years ago when they joined our Friday suppers. They are long-time friends of Marie Claire's. At the time we met, Diane was still getting her strength back from a near-death event.

She had survived a bout of meningitis, pneumonia and septicaemia. This triple-killer developed from a ruptured sinus abscess, which caused purulent matter to leak into her central nervous system, bloodstream, and lungs. She went into a coma and the mark of death was already upon her face. She had blackness around her mouth and cyanotic nails.

Her poor husband was frantic during this time. It looked very possible that he would lose his wife, and he was still in mourning for their son, Marc who died at age 18. Marc had an aggressive cancer, and although he fought hard and underwent the conventional treatments, he only survived for four months, leaving his parents emotionally drained and battered from their roller coaster ride through fear, hope, despair and grief. Now Pierre was facing another death scenario and he was scared. But after a three-day coma, Diane recovered.

I am always surprised at people's resilience. Both Diane and Pierre are happy people. There are times when their eyes well up with tears but both have a ready laugh and they travel and enjoy life and each other, and the loss of their son does not diminish their lifelong interest in children. They are involved parents and grandparents, and Diane often regales us with interesting tidbits from school. She is a teacher, and her husband was the boss before he retired.

I heard about her coma and, as I am curious about these things, I asked if she had any interesting experiences to relate. She stated quite matter-of-factly that she saw Jesus. I said, "So you went down the long tunnel?" She laughed and said, "Not exactly. I went bottom first into a cave."

Diane is a tall woman; statuesque. I had an immediate mental image of her bottoming-out—anyone would. As I had never before heard of such an entry into the afterlife, I asked her to elaborate.

She said she had the sensation of falling, and didn't lift gracefully out of her body as we so often hear described, but rather fell out and down, and into a deep and dark cavern where she apparently landed gently. She heard a voice calling to her from somewhere in the murky depths and it asked for permission to draw near. She was confused about where she was and what was happening to her, and so she yelled back, "That all depends where you're from. If you're from the dark side just stay away from me." She heard responding laughter. Someone found her answer hilarious. She turned towards the sound and saw a warm glow coming towards her. As her vision cleared, this glow became a bright light. In the centre was a form, which she understood to be Jesus. She told me she had no doubt that it was him. She just knew. He radiated love and acceptance and peace. As he stood beside her, she basked in these sensations. She was at once loved and warm, peaceful and pain free. She asked whether it was her time to go and received the answer, "No."

She told me that she begged him to help her, and he placed his hand over her head. And then she noticed they were not alone. Her son was with them, and he told her, "Mom, I've got it covered."

Diane said that her son was the same yet different. He was more mature. He had all of his hair, which he had lost during chemo, and he was now a man who knew his way around. He was there to reassure her—to greet and direct her—and he was at the right hand of Jesus. He was no longer her sick child. He had grown in many ways. She was in awe at the change.

The next awareness that she had was coming out of her coma. She recovered fully, even in spirit. The whole experience left her happy and amused. Her God has a sense of fun and laughter. And how can you grieve a son in such a place of joy! She also realized that even in death we have free will. She could have stayed alone in her cavern. The choice was always all hers.

In looking back on her near-death with the wisdom of hindsight, she has other insights. In her words: "I know my God lives. I know my son lives and his full head of hair tells me that he is whole again, and that his learning continues. When my time comes to cross over, he will be there to say to me, just as he did a few hours before he died, 'Mom in the blink of an eye, I'll welcome you home.'"

And so the roles are reversed. The child teaches and consoles the parent. Her near-death experience was also a learning curve for others. Her medical specialist informed her last June that he now uses the technique developed to clear her meningitis, to laser cancerous growths from the brains of other patients.

Today Diane works with parents who have lost children in death.

Diane's Encounter

Insight:

It is always reassuring to have one's vision confirmed by another person.

Chris, Elena and I were all relaxing after dinner one evening when Diane arrived, eyes alight and brimming with excitement. By all accounts, she'd had a very eventful weekend.

She told us that she and her husband had driven to Durham to see their friends, the Browns. They arrived there mere minutes after a tornado hit, and traumatic as that was, it was not the only mind-blowing experience.

The Browns had just moved into a new residence, and Diane and her husband were seeing it for the first time. She told me that her initial impressions of the 107-year-old residence were positive. It was a graceful three-storey stone building in an old established neighbourhood. It had great street appeal.

As Diane stepped over the threshold of the residence, she saw a middle-aged woman, with a friendly smile, standing alongside her friends. At first she presumed this individual was Amish as her hair was secured in a tight little bun, and she wore an old-fashioned full-length gown, but on closer review, she noticed that the woman's dress was far from plain. As she was not introduced, and no one else acknowledged the woman, Diane surmised that she was from the past. She elected not to mention the apparition to anyone. She wasn't sure how the information would be received, and did not want to create an awkward situation.

The Browns welcomed Diane and her husband, and together they toured the residence from top to bottom. Overall, it was a well-preserved home, with honey coloured hardwood flooring throughout, and Tudor style wainscoting. Although Diane was impressed with the home, she found herself distracted by the female apparition, who was a strong presence.

The group finally made their way to the basement. However, as Diane descended the stairs, she was stricken by an overwhelming pain across her shoulders, which caused an ache right down her back, and in her mind's eye she saw herself carrying a load of coal down the stairway. When she reached the bottom, she saw a young man standing there, in obvious discomfort, with a sack of coal across his shoulders. She felt immediate empathy for him. He didn't seem to know how to put his burden down. His eyes were pain-filled and his face was fraught. She realized that she was seeing another ghostly entity. Again, she elected to say nothing, but she noted that as she left the basement area and the male entity, her pain eased.

As the party moved back to the main floor, the Browns casually mentioned that their friend, Sara, would be joining them for tea. In due course Sara arrived. Diane learned that she was a Reiki Master. Sara further explained that she conducted home cleansings and was frequently called out to clear older dwellings.

Diane felt vindicated when Sara talked of seeing the middle-aged woman and young man. Yet despite this admission, Sara did not elaborate further. Diane had the distinct impression that these two entities were related—perhaps a mother and son. However, Sara made no such assumptions. Her role was simple. There were two entities in the home, and she was there to help them cross over.

Once Sara realized that Diane could also see these ghosts, she asked for her help. She suggested that Diane remain on the main floor with the smiling woman, while she dealt with the young man in the basement. Diane told Sara that she was more than willing to help, but didn't know how. Sara instructed her to mentally invite the entity to sit with her. Diane did and the entity joined her. But then, Diane started to feel strangely ill. She told Sara, who suggested that Diane sit down. After that, Sara assumed control of the cleansing process.

She called out to all entities in the home to move towards the light, and both entities responded. As the smiling entity left her side, Diane immediately felt better. And as both spirits left, the home was cleansed.

When Diane told me this, I was curious about her strong reactions. These were not bad entities, merely people trapped in time, so I didn't understand why these encounters would cause Diane to feel ill or be in pain. There was no doubt in my mind that Diane had faithfully recounted the event, as in retelling her story, she had goose bumps and a case of the shudders. I also noticed that the hair on her arms was raised. She clearly was not fabricating anything.

I think the answer may be that Diane's sixth sense was activated in an expanded context. She saw the entities and felt their emotions. Her visioning was so clear that she was uncertain whether these entities were spirits or people. This is unusual.

In discussing Diane's reaction amongst ourselves, it was suggested that both Diane and the entity would have had to alter their vibration levels in order to communicate. Diane moved out of an observer role and into an interactive one, when she agreed to communicate with the female entity. The resultant change in vibration must have caused her to feel light-headed and disoriented. The pain connection with the young man, I believe, is related to Diane's ability to empathize.

I have some further thoughts on these apparitions. Diane felt the two were related and I agree with her. The woman's dress would suggest that she was a former housekeeper in the residence, and I suspect the other entity was her son. In my view, it would be odd for a deliveryman to carry coal right through the house and down an interior stairway. Coal was generally delivered to an outside coal chute, and then either funnelled into the furnace area or hand-bucketed through. I believe the young man was probably the housekeeper's son who was helping out. I further suspect he died in a fall down the stairs, and then failed to realise he was dead, and when his mother died, she refused to move to the next plane without him.

Diane had another insight. She told us that she had the impression that the female entity was now eager to move to the spiritual plane. As an observer in the Brown household, the mother spirit must have been privy to the Browns' plans to cleanse the premises. She was not only a willing greeter at the front door, but she was fully compliant with Sara's suggestions to leave. In fact, both entities were easily persuaded to go. They just needed to be directed.

Diane told me that she was amazed to see these spirits. Prior to her near-death experience she never saw ghosts. I suspected she was becoming more psychically attuned, which often follows near-death events. It would be a natural development. I also wondered whether the tornado scare earlier that day had put her on high psychic alert or perhaps opened a vibrational window of some sort.

In any case, Diane reported that she was fascinated to watch a house cleansing for the first time and she told me that she felt quite vindicated that Sara saw what she saw, as it is not always easy to be the only seeing person in a family.

Samantha's Visits

Insight:

At death, our soul body may proceed through our auric fields to our purest vibration which resonates with the spiritual plane.

When I was much younger, my close friend Samantha and I worked as court reporters. We covered all courts and tribunals, recording and transcribing evidence. It was captivating work—exacting, taxing, but interesting, especially if you are curious like me. There wasn't a thing that happened in our town that we didn't hear about, and often firsthand. We couldn't wait to meet at lunch and trade stories.

Sam had two children the same ages as mine and because of our similar circumstances, we worked a buddy system, which meant that we would cover for one another in the event of a family emergency. We didn't trade spaces often but we always knew we could, and I felt reassured that her work was indistinguishable from mine. We actually received identical marks in our provincial qualifying exams.

Of course, I got my usual seven-year-itch and eventually took off for greener pastures where I reinvented myself in a new career. Sam remained in position though, and continued to faithfully report all courts until her retirement.

One of the reasons I gave up court reporting was that I noticed the injuries to all reporters senior to me. They usually developed carpal tunnel syndrome or a similar problem. Now, I have never had any desire to be martyred for a job, so of course, the minute I realized the injury correlation, I was off and away, hands intact. Sam, however, stayed put and in due course she succumbed, as most reporters do. She developed arthritis. When the pain in her hands became too much to bear, she made an appointment with the surgeon and before you knew it, she was home again and in recovery. Her thumb had been re-built and it all looked very promising… for a time.

I went to see her on her release from hospital and she showed me some impressive surgery. Her scars were barely visible. Sam, however, was not herself. She said she hadn't felt well since her hospital stay and over the following weeks she got no better. She eventually collapsed and was rushed to hospital in a state of serious dehydration. There, she was diagnosed with C-Difficile. Her husband told us that she might not recover. My husband and I wanted to see her but she was in isolation and visits were restricted to family, and even they had to be masked, gowned and gloved.

After many tense days, Sam was deemed to be in recovery and was released from hospital. Sometime later, we decided that she could probably stand some company and invited ourselves to tea. It was then that Sam told us this story.

She said that she had been lucky to survive her ordeal, and was fairly certain that she'd had a near-death experience. I asked her what happened. She told me that she was aware that she had drifted into another dimension. Her pain had ebbed away, and she found herself floating free. She was out of her body and moving into a tunnel-like space, but her experience was not frightening. This wasn't a tunnel as we usually understand it—long, dark and dank. Instead, she felt as if she was being coddled into a calm and comforting place, and was being moved gently towards a bright light. She had no fear of going towards it because she could see her parents and maternal grandparents welcoming her. She didn't have the nasty experience of being grabbed at, that some people report. It was peaceful in her tunnel.

However, as she met her family group, her mother reached out and placed her palm on her forehead. It was the sort of touch a mother gives a fevered child. She said her mother's hand was cool, comforting and loving. She said to her daughter something like, "It's going to be all right" or "You're going to be all right." With the passage of time, Sam doesn't recall her mother's exact words, just their import. The next thing she knew, she came to in her bed. She doesn't recall retracing her steps or turning around. It was just a touch, an explanation and a return. It was not yet time for Sam to go.

One of the things that an experience like this does is that it takes away one's fear of dying. For Sam, this will never be a traumatic experience, but rather a familiar and comforting one.

I had another thought on these coddling tunnels that she described. I wonder if we don't simply experience leaving our bodies to walk through our own auras or energy fields to the light. These seven-field repeating series that go on forever are the holographic essences of us, and they connect us to our world and beyond. So in a sense we proceed through to the purest vibration of ourselves, which is non-threatening and familiar. These auric fields connect us to those we love, apparently on all planes of existence. We simply follow our connections home. Or at least that's my interpretation of it, from listening to the stories.

Of course, a near-death or death-return experience is life changing for everyone concerned, not only for Sam, but also for her husband, Henry. They both realized they didn't want to waste another precious moment of their lives. They had things to do. They thought about where they wanted to be, and how they wanted to live, and then they redefined their lifestyle. They decided to be more of a presence in their children's and grandchildren's lives, and made plans to sell the family home and move south.

But their decision to do so was not without incident. It seemed their home did not want to cooperate with the sale. Bizarre stuff started to happen. If it wasn't the electrical, it was the plumbing. If it wasn't the plumbing, it was the electrical. There were endless household dramas. They had never experienced anything like this in the 26 years they had lived in the home. The strange thing was that when experts were called in for repairs, they invariably found nothing wrong. Things were just going glitchy all around them.

Sam reminded me that I told her that she probably had a ghost and that she should talk to it and explain things. She said that Henry thought the pair of us quite weird, but in any event desperate times call for desperate measures and so she spoke out loud and said, "You know we're leaving. We loved being here but it's time for us to go. You can come too if you want to. You're always welcome." From that day forward, the dramas stopped; the house settled down; and the place was sold in no time. Whoever it was that lived there with them was grieving their going and apparently a little anxious about changes to come.

Sam and Henry now live closer to their children, in a new dream home of their own design and it's working well for them. Their ghost, however, stayed put.

Cassie's Stories

Insight:

Each of us appreciates the truth as we see it, but on this plane of existence we all have obstructed views.

For a period of time I "temped" at a local office. This was a small firm staffed by the boss and two secretaries, both improbably called Cassandra. To avoid confusion, we called one Cassie and the other Sandra.

I had known Sandra for many years, and when her husband injured his back and was confined to bed rest, she called me in to cover for her. So, in her absence, I worked with Cassie, and Sandra checked in on us from time to time.

The office was unimpressive, located in an architecturally bland and functional building with clean lines, low ceilings, and cheap fittings. For a lone practitioner, our boss was exceptionally busy, and the place had files in and out of cabinets, from one end of the office to the other. It was organized chaos. I needed all the help that Cassie could offer to pick my way through the priorities.

One night as Cassie and I were preparing to close up, I asked that she wait for me. I said I really hated setting alarms and locking up. She misunderstood me. She thought I was afraid to be there alone, whereas my only concern was that I not inadvertently leave a coffee pot on, or some such thing, and burn the place down. She said to me, "Oh, I quite understand; I get scared too." As there was no reason for me to be frightened I leapt to the obvious conclusion, and asked her if the place was haunted. She said she thought so, or at least it had been.

Apparently, one day when she was working alone in the office, she distinctly saw a small black entity arrive at the front desk, and spin past her like a dervish, and move on into the kitchen. She tried to pretend it wasn't there, but it was hard to ignore as it was making whirring sounds in addition to heavy tramping and banging noises. It kept this disruptive behaviour up for the entire day moving from kitchen to hallway to ceiling. Initially, Cassie panicked. She telephoned her sister and pleaded with her to stay on the line. Finally, in exasperation she yelled at the entity, "We both have to share this space, so if you don't bother me, I won't bother you." With that, it calmed down and hasn't visited her since, but she says she still has to fight down fears on the days she has to work alone, mindful that it could come back.

I was curious about her description of this entity because it seemed markedly similar to the ugly black troll things that my sister Rosie had seen. I think these little beings may be what gave rise to the creatures that adorn the doorways of European churches. Those small sub-human *uglies*—the gargoyles—that peer down on you from on high. They appear to have been seen through the ages.

I asked Cassie about the psychics in her family. Although she did not regard herself as being especially psychic, she stated that her daughters and sister are. I told her that in my opinion that would be a most unusual situation; that these things tend to run in families and with this many psychics so closely related to her, it was likely that she was too. She wasn't so sure about that, but over the next couple of weeks she told me her stories.

She was still grieving when I started to work with her. Her mother had died some months prior, and Cassie was trying to sort out the estate and cope with her own personal sadness. In passing one day I asked her if her mother had visited since her death. She looked bemused, and then said she wasn't quite sure. She said her father had come back, and she had no doubt about that, but she wasn't certain about her mom. Now, to me, she either had or had not seen her mother, so I asked her what she meant.

She told me that she and her daughter, Veronica, were going through the old family photos the previous week, and they were having a great time laughing together and recalling good times. In the midst of their laughter, Veronica unexpectedly sobered up with a peculiar expression on her face. Cassie asked her what was up. Her daughter said, "Didn't you see it? There was a ball of bright white light that circled both of us and left." Neither of them knew what to make of it, but I did.

I had heard about this sort of thing before. I said, "That was your mother. She was just checking to make sure you were all right." She told me that she and her daughter were leaning towards that conclusion, but as they had seen

Cassie's father full body, they were confused by her ball of light appearance. So we talked about that.

This is exactly the way that my friend's husband appears to his family. I believe that our spirit moves on when we die, but that it reduces to its purest essence. We know that all the cells in our bodies are holographic and I suspect the same is true of our spirits, so that the part is the whole.

I believe that Veronica and Cassie saw her mother's heart chakra. Her essence was distilled to the finest, purest form of being—a "love" ball of white light. Sometimes this is how our loved ones appear. At other times they reveal their whole being. Cassie's father appeared to her one way, her mother another; but both were valid sightings. There is a reason for the way they appear and in order to understand that, we have to go back to her father's visitation.

Cassie's father died 10 years prior to her mother. Her parents were close in life, so Cassie was not surprised when she saw her father arrive at her mother's deathbed. She knew that he had come to welcome her mother home. He was easily recognizable and wore a suit. He was there not only for his wife, but also as a comfort to his children. Death is a sad and scary time. He wanted to help and he wanted to be seen. Cassie called out to him and told him that she was having a difficult time and asked that he sit and hold her hand, which he immediately did. In appearing full body, he eased everyone's fears, and let them know on no uncertain terms that there is an afterlife and he was there to see to it that her mom was well looked after during her transition.

Cassie's mother's appearance was not in the same vein at all. Her daughter and granddaughter were enjoying a moment. They were laughing together and she came by to check on them. She bounced in, made a quick visit and left, and Veronica, being more psychic than most, saw her.

Cassie then told me about her mother's death. Her mother died in hospital after a lingering bout of cancer, which saw her transferred from hospital to hospital. Cassie said that she was concerned for her mom, and the pain that lay ahead of her. As much as she wanted her to live, she also wanted her to die in peace. Her mother lived longer than expected, and in her last days she kept saying to Cassie, "Hold me. Please just hold me." I told Cassie I understood why she said that. Whenever she felt herself slipping away, she was asking to be grounded or earthed, and the quickest way to achieve this is to be held by someone else. She must have had some residual fear about dying. That is most likely why Cassie's dad made his presence known, but apparently he was not the only one.

When Cassie's daughters came to their nonna's bedside, they commented to their mother that the room was very crowded. Cassie did not understand this remark at all, as for once they were the only family there. Usually the place was filled with extended family and friends. After a time, her daughters had to leave and, as it was evening, Cassie's husband walked them out to their car, leaving Cassie alone at the bedside. By this time her mom was resting quietly, so Cassie eased herself out of her chair and stepped into the corridor for a moment of personal grief. She hadn't had much down time and she was a bit exhausted by it all. Cassie was surprised when she heard some lively chatter in her mother's room, or at least she thought it came from her mother's room. However, when she popped her head around the corner, no one was there. She was confused. She returned to the corridor to wait for her husband.

In due course he arrived and asked, "Who's in with your mom?" Somewhat relieved she said, "So you can hear them too?" "Of course, who's with her?" Cassie said, "Take a look and see." Of course, there was no one. Her husband was mystified; he looked into the room across the hall, and then asked a passing nurse where the noise was coming from—was there a radio or television on somewhere? She told him, no; it was just the angels talking.

When Cassie arrived home that night she talked to her daughters about their "crowded" comment, which now made more sense to her. They told her that there were always happy spirit people at their grandmother's bedside. Her daughters, however, didn't recognise any of them.

So who were these spirits? I suspect they were their nonna's friends and relatives who had previously crossed over, but they may well have been hospital spirits who are there to ease people on their final journey. The girls told Cassie that their grandmother was never alone.

Veronica also told her mother about another encounter she had with these entities. She had been sitting at the bedside holding her nonna's hand when she became overwhelmed by sadness. Even though her grandmother was comatose, she knew that on some level she heard everything going on around her because every now and again, she would squeeze her granddaughter's hand. Rather than upset the others around the sickbed, Veronica decided to take a break. She told her mother later that she felt a presence supporting her as she got up to leave, and that this spirit walked her down to the family room, and sat down beside her. While she didn't actually see the entity, she heard footsteps alongside her own and felt a presence so soothing and comforting that she had no doubt that it was an angel.

All the entities surrounding nonna were happy… except for one solitary instance. On that occasion a fly came into the room. It was a noisy and bothersome fly. It is unusual for flies to be active in winter, and this was an especially cold November. Nonetheless, this fly buzzed people and annoyed everyone. Cassie said she doesn't know why, but she felt compelled to order it out of the room and into the light, and she was only marginally surprised when it left. She felt that some other hospital entity had wandered into her mother's space and so she sent it on its way.

When Cassie's mother eventually passed on, she had all of her family at her side and they all saw her death positively, but differently. Cassie noticed a shining white halo by her mother's crown chakra, which shut down at death and so Cassie knew that her mother had gone. Her sister-in-law, Barb, watched her mother-in-law's spirit detach from the heart area and drift up and away from her body, and so she recognized the moment of death, and Cassie's daughters spoke of seeing the angels leave. They turned to their mother and said, "It's time to go now, mom. The room is empty."

We all see things from our different viewpoints but there is no doubt in my mind that what we see is true. We focus on little shards of truth as the whole scene unfolds around us. We get caught up in the extraordinary and don't have time to back up and take in the whole picture. We become focused, captivated by an aspect, and then the experience is over.

Cassie got her wish. Her mother passed on, supported by friends and family on both the earthly and spiritual planes.

Cassie's Family

Insight:

Once activated, our sixth sense continues to develop, and one supernatural experience usually prompts others.

During the time I "temped" with Cassie, she told me some of her family stories. One of these involved her father who died unexpectedly in hospital. In life, he was a much-loved dad, and a committed family man. His wife and children grieved him deeply when he passed, and regretted the lack of final farewells. He must have understood that, because for the first number of years after his death, they would catch sight of him in his old rocker in the living room, sitting quietly alongside his family, part of it all, yet apart from it. His youngest daughter could even hear him breathing, which she thought was a very non-spirit thing to do. It seemed important to him that his family understand that he was still present in their lives, albeit on a different plane.

After he died, he appeared to Cassie and told her not to worry, he was exactly where he wanted to be, and he sent a dream message to her sister, Marianna, telling her the same thing. He was present at his wife's deathbed and on other occasions too, and is apparently not the only family member to make an after-death appearance.

There was a family tragedy some years back and one of Cassie's young nephews was killed in a horrific boating accident. He was a daredevil in life, and so his aunts were always saying to him, "Alberto, be careful. Alberto, watch yourself" to which his standard response was, "Don't worry; be happy."[8] These words reflected a popular song of the day, and Alberto had adopted them as his credo in life.

The morning after his death Cassie was taking a shower at home. She said she distinctly heard her nephew call out to her, "Don't worry; be happy." She said the voice was not in her head. It was out loud. He used that same refrain when he chatted with his young cousins on the Ouija board. They asked for verification that it was really him, and he used the familiar line to identify himself.

There are other entities that turn up in the extended family homes from time to time. Cassie's youngest daughter, Isabella, was visiting her young cousins and they all watched enthralled as a small circle of light did a walk-through of the home. They have no idea who this entity was. None of them was alarmed by the experience, just intrigued.

In addition to this unknown entity, Marianna, Cassie's sister, has seen another spirit in her home. This one is invisible, yet casts a shadow. Again, it is not frightening, just present. When Marianna first saw it, she called out, "If that's you, dad, you can stay. If it's not, please leave." Occasionally, she hears entities in her home communicating with one another. She said it's like static on a television set and although she can hear the sounds, she cannot make out the words. Of course, spirits don't need to speak aloud to communicate with each other or with us, so why do they do it? Perhaps just to reassure everyone who hears them that life does go on.

Cassie said that once she became aware of supernatural things, she began to experience other psychic phenomena in her life. The first time it happened, she woke up convinced, absolutely certain, that on this day she would be involved in a car accident on her return from work. She was so certain that she relayed this information to her husband, who was less than impressed with her.

On her way home that night she counted off the streets… "Safely past Madison… safely past Queen…" and she thought, "Wow, I'm nearly home. I guess I got it wrong." She stopped at the light and waited to make her left-hand turn, and then the car behind rammed into her. The other driver had come to a complete stop and then unexpectedly his foot slipped and his car shot forward. There was quite a bit of damage to both vehicles and Cassie received treatment for a nasty whiplash.

The next time she had a premonition, it was about her red SUV. She told her husband, "I don't know when or where, but sometime soon this vehicle is going to be in an accident." He was not convinced. A day or so later, he took the SUV to collect their daughter, Veronica, from dancing and he was involved in an accident en route. Fortunately, although there was extensive damage to his vehicle, he was not injured.

These premonitions of Cassie's involve big things and little things. As she was dressing for work one morning, she had the feeling that she should not wear a particular set of earrings because she would lose one. She became irritated, and told herself there was no reason for such a thing to happen. She would not give in to this superstition and she would wear her earrings. She did, and she lost one!

Nowadays she pays closer attention to the messages she gets. Someone is telling her something for a reason.

Our Reflexology Course

Insight:

Not all ghosts are sinister. Some just wander about, maintaining their ties to the earthly plane.

I have been a student of alternative medicine for many years. I am a practitioner in some disciplines and a teacher in another. Some years ago, reflexology captured my interest. There are two Reflexology Colleges in Ontario, each with slightly different practices. I didn't know which to choose, so I had several treatments, selected my preferred discipline, contacted my College of choice, and enrolled in the next class. As luck would have it, the next class was being held some hours away. I knew of one other woman in our area who was interested in taking the course, and she, in turn, had a friend who was interested. We thought it would be fun to study together in the coming months.

There were six people enrolled in the course, and our group of three made arrangements to secure room and board at our teacher's farmhouse, and my husband drove us there.

Our trip was uneventful and we took the opportunity to get to know each other. We were of diverse ages and backgrounds. One of the women was older than me, and the other, younger. We chatted on about kids and jobs and interests, and by the time we arrived, we were quite comfortable in each other's company. My husband took advantage of our trip to visit relatives in the area, and dropped us off and left.

The farmhouse was an 18th century cottage. It had great roadside appeal, and as we drove up to it, I remember thinking that it looked like something out of the English countryside; all it lacked was a thatched roof. Farmhouse is a bit of a misnomer in this case as the building contained two homes. It was in fact an old-fashioned duplex with secret passageways joining the two houses. These passageways were located behind false walls in the bedroom closets and were proudly shown to us by our hosts during our tour of the residence. I couldn't help but wonder who designed these passageways and why and when. There was obviously a history of love and intrigue with the place, or at least I prefer that interpretation.

Eventually we were shown to our quarters, which comprised two adjoining bedrooms. Once upon a time they were probably the master bedroom and en suite dressing room, but in later years, had been converted into children's bedrooms. There were two beds and an inflatable mattress available to us. We tossed a coin to see who would sleep where. I won the toss and got the double bed in the master bedroom; Cheryl won the single bed in the dressing room, and Carla was left with the mattress on the floor in my room.

Immediately after supper we began our studies, which proved intensive. After a long drive and three hours' study, I was ready for bed. I didn't waste any time; I didn't read my book—which is my bedtime ritual. I just climbed into bed, closed my eyes and drifted off to sleep. Because I was raised in a large family, noise does not distract me. It did not bother me that Carla and Cheryl were still chatting, or that Carla took some time to get changed, organized and ready for bed. I simply tuned her out and went to sleep with the light on, leaving her to take care of those details when she was ready.

Sometime later, I was awoken when an older gentleman leaned over my bed and asked me who I was. I started to answer him but then he said, "Never mind; go back to sleep" and left. I found it disconcerting to have a strange man in our bedroom, but realized that he was probably granddad looking for his grandchildren. I drifted back to sleep. I reasoned that he was probably a little confused.

The next morning I awoke early, refreshed and happy. Carla, on the other hand, was in a bad mood. I thought she might be one of those people who don't do well in the mornings, so I gave her a wide berth. Over the following days I noticed that her mood never really lightened, and gone was the woman who was such easy company on our journey down.

In light chitchat with our teacher over lunch the next day, we got around to discussing social matters. We met her husband, and she showed us pictures of her daughters. I was surprised to learn that while grandma occupied the adjoining house, grandpa had been dead for years. It was clear from our conversation that a ghost had just visited me. I was somewhat surprised but I didn't mention it to anyone as I didn't want to offend my hosts. I just made sure that I went to bed at the same time as everyone else, and stayed put once I got there.

We continued our studies over the course of the next two days. Finally, my husband drove up to collect us, and we piled into the car and commenced our journey home. Cheryl and I were chatty; Carla continued to be silent and withdrawn.

In passing, I told my husband that there was a ghost in the home. Carla was in the back seat. She shouted in my ear, "You saw him too?" I told her I did, and she said she had never been so scared.

She then related her tale. That first evening she read for a while before turning out the light, but she no sooner lay her head on the pillow than she noticed an older gentleman in the doorway. He was leaning against the doorframe with his foot on a small trunk, and he stood there for a moment surveying the room. She had time to get a good look at him and he was clearly visible to her. He was tall and slim, and wore blue jeans, a casual shirt, riding boots and a Stetson. She thought he was somewhere around 55-60 years old. He crossed through Cheryl's room and into ours, with a bold swagger. He completely ignored her on the floor, and went directly over to my bed and leaned over me.

Carla didn't know what to do. She had no idea who he was, or what he was doing in our room. She said she lay quietly in her bed trying not to draw attention to herself. She watched me roll over to face the man, and then he straightened up and walked away from me. She heard no exchange between us, and during this whole time, he never acknowledged her. At some point, a car navigated the hill outside, and the headlights flashed into our room and passed right through him. The man then left our room in the same unhurried fashion that he had entered it.

Carla was frozen with terror. She did not usually see ghosts but she knew she saw this one. She dared not close her eyes or take a bathroom break. Instead, she spent a wakeful and agonizing night on the floor. By the time daylight arrived, she had an uncomfortable bladder and experienced real difficulty in getting off her air mattress intact. She told us that she had not slept properly since we arrived and was exhausted.

As she related her story, I caught a mental image of her situation, and started to laugh. At first she was quite annoyed with me, but laughter is infectious and eventually she saw the humour too. Since that time, she has seen other ghosts in other circumstances, but she has never again been so frightened. Subsequently, Carla and I became close friends and continued to study reflexology and other disciplines together. I am pleased to say that her good nature and even temper have returned.

So who was our visitor and what did he want? I believe he was grandpa just checking in on the grandkids—no one scary, but simply someone lost in time.

Taking Ways

Insight:

Ghosts come with all sorts of personalities—as varied in death as they were in life.

I was talking about ghosts to my daughter-in-law Ava one evening and she told me that while she has never seen any, her friends and aunt have, and she doesn't doubt them for a minute. I asked her what their stories were, and she told me.

Her friend Patsy moved into her new apartment on Lee Road. She was happy with it. The location was handy to town and the rent was affordable. The first couple of days there, however, she thought she saw, out of the corner of her eye, a young guy in a t-shirt. She couldn't see his face—just a quick flash—and then he was gone. Initially, she thought it was just an illusion or an unfortunate play of light in the room. But then she found she had difficulty getting to sleep because she couldn't shake the impression that there was someone in her bedroom with her. She rechecked her room thoroughly, under the bed and in the closet, and made sure her locks were securely in place, and then put her head under the blankets and tried not to think about it. A six-month lease is a long time and besides she didn't really believe in ghosts.

Then another strange thing happened. Her underwear went missing, slowly, piece by piece. Every time she washed it and hung it to dry, it would disappear overnight, never to be seen again. It was bizarre.

After she started to run short of undies, she mentioned it to a friend of hers. She didn't mention the ghostly sightings—she was far too embarrassed about that—but she was nervous about who might be coming into her apartment, and when, and stealing her underwear.

Her friend said, "Well, of course, you know where you're staying." Patsy said, "No, what about it?" And her friend told her the story.

Years before, a young man, who was a former tenant in her apartment, became mixed up in the drug scene. He kept unsavoury company and eventually met a sudden and untimely death. He was shot. However, in life he was known to have a penchant for collecting trophy underwear from his women, and after his death, an impressive array was found in his room. The young man's ghost apparently continued this fetish. Patsy was horrified and moved out.

Just by chance, Ava also knew the next tenant in this apartment, and so in due course she asked her, "So, how is your new apartment?" "Well," her friend replied, "it's the strangest thing. My underwear keeps disappearing."

Although I initially found this tale amusing, the recent murders perpetrated by the (former) Colonel Williams[9] (Canada) have persuaded me otherwise.

Ava then told me about her aunt. She said her aunt is a very religious and upright woman who is not given to telling fibs. Her aunt—let's call her Emma—moved into her new home on the Prairies. There was nothing about the place to indicate anything was wrong when she bought it and there was no disclosure by the realtor, but not long after she moved in, she found herself disturbed by some nightly goings-on in her kitchen. Apparently, the kitchen cupboards would come alive with doors opening and closing and banging. It was a great cacophony. As there were no drafts to warrant this, she couldn't understand it. She was beginning to suspect that these events involved the paranormal. Then, inexplicably, things intensified. She started to have fires in her kitchen. Fires may happen once, maybe, if you're careless, but twice? That was enough for her; she moved out!

From what I understand, life has now returned to normal for Emma. The ghost did not follow her to her new residence, and she is no longer on fire alert.

Although this is a simple story, it is not an easy one to understand. I suspect that this ghost was attached to the location. This entity would apparently rather burn the home than have some people in it. If noise won't drive them out, a fire surely will. It makes one curious to know the history of the place. Who was this ghost and why was she or he so angry?

At the Hairdresser

Insight:

*Some ghosts think they own the place and that
people are just there by grace and favour.*

I enjoy having my hair done. I go religiously every four weeks and have done so
since I was 12. I think it is one of the greatest pleasures in life. You go in looking
drab and come out feeling wonderful. I could say looking wonderful, but that
would be a gross exaggeration of the facts. For many years I went to the salon
on Front Street. This was housed in a three-storey turn-of-the-century home.
Over the years I have been on each level of the house.

The first floor always felt welcoming to me. It housed the original front
parlour, dining room, kitchen and pantry. Initially, I had my hair done in
the dining room and the parlour was set up as a reception area. As the salon
expanded and more hairdressers came on board, my hairdresser relocated to
the second floor or bedroom area. A masseuse had treatment rooms on the
third floor, and the basement was reserved for salon supplies and break rooms
for the staff.

After I moved up to the second floor, I started to feel uncomfortable. I
found that I could sit in the master bedroom to have my hair done, but was
most anxious whenever I sat in the basin area, which was located in the former
bathroom. I wouldn't stay in that room alone and I hated getting my hair washed
in there. I always sensed a presence and it gave me the creeps. It seemed to
hover behind me.

For a time I made excuses about where I wanted to sit and why, and then
finally Richard, my hairdresser, asked me what was going on. I didn't want to
lie to the man so I said that the room just felt bad to me. He said, "Isn't that
interesting. An old couple used to live in this home, and I'm told the old man

died in there." I said to him, "I don't think he just died, I think he committed suicide." Richard didn't know anything about that, but he did say that the wife had also died in the home. He said he often felt her presence downstairs, and that she frequently rearranged the knickknacks and photographs, and sometimes even the chairs, in the waiting area. He found her to be a tasteful individual. Her little decorating touches were often an improvement. I didn't feel that the old gentleman was as pleasant a personality.

Years went by. I continued to have my hair done, and Richard ensured that I was comfortable. Then a new student came to the salon. It was her job to work on the second floor with Richard, and to carry supplies from the basement to the masseuse on the third floor. She was also responsible for cleaning up and locking up at night. She seemed to be a sensible girl.

One evening she refused to work above the first floor. Richard argued with her, telling her that was her job. She was adamant. She told him that "Michael James," the ghost on the second floor, had told her to stay away, and she had no intention of confronting him, or of invading his territory.

Richard had never mentioned the ghost to her. In fact, he never mentioned the ghost to anyone as it would have been bad for business. He only told me because I felt it anyway.

Obviously, the student couldn't stay, or more accurately, wouldn't stay. She lasted three weeks and then left. But Richard was curious. He wondered about the name the student had mentioned. Who was Michael James and why was he there? A title search revealed that he was a previous owner of the premises—one who had never moved on.

Over time, Michael became less confrontational with the people in his shared space. He began to communicate directly with Richard and let him know that he was satisfied with the improvements that Richard had made to his home. One could almost view him as a permanent "overseer" of the property... that is, until he can be persuaded to be otherwise.

The Office on Main Street

Insight:

It is easier to admit an experience than to block it out.

I have enjoyed a number of careers through my lifetime—everything from broadcaster to court reporter. It seems that approximately every seven years, I would shed my skin, reinvent myself and try something new. In my younger years I was a secretary, and for some of those years our office was housed in a three-storey building on Main Street.

It was a well-attended building. A popular pizza parlour and video shop occupied the first floor, and our firm was on the upper two floors. At one time the office had teemed with staff, but my boss had cut back and only four of us remained. Colleen, the receptionist, and I worked on the second floor, and my co-worker, Miranda, worked alone on the third floor. Our boss, Stephanie, also had an office on the second floor, but, in truth, was rarely there, preferring to work from home. To a large extent, we all worked alone, submitted our work to Stephanie via fax at the end of the day, and went home. Because of the isolated nature of our work, we didn't really function as an interactive team. I worked on different projects than Miranda and Colleen, and there was no need to share information.

I had a lot going on in my personal life at that time. Both my parents were ill, and I was receiving daily bulletins on their failing health. I felt dragged out and low and I had a never-ending migraine headache that I learned to work around. Miranda had her own worries and concerns, but as we never shared personal information, I wasn't aware of these at the time.

On the rare occasion when Stephanie came to work, we would all get together for strategy sessions and coffee. She was moving the firm in a new direction. It was on one such day that I fell down the office stairs. Now, this might not seem like much to you, but it was to me, because I was raised in a mountainous country with stairs everywhere, and I had never fallen down any of them. On this day I know I did not trip; I did not stumble; I simply fell, and even more amazing to me was that my full cup of coffee was still intact in my hand at the bottom of the staircase.

Of course, I never do anything quietly and I did not fall down the stairs lightly. I sounded like a herd of elephants and everyone came running to find me in an untidy heap at the bottom, with an ankle that was fast swelling and turning blue. My boss asked me what happened. I told her I had no idea. She told me that people often fell down that staircase, and I found that odd.

Later, when my ankle was less sore, I made my way back up the stairs to check to see if they were all standard width. I thought that perhaps, as it was an older building, they might not be up to code, but that was not the case. They were an ordinary standard set of risers. So I went back into my office and sat down. I never liked those stairs and because of that, I confined my visits to the third floor to trips of necessity.

Our office was dated both in furnishings and decor. We had drab carpets and institutional off-white paint. Years before, the premises had been a family home but had long since been converted to office space. The building was a strange design. I think the second floor, my floor, originally housed the bedrooms, and there were three small rooms and one larger one. The third floor may have been for storage, or perhaps housed the servants' quarters. There were two large rooms and each had a wall-to-wall closet. These shoulder-height closets actually connected to each other, like a hidden passageway, and ran the length of the back of the house. It was hard to imagine what people would have kept there, as they were too short to hang clothes in and much too large for trunk or suitcase storage. We rarely opened them as we believed they housed a thriving mouse population. Sometimes one made it out into the general office and caused us great consternation.

At around this time, I remember that the receptionist started to complain that her computer was already on when she arrived in the morning, and that she always turned it off before she left at night. The same thing was happening with Miranda's typewriter. Then Miranda complained that someone was constantly adjusting the height of her steno chair and had taken her reference book off her desk. While nothing was happening in my room, I had noticed that our hallway blinds were open every morning, when I knew that we closed them before leaving at night. With everyone complaining and no one taking responsibility, I felt it was time to call the boss.

We asked for an office meeting and laid out our concerns to Stephanie. At that time we felt that someone might be going through our office files after hours and that would constitute a serious privacy issue. Stephanie placed a call to the police. In no time they arrived and reviewed our practices with us. They told us that it would be difficult for them to pick out a suspicious vehicle in the car park because of the ever-present traffic. However, they offered to keep an eye on the place, and suggested that we arrive and leave on time and never work alone in the office.

We were all sitting in Stephanie's office during this meeting and just in passing, she absent-mindedly picked up her clock and rewound it. She asked if any of us knew of a good clock repair person because, for no apparent reason, her clock kept stopping at 3:15. That time spooked me. I have always regarded "3" to be an inauspicious time. I quietly revised my opinion about what might be in our office after hours.

I continued to work as usual over the following weeks. My work was solitary. I met with clients and drafted their documents. For every hour I spent with them, I spent eight hours alone. I had a small printer which tended to malfunction. One afternoon, I unplugged it with the intention of rebooting it. As I pulled out the plug, my bracelet touched the outlet and I received an electric jolt. It was substantial enough to deposit black soot from my fingertips to my elbow, and it gouged a deep line in my gold bracelet. I was so upset that I left work and drove home before I remembered to tell my boss that I was leaving. I don't remember most of the trip—I think I was on autopilot. When I finally remembered to call her, I requested that she check the building's electrical as I was sure it was faulty.

She called the electrician the following day. However, after checking the outlet and hearing my story, he was incredulous. He kept insisting that there was nothing wrong with the electrical wiring and that I simply could not have sustained a shock in the manner I alleged. I found this irritating, especially as I had to foot the bill to repair my bracelet and furthermore, Colleen was my witness, and had seen the soot on my arm. Later, though, when I calmed down, I wondered, "Well, what if he's right? What does that mean?" I picked up two wooden rulers and made a cross with a rubber band and told myself that if there was something peculiar going on, I didn't want any part of it. I put my makeshift cross on my bookshelf.

A few days later, I sat down to talk to Miranda. I wondered if she had ever felt anything ghostly in the office. She did not welcome this conversation at all and was adamant—she did not believe in ghosts; they were a product of people's overactive imaginations. I didn't argue with her, but I did state that my experience had led me to believe otherwise. As I made my way across the room to the doorway, I told her that I had nicknamed our nocturnal visitor, be it real or imaginary, "Annabel." This annoyed her even more. She insisted there were no ghosts and that if there were such a presence, it should make itself known and not just make a nuisance of itself.

I was disturbed by her words, and froze in the doorway. I was even more alarmed when a heavy electrical box flew off the desk behind her and hit the opposite wall with a very loud thud. That did it for me; I did not stick around. I flew down those stairs, and as fast as I went, Miranda was moving faster. She had her hand on my back, between my shoulder blades, and she was pushing me on. Had I tripped, she would have run right over me. If I was frightened, then she was terrified. There were two flights of stairs and we both cleared them in seconds. When we reached the safety of my office I said, "Why on earth would you say a thing like that? Now you've challenged it." She repeated that she did not believe in ghosts and I told her that in the normal course, transformers don't fly.

My room felt safe and eventually I settled down enough to return to work. Miranda, poor woman, had to return back upstairs to her office. I don't know how she did it, but we both had deadlines to meet and our jobs were dependant on that.

After that, I avoided all ghost-talk with her and the next week or so passed by. Blinds continued to be altered. Chairs continued to change heights. Computers and typewriters were on when we arrived at work and the clock continued to read 3:15. Miranda ignored it all.

Colleen became fed up. She quit her reception duties and was not replaced. She said she felt unsafe and, anyway, the place smelled. I asked her what she meant and she told me that she often got a whiff of gas at her desk and thought the whole environment was unhealthy for more reasons than one.

That left Miranda and me. Eventually, I took a day off—I can't remember if it was a holiday or if I was at home sick, but in the early afternoon I received a panicked call from Miranda. She had never before called me at home. She asked me what I could hear. I didn't know what she was asking me. I said, "I hear you, of course." She said, "What else?" I said I heard the typewriter. She said, "Well, I'm the only one here, and I'm at my desk." That stopped me in my tracks. It was impossible. The typewriter was located approximately 3 metres from her desk, and yet it was beating a steady and unmistakable tattoo. Someone was definitely typing. She said, "I can't take this anymore; I'm leaving." She phoned our boss and left.

The next morning my boss called an emergency meeting with both of us. We discussed the event and what to do about it. Someone suggested that we put a page in the typewriter and see if there was a message, but I was against it. I felt the dead should stay dead and we should not communicate with them.

Stephanie decided to call in a local healer to smudge the offices. He came, smudged and left, but nothing changed. The rooms did not feel different to me, and the clock, blinds, chairs and computers still had the same interference. Apparently, our spirit was not responsive to First Nations' rites.

Our building had been in the ownership of the same family for generations and I wondered aloud if they might know who was haunting us. I had the feeling that it was a young teenage female who was more boisterous than malicious; someone who wanted to be noticed but not seen; whose mission was to scare us and disrupt our work. Then again, I'm no expert. I wanted to question our landlord as to whether any of the family had noticed this entity but my boss vetoed the idea. She felt her credibility as a professional would be called into question and even ridicule. She just wanted to end her lease and leave. Stephanie promised us that until we moved, no one would work alone, and for a time she came to the office every day.

One morning I arrived bright and early and I noticed the smell of gas. Although Colleen had complained of this, I had never before noticed it. On this occasion it was so bad that I felt weak at the knees and I noticed that my headache had returned with a vengeance. We called the fire brigade. When they came, in spite of the fact that we had opened all windows and doors some ten minutes prior, they deemed the place pre-explosion, and a citation was issued to the owner. We lost half a day's work waiting for the fumes to clear.

We experienced repeated gaseous events over the next few weeks, which prompted more calls to the fire department. This was a worry. Should there be a fire in the stairwell, I had a window and outside door to escape from, but Miranda was up on the third floor, high above the outside concrete, with a broken and non-functioning fire escape. She would have no way out. Her husband took matters into his own hands and attempted to repair the fire escape. My husband reported the code violation to the city.

After yet another gaseous occurrence, I informed Stephanie that I was leaving until she had located a safer work venue for us. That day, she made arrangements to move our firm to a building across town.

And then, finally, it was moving day. Miranda and I were to box everything, and the movers were responsible for transporting file boxes and equipment. I packed up quickly, and it was time to help Miranda. I went upstairs and found her sitting white-faced at her computer. The cupboard door beside her was repeatedly opening and closing. It could not have been the wind. I have never seen anything like it. Open/close; open/close... It was a rapid rhythmic action that could only be achieved by someone actually manhandling it. I said, "What on earth...?" And she said, "I'm not looking at it. I don't see it." Even then she wouldn't acknowledge the possibility of ghosts and I knew better than to argue with her. How she justified these happenings, I have no idea. I got up to leave, but she pleaded with me to stay and I did because she looked so wretched sitting there all by herself. Interestingly enough, I was not upset. It seems that it is far easier to admit what you're seeing than to try and block it from your mind.

As soon as Miranda packed her files, we drove over to our new workplace. Soon afterwards, the movers arrived with the keys to our former office. We had asked that they lock the premises and bring us the keys. However, when they arrived, they told us that they had not been able to lock up as there was still someone in the closet packing. I don't know who they thought they saw but it wasn't one of us; we were all accounted for. I did not volunteer to return to lock the office and neither did Miranda.

Since that time I've often wondered what the point of the whole thing was. I've now come to believe that the ghost wanted to protect us from the gas. Gas leaks are insidious things, yet no one was taking them seriously and the danger was very real. During our time in that office both Miranda and I became ill, yet neither of us thought to mention it. I put my headaches down to my worry about my parents, and Miranda had her own concerns, and in retrospect, I think the ghost was trying to get us out of there.

At the Centres

Insight:

*There are many reasons why ghosts stick around—
attachments to people, places or things; and sometimes
they don't realize that they are dead.*

Two of my friends and I decided to have lunch in town. Technically, this involved a little bit of hookey on their part, but I prefer to think of it as a mental health break. Everyone needs a little downtime and this was ours. Trish was having a difficult time following her recent surgery and Betsy and I, like two mother hens, were there to provide moral support.

After we discussed work scenarios and strategies, it was time to relax. I had just eaten the most sumptuous pot roast followed by cherry pie. It was blustery and cold outside and I felt the need of comfort food. What could be more satisfying? The other two were more abstemious—forgoing dessert, and selecting a salad entrée. At times I wonder about my friends and me—we are so very different. There are occasions when I like to kick over the traces and try everything to excess. My friends are invariably more moderate in their lifestyles.

We inevitably got into a discussion of what next? I am the oldest of the three and have just retired. The other two are success stories at the peak of their careers. They were interested to know how I was handling retirement, as it is such a change from full on to full stop. But I like change. All of my life I have embraced it. I told them that I was having a ball and was still undecided whether to retire completely, or to take up some sort of part-time occupation down the road. I said I would give myself a period of rest and relaxation before making a decision either way. In the meantime, I was enjoying writing and painting.

"Writing what?" Trish asked. "Ghost stories," I replied." What fun!" she said. "I have one for you." And she told me this tale.

Now, to give you some background, Trish is a social worker. She oversees a series of live-in centres for people who are trying to turn their lives around. She's good at her job and has designed many in-house programs that have been adopted nationwide. You could say she is cutting-edge in her field—full of imagination and initiative. Her programs appear in television documentaries.

She has never seen a ghost herself but many of her staff and guests have, and she is not about to deny them their experiences. She told me that the stories are too similar, happen too often, and affect too many people to be written off. She routinely has the centres smudged and blessed to cover all bases, but nonetheless there are three resident entities in the Centre I will call "Mount Pleasant" and one at the Centre I will call "Mount Hope." They are all distinct in nature and tend to turn up in the late afternoon and evening. Generally speaking, long-term guests check in at Mount Hope with short-term guests at Mount Pleasant. There is always a revolving door of patrons in and out and sometimes back again.

The first entity at Mount Pleasant is the man in the plaid shirt. He is an older gentleman. He visits the centre and just checks things out. Yet in all the years of operation at that site, this old chap has never scared anyone. He drops in, walks about and then leaves. He's friendly and I tend to think that he is attached to the location. Trish tells me that he was never associated with the premises either as a guest or prior owner and I think that perhaps he once owned or worked on the land the centre is built on. Plaid shirts generally denote work shirts. I suspect he might have been an old time lumberjack. After all, St Anne's was once a lumber town.

The next entity at Mount Pleasant is a woman. Like the old gentleman, she is no threat to anyone and just drops in from time to time. She has a long white gown, which again would suggest a yesteryear existence. She brings with her a sense of quietness and calm. No one objects to her presence. She always appears around the same time as the third entity.

The third entity is the reason that Trish gets the place blessed and smudged. This creature is a black mass that appears, annoys, terrifies and leaves. It has no definite shape. It conveys no idea of personhood. From her description, I imagine it to be a menacing him. His actions don't portray him as evil per se, but he is definitely not happy.

He appears when people are at their most vulnerable—when clients are alone in their rooms, or staff are on solo duty at the desk. He isn't quiet. He won't be ignored. He interrupts and disrupts. If clients attempt to sleep, he will frighten them into wakefulness by dropping things, moving things or hovering over them; and if staff attempt to work, he will throw their work on the floor. He is intimidating and conveys a sense of violence. He does, however, respond to being told to get lost even though he will not stay gone for long.

So what is this entity? Trish had never had any experience with anything like this, so she asked a visiting elder what his thoughts were. He was of the opinion that the clients, in their pain and adversity, inadvertently attract him.

I thought about his explanation and I believe he's right. Guests arrive at their lowest personal ebbs—in deep emotional and physical pain. They require help because they can no longer go it alone. Naturally, their auras would reflect their physical and emotional state, and would be murky. The black entity would be comfortable with that. Anything dark is familiar territory for him. Every time there is a new arrival—a new fraught client, a new pain, a new sorrow, a new grief—this darker creature is drawn out. He identifies with negative emotions.

The female entity, the elder believed, arrived to counterbalance the dark one and provide a level of protection to those in need; and the third one, well, the man in the plaid shirt just hasn't moved on. Maybe he doesn't know that he is dead.

Trish and I talked about these entities at some length. I thought she ought to discuss them further with a minister friend of hers because this is one instance where I believe that perhaps something more than a blessing is required. I would like to know that the old gentleman in the plaid shirt, who does no harm to anyone, had been informed of his true status and invited to walk into the light. The dark entity is more problematic. I don't think he could accept the light. It would not be comfortable for him at all. But he might—just might—be persuaded to take himself off elsewhere. And once he's gone, the protective one will move on as well.

Mount Hope's entity is totally different. Guests come to Mount H as it's known locally, for rest and recuperation. Physical pain is largely behind them, although emotional scars may persist. They are at Mount H to receive support and encouragement. It is an upbeat place. I would expect by this stage that the guests' auras are improving as they are reflective of their state of being. Not surprisingly, the entity there is light and mischievous. Staff and patrons recognise it as a female entity. She's playful and delights in hiding things—which is irritating and a nuisance. Guests will place an item in one location and find it moved somewhere totally different. The entity involves them in a game of hide and seek.

This is the sort of thing that children like to do. I suspect that this is a young female entity who is attached to the location. She probably does not realise that she is dead and simply wants acknowledgment of her existence. When she finds herself ignored by those around her, she tries to engage them. She is not sinister, just lost.

The staff, however, have a slightly different view. They believe the entity once lived at Mount H, where she was happy... and so she returns.

The Smallest Seer

Insight:

*Children are placed at risk when we don't
acknowledge a dangerous situation.*

In one of my careers I worked with a delightful girl whom I'll call Sarah. Sarah and her husband have two children, the youngest of whom is Jamie. At the time of the incident, he was around three years old.

Sarah and her husband Jake are a genuinely happy couple and very family-oriented. Sarah always came to work in a good mood with humorous, loving stories about her children. They were her life. Most times I am not interested in hearing about other people's kids but Sarah was different. She was quite literally the happiness person in the office. When she came to work in the morning, the atmosphere lightened around her. She was a joy to be with; we all loved her, and by extension, her family.

However, one day she arrived quite distraught. She told us that her son was seeing dead people. Of course, that caught our attention. Most of us had seen "The Sixth Sense"[10] and we couldn't wait to hear more.

We learned that Jamie, like many youngsters, talked to an invisible friend. Although surprised by this development, initially, Sarah and Jake were not troubled. They recognized that their son was not only creative and imaginative, but also a happy well-adjusted child who enjoyed close relationships with friends and family.

However, Jamie's friendship with his special friend was evolving, and this friend seemed to be commanding more and more of his time and attention. Although their friendship started off quite pleasantly, the tenor of their conversation had changed, and Sarah was now uneasy. Jamie reported that his friend promised not to hurt him if he did what he was told. The friend was establishing an alpha-relationship with the child. Sarah was beginning to fear that, whether or not the imaginary friend existed, this was not a healthy development for their son. She tried to dissuade him from continuing the friendship, and invited other little friends over to distract him, but the invisible friend seemed to have a strong hold on the child and his imagination. Jamie saw him as real, although he seemed to understand and appreciate that no one else could see him.

Sarah started to pay close attention. She noticed something else that was strange. For no good reason, their family pet, a cat, had started to prance on stiff legs, back arched and fur raised. This always happened near where Jamie and his friend were playing. Sarah started to wonder if perhaps the imaginary friend wasn't so imaginary after all.

She asked us what we thought. I believe there are ghosts and said so. The others were divided 50/50, some believing and some not, but we were all in agreement that it was an unhealthy situation for Jamie to be in.

Sarah tried discussing the situation with her husband, but he didn't want to hear about it. Truth be told, it freaked him out. He kept telling Sarah, "Tell him to stop" whenever the subject arose. This invisible thing was now causing a lot of discord in the home. And the minute there was mention of getting rid of the friend, other things started to happen. Lights went out at inconvenient times; Jake fell down the stairs not once, but a number of times; and Jamie's friend seemed to be more insistent on time being spent with him, and with him alone, and upon things being done his way—or else.

When Sarah brought these stories to work, we all became concerned. Peter, an intuitive co-worker, told Sarah that she should leave the house. He said, "Sell up and move—take a financial loss if need be—but just get out." He reminded her that none of her family had been well since they moved in and suggested that things would only get worse. He advised as an interim measure, that she place salt around the perimeter of her home. I am not sure of the significance of salt, but in any event, it did not work. The friend continued to engage and threaten, and Jake kept falling down flights of stairs. I agreed with Peter. I felt the family should move out.

I asked Sarah if her husband was usually a klutz. She said not that she had noticed—and, of course, she would know as they had been married for 10 or more years. She told me that occasionally she was clumsy but her husband was not. I asked her to consider why it was that he had started to fall down the stairs—did he need his eyes examined? were the stairs not built to code? or was he being pushed? She decided to check it out. Jake's eyes were fine, and the stairs were standard. The situation, for them, defied explanation. Peter and I had one, but not one that they were prepared to hear.

Meanwhile, life went on. One day Sarah took a number of photographs of the house. She photographed the children, the living room, the kitchen and the stairs. When the pictures were developed, one clearly captured an apparition on the stairway.

Sarah and Jake sold their house. They moved to one in a neighbouring street. I am told that they took quite a financial loss but at least Jamie said goodbye to his imaginary friend for good. The little family are now ensconced in their new home and I have it on good authority that Jake has stopped falling down the stairs.

But the story has taken an interesting turn. It appears that Jamie is not the only person in the family to experience psychic happenings. Sarah's sixth sense has activated—perhaps in protection of her son, and perhaps not. Her special awareness, however, does not confine itself to family matters. Her scope of "insider" knowledge has become much broader than that.

The Easter Bunny

Insight:

Children often see other planes.

Anna is another one of our Friday night supper crowd. She works in the medical field, and shares my passion for travel. She is very good company with a broad range of interests, and she and her husband regale us with wonderful travel stories each time they return from one of their many jaunts abroad.

Prior to her joining our supper crowd, we had met. I didn't know her well but our paths seemed to cross at various seminars over the years. She turned out to be a close friend of Marie Claire's, who invited her to join us. It really is a small world!

As we were walking out the restaurant door one evening, she overheard me discussing a story with Cate and asked what we were talking about. I told her I was collecting ghost stories and she said, "Oh, well, I have a few to tell you about." As the evening was already late we promised each other that we would get together soon for a good old fashioned story-tell, but before she left that night she told me this little tidbit of a tale.

When she was young, she remembers anxiously awaiting the arrival of the Easter Bunny. She could barely contain her excitement. She had been promised Easter eggs and chocolate, and like all small children, she simply couldn't wait. She hurried off to bed early, willing the morning to arrive, and awoke pre-dawn. The household was still quiet and all was in darkness. She crept out to the staircase and peeked through the railing into the living room. She wanted to see the Easter Bunny. With all the determination of a small child, she watched and waited and her eyes gradually adjusted to the creeping dawn.

She was surprised when she saw a tall man in funny clothes standing in the living room. He was checking out the Easter candies, and so she thought, "Well, that must be the Easter Bunny but he doesn't look like a bunny." However, misnomer aside, she was satisfied. He had come, the candies were there and all was well with her world. She crept back to her room thrilled with her secret escapade.

Some hours later the household awoke. Anna is one of four children, so you can imagine the hustle and bustle and excitement as each discovered their candies. She told her mom that she had seen the Easter Bunny. "Really?" her mother sounded most impressed. "Yes, I did, but why do you call him a bunny? He's not a bunny; he's a man." Her mother looked a bit confused. "What did he look like, dear?" "Well," said Anna, "he had funny pants on and boots that came all the way up to here" indicating her knee. "What was funny about his pants?" her mother asked. Anna pointed to her thigh and explained that, "They were fat and baggy here." Her mother nodded and walked over to the cabinet. She returned a few seconds later with an old photo album. She flicked through the pages before removing one of the pictures and showing it to her daughter. "Is this the man you saw, dear?" "Yes, that's him; that's the Easter Bunny." "No, dear," replied her mother, "that's your grandfather."

The explanation really didn't mean much to Anna that day. She didn't know her grandfather; she'd never met him. She didn't even know he was dead. The man she saw that day was dressed in jodhpurs and riding boots. Anna didn't know anything about those then either. The penny didn't drop with her until many years later.

Great-Uncle August

Insight:

Interpersonal ties bind planes of existence.

Anna had one other tale to tell. This one involved her great-uncle August. When she was young, she spent a lot of time sitting around the fire listening to family stories. Television was in its infancy in those years and family times involved reading and story times. Some of these stories involved otherworldly experiences and this one, in particular, captured her imagination. It was set in the trenches in France during World War I.

The war broke out when her grandfather and great-uncle August were young men in their prime. August joined the Army and was eventually posted to France. August's buddy, Sam was in the same regiment, and they were in the trenches together. Sometimes they fought side by side and at other times they were stationed apart. These trenches were hideous places. If the gas didn't get you, a bullet would. They were dark, muddy, smelly death traps and the only way to defend them was to stick your head up and hope that no one shot it off in an exchange of gunfire.

During one long, arduous battle, August and Sam were at different ends of the trench, but within hailing distance. After every skirmish, each would check to see that the other had made it through. Then the unthinkable happened—Sam was fatally shot. August saw him fall. He drew some consolation from the fact that at least Sam's death was quick and he didn't suffer. In war, you are grateful for these small mercies. If you couldn't manage to live, then the next best thing was a quick death. Too many men died agonizing deaths, and it was torture to hear their screams.

The battle continued. August manned his position and the skirmishes went long into the night. Volley upon volley; round upon round. The scream of bullets too close to his head... It was relentless. Then above it all, he distinctly heard Sam's voice shouting at him, "Get out, Oggie, now. Move. Run." August didn't question it. He didn't hesitate. He took off running down the trench as the earth exploded all around him. Someone had lobbed a grenade at the spot where he had been standing.

August continued to fight that night, and the next, and the next after that. Eventually the war ended and he returned safely home to Canada. He had Sam to thank for that.

Louise's Encounter

Insight:

Sometimes our life choices cause our angels to mourn our decisions.

Louise and her husband John often join us on Friday night. Louise is a settled, happily married woman, who has enjoyed a most unusual life. She grew up on the prairies where she trained as a nurse. In her 20s, she worked in hospital administration in the Canadian far north. Later, she changed careers and locations, and moved south to Ontario where she took a supervisory position with a large international corporation. If you had to use one word to describe Louise, it would be "capable." Throughout her life, she has travelled extensively. It is one of her passions, and her husband shares her interest.

Louise and I took a trip together, and she told me about her encounter with the supernatural. She said that when she was younger, she and two friends set off on an extended trip through the South Pacific. There they spent time in both New Zealand and Australia.

During their time in Sydney, the three women stayed in a hostel. Because there were only two beds to a room, her friends shared one room, and she was assigned another room, with a stranger.

Louise and her friends spent their days exploring Sydney, and returned to their rooms at the last possible moment at night. Sydney is an exciting city and they didn't want to miss any of it. In hostel life, there's not usually a lot of time between house curfew and lights out, so she didn't really have the opportunity to meet her roommate, just a "Hi there," sort of thing. Louise had the impression that her roommate was just another traveller—perhaps a little bolder than most because she was travelling solo—but she said that she really didn't pay too much attention to her at the time. She simply ran in at night, changed, and hopped into bed before lights out.

That first night Louise fell asleep quickly. She was tired and her legs were sore from walking the endless Sydney hills—which are quite challenging for someone raised on the prairies. You discover muscles you never knew existed, and you know about them for a few months to come.

Sometime in the night, she awoke to the sound of sobbing. These were deep, heartfelt, racking sobs—not the sniffly sort you expect from a person with a case of homesickness. Whatever was wrong, was major. As it was the wee hours of the morning, her room was quite dark, but despite the enveloping gloom, she was easily able to make out a figure sitting on the end of the other bed. Of course, she immediately assumed it was her roommate, and went over to see if she could help.

She paid much more attention to the woman than she had earlier in the evening. Then, she had been no more than a head on a pillow with blankets to her chin. Now she saw that the young woman had long fair hair tumbling down her back. Her face was hidden from view and cupped in her hands, and she was dressed in a long gown that Louise presumed was her nightie. She was absolutely bereft.

Louise reached out to touch her shoulder to let her know she was there. As she reached out, her hand passed through the woman's shoulder, and then, to her absolute astonishment, the young woman faded from sight, and the sound of her sobbing ebbed away.

By this time Louise's roommate was sitting up in bed, watching. Apparently she, too, had been awoken by the crying apparition at the end of her bed, but unlike Louise, she was totally unfazed by it. Louise had never seen anything like this in her life. She was now wide-awake with adrenaline pumping but her roommate was strangely unaffected. She took it all in stride. Louise wanted answers. She wanted a discussion. She wanted to talk—but her roommate simply shrugged off her questions, rolled over and went back to sleep. She had no inclination to discuss the incident at all. Louise found her reactions bizarre.

I asked Louise what the entity looked like. She said that although the room was dim, the woman appeared to her to be quite brightly lit, however, that anomaly didn't hit her at the time because she was so focused on helping. So I asked her, "Well, then, was it a ghost or an angel?" She said, "Well, do angels cry?" I must confess that I don't know for sure—but if not, why not? I said that I didn't think that ghosts were so brightly lit.

She said she lay awake for the rest of the night trying to make sense of it all. Was the entity there for her, or for her roommate, or was she just someone attached to the room? I asked her whether the apparition appeared to be in real time or olden time. She thought she was in real time. She reasoned that the being had nothing to do with her own life. She did not recognise her, and her own life was happy. There was no reason for tears. However, she was not so certain about her roommate.

I asked her about her roommate, but because they were strangers, she knew virtually nothing about her. They had only shared light pleasantries.

From what Louise told me, I suspect the being was an angel associated with the young traveller. This entity did not hide her presence and she did not hide her grief. She wanted to be seen, heard and understood. It was unusual in those years for a young woman to travel alone, and I think there was a story behind that. I think her angel was crying for her. The young woman appeared not to be surprised by the entity's appearance, which leads me to believe that she had seen her before, and knew full well who she was and why she was there. Otherwise wouldn't it be human nature to talk about it? Wouldn't you? Thirty years later, Louise is.

I asked her to proofread her story for accuracy, and she wrote back "The passing of time has not made the event lose any of its realism. It has not faded and this seems unusual. I don't even consider whether I saw something. I know I saw something."

The Psychic

Insight:

Ghosts can be protective—or was this actually a guide?

All things psychic intrigue me. An old friend was in town and he introduced me to an interesting couple. The husband, a man in his 50's, had in earlier years been a seer. He worked in a section of the military that most people don't know about. He and his team saw situations and developed strategies. They were apparently pretty good at it. He never lost a man, not even on frontline duty. He told me his was the only team with a perfect record.

We were invited to supper at his house, and I couldn't wait to go. His wife invited us. She said that her husband was hoping to develop happier psychic experiences, and at that time I was enjoying my angel cards which she saw as good. Her husband's psychic experiences had been fraught, involving matters of life and death. She felt he had a gift, which should be a positive thing, not a nightmare.

I knew that he was a gifted seer, and hoped that he would read me. I had just had some interesting Kirlian[11] photography done and some of the pictures were difficult for me to interpret. Generally, I have a turquoise aura. I have tracked it over a number of years with several different photographers. It's nearly always the same. I vibrate between green and blue. However, one of my pictures showed an indigo figure standing directly behind me—or so I thought—when there was no one actually there. Indigo, to me, is a high vibration. I brought my pictures to him to analyze. I thought he might be able to do this for me.

His actual skills were in remote reviewing. He could determine a best course of action. In the military he worked with a mentor—one who reviewed the information he received and his conclusions. He did not usually work alone. However, he was confident, and he told me that he could also read people through articles that held their vibration. I gave him my ring, but he was reluctant to read me that night and seemed ill at ease.

I found him distracted and somewhat difficult to talk to, so I brought the conversation around to him and his skills and abilities. I find that nervous or remote people will often talk about themselves, and that it's usually a safe subject for them. They don't have to try too hard. He told me about his military experiences, and I asked him how he honed his psychic skills. He brought me a cork with a needle and thread. He inserted the threaded needle into the centre of the cork, and then mentally directed it. The needle swung in every direction he dictated, at differing speeds, all of which he controlled with his mind. He told me that he practiced this simple task every night.

We then talked about mind activities. I have bent spoons and keys with my mind, but the nuisance of it is that while I have done it, and done it a few times, I can't control it. Sometimes I can do it and other times I can't. I can't seem to summon the skill at will. In order to do it at all, I have to meditate first. My friend Nicky, on the other hand, merely states what she intends to do and does it. No special preparation is required. She can clearly access the part of her mind that controls this much more easily than me. I want to know how to do this. To bend metal to one's will is amazing and it is possible to tie the spoons in knots.

We discussed this and other mental phenomena and then, finally, the psychic told me why he felt ill at ease. Our arrival at his home seemed to send out a challenge. He immediately experienced trouble with the electrical circuits in his home, which preoccupied him until he was able to resolve the situation in his mind. He later came to view these happenings as coincidental, but at the time they confused him.

I know that I am a good person, and that I did not bear him ill will or bring any negative feelings into his home, but someone was there protecting him, and that person was leery of me. It was then that he and I both saw her walking on their balcony.

At first glance, I thought I saw a neighbour coming to the patio door, and I drew his attention to it. He told me that his balcony was 3 metres off the ground with no stairway down. It only opened off their living room. There was no doubt what I was seeing—it was a "her." I asked him if he saw her too, and he acknowledged that he did. She did not join us in the living room but she certainly made her presence known. She paced the length of the balcony—nervously—to and fro, to and fro... It was like: I see you and I'm watching you.

Neither his wife nor my husband could see any of this happening. They were entirely comfortable chatting away in their corner of the living room.

Neither read the situation that was unfolding around us. It was interesting to me that both the psychic and I had married similar people—both are grounded individuals.

After the female entity determined that I was not actually a discordant personality and posed no threat to the household or to the psychic, she dematerialized and the electrical situation resolved.

I did not feel uncomfortable with this presence. It did not scare me. It was definitely not a bad spirit, merely a protective one. She is probably one that has been with him a long, long time, and has protected him through many situations. When she appeared, it was like a red flag for him. When she left, he relaxed. But why did she appear? What made her nervous? Was the psychic not used to visitors in his home?

Two explanations spring to mind: one is that I startled the entity who sent a warning to the psychic by way of electrical interference; the other is that the psychic's energy and mine were initially so at odds and out of sync that they interfered with the home electronics and prompted a visit from her.

When things settled back to normal in the home, the psychic looked at my pictures. He agreed with me that the indigo figure was not a figment of my imagination. He told me it was someone I knew well, who had recently died from cancer. He saw cancer in the lung area. I knew straight away it was my mother. He said he knew that it was someone who cared deeply for me, as she had an attitude of compassion with her hand on my shoulder. He asked whether I had been upset on the day the picture was taken as she appeared to be comforting me. I thought back. I remembered that I was at the psychic fair with my friend and I was concerned for her.

The psychic read all of my photos for me and explained them in detail. His observations on past events were sound. He was certainly gifted. One of my pictures showed a number of green orbs and I have always wondered what they were. They were all around me. He told me that I was surrounded by angels. I liked the sound of that. I feel that too.

Addendum ~

There is one further piece to this story.

The friend I was worried about did receive a clear analysis of her situation by the seer at the psychic fair. While he did not offer her solutions, he brought clarity to her personal dilemma. I think that is why my mother was reassuring me. There was no need for worry after all.

Electrical Interference

Insight:
Our field of influence is larger than we know.

My experience with the seer in "The Psychic" and other events has convinced me that human/electrical interference happens. In our family it has happened with a few of us. My sister for many years could not wear a watch as no matter what brand she tried, the watch would simply stop. I have since heard of others who attract this reaction.

When my father came to visit me many years ago, my husband took him to visit a science museum. At the time there was an interactive experiment that was quite popular. If you held a wand, your hair would stand on end. Dad joined the line-up. Everyone was having fun laughing at how ridiculous they looked. Then it was Dad's turn. He grasped the wand and found himself thrown across the room. He was not impressed.

So what happened there? What was it about his energy that intensified the electrical charge around him? Or was this just a power surge?

In my case, in my late 20s I developed the very unhelpful habit of stopping machinery. When it first occurred, I was a court reporter and used the standard government-issued X-brand typewriters. I had one machine at work and wanted to purchase another for home, but after I had broken a series of brand new typewriters, the sales clerk suggested that I purchase from another company as their machinery was not designed for my speed of operation. So I purchased brand Y, which functioned somewhat better, but not perfectly. My machinery always seemed to end up in the shop at the most inconvenient times, and then I began to be aware of a correlation. Whenever I had a certain feeling, my typewriter would break down shortly afterwards. The pattern was so apparent that I came to understand that one thing invariably meant the other, so I would proactively make an appointment for my typewriter. The conversation went something like this, "Good morning, I would like to make an appointment for my typewriter to be repaired tomorrow." "Certainly, and what is the problem with it?" "I'm not sure, but I need to have it repaired tomorrow." "Yes, but what part is not functioning now?" "Oh, it is functioning now but it will be broken by tomorrow."

The receptionist didn't argue; she just sent the repairperson out the next day, but after a time she and I became quite friendly and eventually she said to me, "Our guys are curious. They would like to come out immediately when you call, and not wait a day. They want to see what you're noticing." I assured her that there was nothing to see but that they were welcome to come. They came. They examined my typewriter, proclaimed it to be in perfect working order, and left. The next day they had to return to repair it. I never made a false call and the breakdowns were all dissimilar. Back then I didn't understand how I knew that my typewriter would break, but now I think I do.

The next development followed when I moved to an office setting. I worked for an individual who did everything at the last minute. I would find myself racing from photocopier to fax, and the more important the document, the more certain I could be that one or both of the machines would malfunction... but only for me. If I had the receptionist photocopy or fax for me, the equipment would be fine. It became a joke in the office that if someone else had an important deadline to meet, I should stay away from the equipment. At the time we all regarded it as pure coincidence.

However, when I moved to my next office, I became aware of an offsetting feature. The fax machine would be producing steadily until I passed by, and then the sound and speed would alter, and then resume normal operations once I had moved on. I tried an experiment. I determined where my field of influence lay, and stepped in and out of the field. The equipment functioned and malfunctioned accordingly. So the next time my computer malfunctioned, I called over another operator and asked her to stand in my cubicle for a moment. The machinery would then reset and all would be well. It then became apparent to me that my state of mind had a direct bearing on my equipment.

In my court reporting years, I had simply believed that it was a case of Murphy's Law.[12] If the transcript was important, then the machinery would break down. Now I realized that if I experienced any anxiety about the transcript I was working on, or felt any pressure from deadlines or any causes, then the machinery would break down. It seemed that my vibrations would go out of sync and cause a disruption in my field. My feelings had consequences. They affected my vibrations, which, in turn, affected everything around me.

In recent years, I have become interested in vibrational energy and frequently have energy treatments. Whenever I am feeling really stressed, my energy field reflects this. As practitioners pass their hands though my field, they report an electrical sensation, and on occasion have seen sparks and heard a "zzzzzzz" sound.

While my interactions can be annoying, at least their impacts have been relatively minor. A friend confided to me that her daughter was having some strange occurrences in her life. Whenever she was upset and stormed along a roadway, the streetlights would blow out in her wake. How embarrassing is that!

Apparently, we are not only connected to each other and all living things but also to all things, even inanimate objects. We are more powerful than we realise.

The Medium

Insight:

*Prepare for the task at hand, and protect yourself
when dealing with the unknown.*

It is always interesting to watch a medium at work. I've seen a few of them in action over the years—John Edward, John Holland, Sylvia Browne—and more recently I attended a world-class conference with two friends, and observed a new one, someone I was not at all familiar with.

This lady, whom I call "Betty" was attractive, with long raven-dark hair, which gave her a striking Eurasian appearance. The first day I watched her, her skill level greatly impressed me. She appeared to be happy, efficient and accurate. She managed the audience of 1500 with ease, and kept things moving along nicely. In all, it was an up-beat event and I looked forward to attending a second session with her the following day.

However, when I arrived in the auditorium the next morning, things looked off to me. When Betty walked out to the stage, I was not sure I was seeing the same person. Her face was not set in the happy contours of the previous day and her body language was stiff. However, while Elena and I noticed these details, our other friend noticed nothing amiss.

Betty was a professional, and the session proceeded in much the same vein as the previous day. She really was an outstanding medium. About midway through the program, Betty decided to lead us in a healing meditation. She asked us to open our hearts, and to bring to mind someone we were not fond of. The object of the exercise is to heal the rift between people. Everyone in the auditorium settled in to follow her lead.

I have done this type of meditation before, and taught it in my classes. It is well known and is designed to help you look at a discordant personality with compassion. It is actually a double-healer. You send good wishes to the person you don't like, and change the negative way you feel about them, thus improving yourself and them.

At Betty's instruction, we sat comfortably on our chairs, placed our feet firmly on the floor, and rested our hands palms-up on our knees. She began the guided meditation. Then I heard Betty start to cough. Once she started, she could not stop. She coughed incessantly. I saw her reach for an inhaler that did not appear to work, and I was alarmed as I watched her struggle for breath. All the while her aura grew huge and purple—which signifies impending death to me.

Someone in the front few rows handed Betty another inhaler, and I was relieved when it brought her coughing fit under control. By this time, Betty was in shock and appeared weak at the knees, prompting a brief adjournment of our session. My friends and I looked at each other and said, "Psychic attack."

Betty resumed her position on stage some 15 or 20 minutes later and told us what had happened. She asked if anyone in the auditorium had called upon a really nasty individual who was also an asthmatic. An older woman put up her hand. Betty asked her a few questions, and then indicated that this nasty entity had actually jumped into her body where he caused her to have a serious asthma attack. She said she had never experienced anything like this in her 17 years as a medium, and that it had been 12 years or more since she had suffered from asthma.

In watching the exchange between medium and student, it was apparent that the student recognized the attack immediately for what it was, and it did not surprise her. She said the nasty one was her father, and that he'd been narcissistic and abusive in life. She did not say psychopathic but the impression was there, and I suspect that's exactly what he was because he had made a clear attempt on this medium's life and he chose centre stage for his action. He was relentless. He tried a further attack after she recovered from the first one. Fortunately, the second time round the medium was more wary and protected herself. She did not indicate to us how she did this, but there are various methods. One is to mind-place a protective shield around yourself that nothing can enter.

The woman in the audience indicated that she was troubled by the attack on Betty, so had sent some healing thoughts. I remember thinking that her words didn't match her demeanour and I had difficulty believing her. The medium had one rather unsettling message to relay. The nasty one was proud of his daughter. Really! For what, precisely?

The seminar continued and for a time, our attention went to other things. However, even hours afterwards, my friends and I felt distressed, and despite the fact that we had made plans to go out for dinner, we felt incapable of leaving the hotel until we had made some sense of the incident. Jody's legs collapsed under her on our way back to our room, and Elena experienced a strange set of incidents where doors slammed on her bruising her arm, and hitting her on her backside. More than one of these doors was a sensor-type, and should have swung open not closed. She said that the other doors all felt strangely weighted, and interestingly, that weight was not in evidence the following day. Whatever had attacked Betty, had upset the ambiance of the place.

In talking about the incident, I felt that perhaps Betty had not centred or protected herself, and had left herself vulnerable. Jody wondered whether the nasty one's daughter was somehow complicit in the situation. I remembered my own reaction to her, and an inadvertent remark I had made calling her "that dreadful woman." Initially when those words came out of my mouth, I was ashamed of myself. The words spilled out without any thought behind them. That's not like me. Of course, these were just our impressions. We didn't know the woman in question, and she could well have been innocent of all sinister involvement.

The next morning, at a different class, we recognised many of the students from the previous day, and it was apparent that some were still confused and upset. One of them raised the incident with our new presenter. He had heard about the situation and told us that he had never seen such a thing before, or heard tell of it. He said that he had given the matter some thought and it was his impression that perhaps the entity was attracted to the presenter because of her disposition at that precise moment. This made absolute sense to me. We already knew that Betty was having an off day—we saw it—and the entity took advantage of her when her defences were down. I have noticed this before. If no protective measures are engaged, negative thoughts or feelings can attract the worst of entities.

This situation was a wakeup call for me. I used to quite blithely tell students to, "Think of someone you don't like." Now, I'll be much more careful to say, "Think of someone whom you respect and regret arguing with…" I don't want to invite any of these nasties into my life, or provide them with a stage to work on. It was also a forceful reminder to everyone at that seminar that it doesn't matter how experienced you are, things can go very wrong if you don't properly prepare for the task at hand.

In a class of 1500 people, there are bound to be people with attachments. And as we have seen in many of the evil entity stories, these things can attack, hurt, and possibly kill. A psychopath is a psychopath wherever they end up.

Marie Claire's Houses

Insight:

Childhood traumatic experiences are built into the child's sense of "norm" and their sixth sense is activated.

There are times in my life when everything is calm—no ghosts, and no need for my intuition to kick in. At these times my life settles into a happy routine, and I can just be. My sixth sense is turned off and life dials down a notch. Invariably during these periods my own family is thriving, my extended family is well and happy, and I am not worried about anyone or anything. Some would call that bliss—I know I do.

During one such calm period, I was invited over to Marie Claire's for a party. Her birth father was in town for the first time, and she was introducing him to her parents and friends. By this time Marie Claire had met both birth parents, and her father was eager to see how his daughter lived and where.

Of course, I couldn't wait to meet her father. I personally found the circumstances surrounding Marie Claire's adoption fascinating. They were tantamount to a legal kidnapping and I was surprised that such a thing was countenanced in a country like Canada—but of course, at that time I had no knowledge of the residential schools' fiasco where there was wholesale resettling of children. It was also intriguing to me how little value we, as a society, place on a baby's feelings and on bonding between parents and child. Marie Claire fell asleep in her birth mother's arms, safe and secure, and awoke some hours later in the arms of strangers. She was not to see either of her birth parents again for 36 years.

In our society, we think that these early separations don't matter, that children will rebound and respond to love from any source, but apparently it does matter. While it is true that children respond to love, it is equally true that they respond to loss, and there is a bonding that takes place between mother and child long before the child is born. Their hearts beat side by side for months. The two are bound together in so many ways—and not just on a physical level. There is a familiarity, a bonding, a belonging, and a longing. The sudden loss of these sensations can be so devastating to a child that I believe it can leave them feeling bereft and disoriented their whole life, despite relocation into a happy home.

There is also a bonding of a different sort with the father if he is still in the mother's orbit. He presents a familiar sound and perhaps a touch. Marie Claire's father was very much in the picture back in those early days, and would have been a familiar presence to his unborn and newborn daughter.

After the infant Marie Claire was taken from her mother's arms, she never again allowed herself to fall asleep in anyone's arms and would only settle in her crib. She would accept cuddles from her new family in the right circumstances, but her early parental loss clearly had an impact. At around age two Marie Claire endured surgery for appendicitis that was perhaps brought on by infant stress. She had an attendant near-death experience. The child spent her babyhood on high alert, leaving her new mom at a loss to know how to make things right for her. Marie Claire's birth father and adoptive mom had lots to talk about when they finally met and were able to put the whole picture together.

The night of the "meet the dad party" everyone was happy. When my husband and I arrived, the party was already in full swing. It was a huge celebratory affair—the coming together of family who had searched for each other their whole lives. Marie Claire's adoptive parents were generously welcoming to her birth dad. They were secure in their daughter's love, and the whole introductory experience was enhanced by their graciousness. The atmosphere that night was good and happy, so I not expecting, in these joyous circumstances, to find myself face to face with a ghost.

Marie Claire lived in an older home, probably circa 1920. It was a quaint little place downtown on Bay Street. The house had a chequered history. It was once an elegant family home which was later remodelled into a boarding house. The then-proprietor was strict and inflexible. She was a well-known character in her day, who ran her boarding house like none other in the area. In more recent times, the premises again became a family home.

At some time during the evening, I went upstairs to the washroom, which was tiny, yet functional. It probably started off as a hall closet which was later converted. I had no sooner shut the bathroom door when I realized that I wasn't alone. There was an older woman in there with me. She was my height with grey hair and she stood nonchalantly by the hand basin. She was misty and obviously a ghost. She gave me a long stare. Although she didn't stay and was actually not threatening, she did, nonetheless unnerve me. I did not welcome her presence. I found it intrusive. However, I had no choice; I had to use the facilities.

Later, as I left the room, I all but collided with Peter, Marie Claire's husband. He took one look at me and asked what was wrong, and I told him about this visitor. It did not surprise him at all. He reassured me, and told me that while he had never seen the ghost personally, he was aware of her presence in their home as he often heard her feet tap-tapping on the stairs. He felt sure that the entity was the previous owner of the boarding house, and suggested that she was likely just ensuring that everything was in order for the guests. After all, she was known for her high standards.

Some weeks later, Marie Claire and I discussed my encounter and she said that their residences were often inhabited but that these entities were never threatening to them, just present. She indicated that a man had died in their home some years back, and she wondered whether it was his spirit that I saw. I told her no; that I definitely met a female entity upstairs.

I asked Marie Claire about her other hauntings. She said that the first one manifested when Peter and she were newly-weds in their first home. When they first married, Marie Claire and Peter went through what they now call their "Greenacres" hippy period where they relocated briefly to the country to live off the land. There, Marie Claire gave birth to the first of their three children. During this period, she was thoroughly engrossed in her new role as country wife and mother. She appreciated the pace of country living and the natural beauty of the surrounding countryside.

One day as she sat breastfeeding her young son in her warm and comfortable farmhouse kitchen, she became aware of another presence. An older woman manifested and came over and sat down quietly in the rocker beside her. Marie Claire's own reaction surprised her. She found that she was not at all perturbed by the presence—although she was admittedly curious as to who the entity was and why she was there.

Her questions were answered sometime later when she received an unexpected caller. An old gentleman came knocking at the door. He told Marie Claire that he and his wife had once lived in her home and he would like to come in and look around for old time's sake. He missed his former home. Marie Claire welcomed him in, and over a cup of tea, he told her about his late wife, and her penchant for sitting in the kitchen, rocking in her chair and dreaming her dreams. He said that his wife had loved children, and when Marie

Claire described the ghostly presence she had seen, the old man nodded in recognition. That would be his wife, he said. She apparently loved babies and would enjoy seeing a new baby in "her" home. He told Marie Claire that he and his wife enjoyed a wonderful marriage, and he had the sense that she was just waiting in the wings for the day when he would join her. She'd been happy in this home and he was not surprised to learn that she continued to drop in from time to time. The old fellow was reassured when he left. He knew his wife lived on, with happy memories of the life they'd once shared.

There were other ghostly tales that Marie Claire told me that day, and I found it intriguing that she and her husband had shared so many encounters. Like my parents, they had unwittingly settled in inhabited places, or was it just that they were more aware than most of other planes of existence? I wondered about their lives and their histories, and what allowed them to take these manifestations in stride. Marie Claire clarified this for me.

Like his wife, Peter had also endured a traumatic childhood, complete with a near-death experience at age 12 when he was run over by a car. He died and was revived at the scene, and spent many months in recovery.

It appears that when childhood traumas occur, the child's sentient range is immediately broadened as the sixth sense kicks in. This sense may remain dormant but will be actionable throughout their lives. Their encounter with death and trauma adds a whole new skill-set to their toolbox and redefines their "norm." Their heightened awareness is incorporated into their personalities and lifestyles.

I recall attending a psychic fair with Marie Claire years later. This experience also provided an overlay of understanding for me and for Marie Claire.

I like to go to these events—sometimes they're good and sometimes they're unimpressive. On this occasion I found my reading to be accurate and so I persuaded Marie Claire to have one done by the same seer. As her session was conducted in rapid French I was unable to follow it, but I did note the impact upon my friend. By the time the reading was over, she was pale and drawn. She did not disclose everything that was said to her that day, but she did tell me that the psychic had indicated to her that she had been depressed since birth. Her auric picture confirmed the psychic's opinion.

The suggestion that she was depressed surprised Marie Claire, but while she was clearly thrown by it, I realized that it was probably true. I told her that the upheaval she sustained during early childhood could well have triggered depression, which may have lingered on to a greater or lesser degree. My comment startled her, but on reflection, and when put in that context, Marie

Claire allowed that it might be true. She just needed some alone time to think about that and process the possibility. In truth, she was somewhat surprised to find herself described in such a manner as it did not fit her mental image of herself.

We all have a self-image but we never see ourselves quite as others do. We see others in context against a common backdrop, but it is not so easy to see ourselves. And if your earliest memories are of grief and sadness, those feelings would be absolutely normal to you and become your frame of reference. It's what you know. Marie Claire's early childhood trauma had robbed her of her infant serenity, and that loss had an attendant impact on her whole life.

There was one further compounding factor. As a young woman, Marie Claire learned to her surprise that she was a surviving twin. She had endured yet another early infant loss. It is my belief that on some level, she always knew this.

I then took a mental step back and looked closer at Marie Claire's friends. Most had endured a serious shock or loss in their lives—the death of a child, the death of a spouse, a serious illness, a near-death experience, a divorce… Now I am not suggesting that these people are all depressives and miserable, but they do understand pain, shock and loss to a greater extent than most, and have become compassionate and supportive as a result. Most of her friends are caregivers of one type or another—social workers, teachers, nurses, or counsellors. Marie Claire and Peter had inadvertently surrounded themselves by people of a similar background.

Again I am reminded of vibrational levels. While Marie Claire has joy in her life, she has also endured a lifelong underlying sorrow. It is this vibration that resonates with our friends on the other plane, and it is in these fleetingly sad moments that they manifest.

And again, I am reminded of Fr. John's words, that these things cannot exist around happiness. It is just unfortunate that happiness on this plane is a variable. Like the tides, it has a natural ebb and flow, with peaks, lulls and every level in between.

In later life Marie Claire moved completely into help-mode. She spent the latter part of her career in the mental health field helping others with their emotional journeys. In reconnecting the broken links of her childhood, she developed a greater understanding of who she is and why. I imagine that she and Peter will always share their lives with ghosts. Their life experiences and vibrations simply define them that way.

Hal

Insight:

Caring spouses remain ever protective of each other.

We live in a tightly knit community. Most of us moved in as young married couples and we have raised our kids together. Those ties bind. We have seen each other through the best of times and the worst.

An old friend dropped by the other night, Harold, or Hal as we call him. Although he no longer lives in the neighbourhood, we still maintain our friendship. His wife died of cancer after a long and painful illness. The thing I remember most about those years is his frustration in trying to ease her pain. Back then the medical profession had a concern that she would become addicted to painkillers and rationed them. As she was terminal, we could not understand their reasoning. Why not keep her comfortable?

Before that time he was just another neighbourhood dad, but after watching his care of his wife, he became someone we were proud to know. If I were dying, I would want him in my corner. As her cancer was discovered late, there was never any doubt that she would die. In the early stages, her cancer was symptom-free but, unfortunately, the end stages were a different story.

We got around to talking about her during the evening. Her name was Babs. I remember her as being an attractive woman—friendly, outgoing and full of energy. She held down a full time management position, raised two sons, and became involved in church activities. Before she died she told her husband to get on with his life and marry again. In the decade or so since her death, he's tried but she's been hard to replace.

Hal recently had a run in with cancer himself. He told us that he credits Babs with saving his life. "Really," I said, "how?" He said that she often would send him little messages in his dreams. These happened more frequently in the early years following her death, and then unexpectedly six months ago, they started up again. Babs was insistent that he get an ultrasound... now! She said there was something wrong with his bladder.

Hal went to his doctor who asked the usual questions—"Is it painful to urinate? Have you noticed any changes?" You know the drill. Hal told him no, but nonetheless he wanted an ultrasound. He's not the sort of man who complains of illness, nor is he a whiner. When faced with Hal's quietly insistent request for an ultrasound, the doctor agreed. The test showed an abnormality. Hal then saw a specialist who scheduled surgery.

His surgeon told him afterwards that he was lucky to have caught the tumour in the early stages. Of course, Hal never had any doubt about the outcome. Babs had tipped him off and she wouldn't have done that for nothing.

I asked Hal if he had ever seen her since her death, and he said no, but that she had made her presence known in all sorts of little ways, and one of them was most unusual. I was interested to hear more.

Before her death, Hal and Babs enjoyed their summer home up north. It was large enough for family and friends, and together with their boys, they spent time there whenever they could. Their home is situated on a beautiful northern lake. Where once Hal and Babs spent considerable money, time and energy preparing the place for their retirement, Hal now pursues that dream alone.

On this occasion, Hal told us, he had met someone new and they had planned a romantic interlude at his home on the lake. He said they settled in for a comfortable evening with a glass or two of wine.

Before going to bed, Hal took the wineglasses to the kitchen sink to rinse them out. They were special 25th Anniversary glasses—not crystal but special nonetheless. Because they were important to him, he was always careful in his handling of them. They never saw the inside of a dishwasher, instead he washed them by hand in moderately warm water. Despite his care, however, one shattered in his hand. He wasn't cut, but he was surprised. He wondered, "Now, how did that happen?" He picked up the second glass. This time he was super cautious as he only had one glass left of the two-piece set. Again, the same thing happened. He got the message: don't use my glasses on that woman.

Babs had never been a jealous woman. She wanted nothing more than for her husband to move on and be happy, so if she was sending this strong a message, there was a good reason for it. He returned his new lady-friend to her home just as soon as he could gracefully do so. He has entertained other women since that night but has never again attracted the strong negative reaction displayed on this night with this particular one. I guess his taste must be improving—or at least Babs thinks so.

Healing Surprises

Insight:

Energy healing is a new frontier. Let's see how far it can take us!

All of my life I have had an interest in complementary medicine, and I have seen some pretty amazing results over the years. My sister is alive thanks to First Nations' knowledge, and my youngest brother owes his life to Samoan healing practices.

One of my friends, Judith, co-teaches with me in the field of healing energy. We complement each other. I focus on the theory of healing, and she is a gifted practitioner. In addition to being the daughter of a minister, Judith has a background in social work. She has enormous empathy for people and her treatments are special. She has a keen interest in both palliative care and birthing. In her practice she assists at both the beginning and end of life.

Energy work is reasonably simple and anyone can do it. It taps into our innate human abilities. The theory is that in a state of wellness, energy flows symmetrically through the body in an unimpeded fashion. In a state of disease or sickness, the energy flow may be weakened or blocked. The goal, then, is to restore the energy balance so that the body will move itself towards a state of wellness. An energy practitioner does not heal. He or she merely re-establishes the energy flow and balance in order for the wellness process to begin. Some of the benefits of a balanced field are immediate. The client gets a sense of relaxation, and a perception of a reduced level of pain. There are other clinical improvements as well.

Judith is a seer and I find her insights and reports invaluable—especially those on dying, and I have begged her to get them into print but she is one of those over-committed women who works full time, treats clients, teaches with me, and is involved with amateur theatre. Additionally, she takes good care of her husband who has a medical condition. She doesn't have much free time for writing. We get together with our practice group about once a month to trade treatments, review theory, and discuss any situations that may arise.

At one of our evenings Judith arrived out of sorts. Usually she is outgoing and vivacious and bounces in to join us. However, this night, she was unusually quiet. Tactfully, I tried to draw her out, to find out what the problem was, but she simply whispered, "I'll tell you later," and I had to be content with that. As team leader I had to put my curiosity aside for the time being and focus on the group.

Finally, the meeting wound down and the others left. I sat her down, "Now tell me." "Something awful happened today," she said, "and I don't know how to deal with it." She went on to say that she had been called to the hospital to assist a dying patient who had a brain tumour and only a few weeks to live. Judith's role was to guide the family through the dying process, and to ease the patient's residual pain with non-drug therapy. The patient, whom I'll call "Jill" had already been operated on and the surgeon had done all he could, however, he had been unable to completely remove the tumour. The operation had left Jill paralysed on one side and with impaired function on the other.

Judith went to the hospital, met the family and talked with Jill. They had an immediate rapport. She decided to use a blend of energy disciplines and discussed this with the family. Her intention was to help Jill, through a process of guided relaxation, to attain a more comfortable existence. Usually, following a treatment, the recipient sighs deeply and relaxes, and is left with a sense of peace and calmness.

Judith began her treatment in the normal way. She was aghast when Jill's right arm started to move and thresh around the bed in an uncontrolled fashion. The family told her that Jill's arm was paralysed. Judith didn't know what to say; she had no explanation. Jill's arm was clearly moving, paralysed or not, and no one knew why. She wound up her treatment as quickly as possible and left the hospital. She was still visibly shaken when she attended our group. Jill's reaction was neither peaceful nor calm; it was energetic and active, and very alarming for Judith.

I asked, "Why did you stop?" She told me that she didn't understand what was happening and thought it safer not to proceed. I enquired whether the arm movement caused Jill any pain, and she said, no, it didn't appear to. I said to her, "So go back and continue your treatments. See what happens." She said she couldn't; she had no explanation for what was happening. I said, "I do."

I reminded her that our brains are amazing and that energy work is relatively new. I told her that we are still working in uncharted waters. I said, "Your treatment may have prompted Jill's brain to generate a new nerve pathway to her arm, or repair a damaged one. As long as you don't cause pain, follow through with your normal treatment." So she did.

Jill's wild and uncoordinated arm movements became more controlled, and it took her a mere three days to relearn how to manage her arm. In the end, she actually re-established fine motor control and was able to scratch her nose and turn the pages of her book. These are small improvements but they mean the world to a bedridden patient. Over the time that Judith treated her, Jill regained movement in her right side and left arm. It was a much better outcome than she had believed possible.

Jill's surgeon, however, was not at all comfortable with these results. Initially he asked to meet Judith—then changed his mind, then changed it back, and finally decided to let it go. He had no explanation for this turn of events, and he was uncertain whether to hear any explanation that Judith might have to offer.

In due course Jill died and Judith was there with her. She told me that Jill had a peaceful death and that she was lucid to the end. She told Judith that the room was filling up with smiling "cocooned" people and that they wanted her to go with them. Although she did not understand the reference to cocooned people, Judith reassured her that the smiling people were her guides and she should follow them into the light. As she lay dying, Jill's crown chakra turned the most beautiful shade of mauve.

Judith's treatment did not diminish the tumour but did assist with Jill's pain management and quality of life, and her family was content.

At the end of the day, though, we're left with the question—can energy work re-generate or grow nerve pathways? If so, shouldn't we be looking into this a bit more? When doctors are faced with unexpected results, is it not incumbent upon them to explore the matter further or at least report the situation so a medical researcher can? Jill's results may be medically significant. I would hate to see them ignored just because Judith doesn't have MD after her name.

Judith was involved in another incident which I found fascinating, and this one involved a pet. Judith is an avid pet lover. Her household has included cats and dogs and, on one occasion, a rescued baby chimpanzee. One afternoon last summer, a woman in Alberta contacted her. Although they had never met, "Lara," had heard all about Judith. She wondered whether Judith worked with animals. Judith told her that they were not part of her normal practice, and that she had only ever worked on her own pets.

Lara told her that she was at the veterinarian's office. Her dog was in pre-op care awaiting surgery which was scheduled to begin within the hour. She told Judith that she had misgivings about the surgery. She said her dog had a bowel obstruction and she wondered whether Judith could see her pet and provide any insights about his condition. Judith explained that she didn't usually do that sort of work, but the woman pleaded with her to try. Judith asked Lara to describe her pet, and tell her the animal's name. Lara did. Judith centred, and in her mind she called the pet. She thought she found him. She then entered into a communication with the dog. He indicated that he did not require surgery. He acknowledged his pain, but insisted that he just needed to be walked.

Judith relayed his message to Lara, who told the vet. He was understandably furious. By this time the dog was already hooked up to an IV. He told Lara in no uncertain terms that the dog would not be able to pass the sizable obstruction in its bowel without medical intervention. In his mind there was no way around it; the dog required surgery. Lara argued with him. She reminded him that she was the client, and informed him that she would take her dog for a walk—just in case—before proceeding with surgery.

The vet reluctantly agreed and unhooked the IV. Lara took the animal out to the yard and walked him. He passed the obstruction. Lara walked him back inside and told the vet. He was so disbelieving that he went out to the yard to inspect for himself.

On this occasion, Judith was able to mind-cross with the dog, and the animal knew exactly what was required to get well. My friend had become a distance dog whisperer. I suspect that Lara also experienced a mind-connection with her pet otherwise she would not have sought Judith's advice. This situation, and especially the species' mind-cross, was extraordinary.

Judith's Ring

Insight:

Negative energy attaches to people, places and things.

My friend Elena and I were having coffee at Starbucks recently when Judith happened by. We invited her to join us. She told me that she was pleased she had run into me as she had intended to call for several days. Something had come up and she didn't know what to make of it.

Talk about sitting forward in your chair—I was all ears. Judith is anything but boring and her 'somethings' are usually fascinating.

She told us that as the only daughter in the family, she had inherited all of her mother's jewellery, including her mother's engagement ring. She said it was a beautiful ring, comprising a centre diamond belonging to her great-great grandmother, and four supporting stones that had been added in later years. The original ring came from Germany, and the setting had been changed to modernize it. However, despite the beauty of its stones, Judith said she was beginning to feel it was cursed. I asked her why. She told me that every time she wore the ring, something bizarre happened. She wanted me to know she wasn't just imagining it. Her husband and her friend, Marla had also commented on the coincidence. I asked, "What awful things?" She said the last time she wore the ring, her car was rear-ended. Well, that wasn't so unusual to me. These things happen, and in our city, all too frequently. She continued with her story.

The first time she wore the ring she was on her way into the city, when she took a side trip to the next township to pick up a few specialty items. She was driving her red van and her dog was in her vehicle with her. She pulled into the parking lot, and that's the last thing she remembers. She came to lying on her back on the front seat of her van, with her door wide open, and her dog barking frantically beside her. There was a man straddling her body with his hand at her throat. She screamed and yelled, kicked and bit, and scratched and hit. She wasn't going to go down lightly—she would fight—and she did. She fought him off valiantly. The man kept telling her to calm down, that he was there to help, and all the while she yelled for the police at the top of her lungs. The man's wife came rushing over to the car. "What's on earth's happening?" "She passed out and I came to help," he replied. "Call the police," yelled Judith. "Rape."

Eventually it was sorted out. Judith had inexplicably banged her head as she was exiting her vehicle and knocked herself out. The good Samaritan was out shopping with his wife, when he noticed her lying inert on her seat and came to her assistance. He was looking for a pulse in her neck when Judith leapt to the conclusion that he was choking her and was a rapist or murderer or both.

By now, she was embarrassed and he was sore. Judith is not a diminutive girl. She would pack quite the kick—especially a well aimed one—and he was standing in a vulnerable position. The poor fellow was in a terrible situation. Had he run away, he would have looked guilty, and by staying, he had done himself no favours.

Because Judith had experienced a shock, and had a sizable lump on her head, it was suggested that she rest quietly in her vehicle before resuming her trip. She did. She sat there for a good 15 minutes before driving on.

Twenty kilometres later, she pulled into the grocery store parking lot. She doesn't know what happened next, but apparently it took four men to detach the grocery cart from underneath her vehicle. It just wasn't her day. She took her ring off and slipped it into her pocket. Enough already!

The next time she wore the ring, it became too hot for comfort and scorched her finger. The next incident involved a nasty fall, and the one after that resulted in a migraine headache that didn't release until the ring was off her finger. She suffered trips, falls, bangs, and bad days. Every incident coincided with a "ring" day. After watching this trend, her husband suggested that she put the thing away and never go near it.

"So," she said, "do you think my ring's cursed?" Elena and I agreed it could be. We told her that entities can attach to jewellery; it's well known. We discussed psychometry, and the history of her ring. She didn't know her great-great-grandmother, but she did have a great relationship with her grandmother, and a less than stellar one with her mother. She said she had taken the ring to a psychic who told her that it had previously belonged to an unhappy woman. That ring had been on her mother's finger from the day she got engaged until the day she died. We wondered if the ring had made her mother unhappy, or vice versa. It was Judith's impression that her mother had always been unhappy and the ring merely reflected that fact.

Judith decided to take the ring apart and redesign it and make it hers. She hoped that would change the energy. She took it to a jeweller and had a new shank constructed from a conglomeration of gold rings that previously belonged to her mother and grandmothers. The diamonds from the original ring were fitted on top of the new shank in exactly the same configuration that her father had designed for her mother.

Her new ring was finally ready and Judith came to pick it up, but although her jeweller had carefully sized it, she could not get it on her finger. The ring simply wouldn't fit. The jeweller checked and rechecked the sizing. He couldn't explain it, and he certainly didn't bill her for it. He reworked the ring and eventually Judith was able to get it on. She left the store and set out for home. Her car was rear-ended en route. Nothing had changed.

She asked me if I would take a look at her ring and see if I could change the attachment. I said I would, but that in her shoes, I would probably dunk the thing in holy water and have it blessed. Elena agreed with me. Judith said she would like to try an energy change first and have the blessing as a fallback position. She would rather not believe that her mother's spirit required such heavy duty cleansing, and I couldn't blame her for that.

I dropped by and saw her the following week. She brought the ring to me and I put it in the palm of my hand. I am not a psychometrist but even I was aware of the discordant energy in my palm. It felt like a prickly hedgehog. I soothed it. It grew hot. I soothed it some more and all the while Judith talked about her mother's life, trying to put it into the context of difficult times, and gradually the heat and static eased. I worked on the ring for about 30 minutes, calming it and soothing it. Then I worked on the jewellery box that it was stored in, because that too had a discordant energy—heavy, draggy almost. I literally had to pull the energy out of the box, and Judith could not believe the difference afterwards. She said the weight of the box had completely changed and it was much lighter.

Then I asked Judith to talk directly to her mother and tell her that while she had never understood her in life, she had always loved her, and would treasure her mother's ring as a symbol of the love that her parents had for each other. We then invited her mother to release the ring. I suggested to Judith that she wash the ring in cold water[13] and wrap it in natural fibres[14] of a well-loved item—like a favourite cotton T-shirt—and place it near an amethyst geode to dissipate any negative energies. I thought she should leave it absorbing happy energy for at least a week. Judith decided to leave it in place for much longer.

I am not sure if our little ceremony will do the trick and we may have to resort to Plan B. I found this situation most interesting because although I knew in theory that jewellery could take on different energies and memory vibrations, I had never before experienced such a thing.

Judith's Dad

Insight:

Communications are difficult between different planes of existence.

At times apparitions try to communicate with us, but these interactions are never easy and are subject to error. When spirits reach us telepathically, communications are somewhat successful, but if they revert to words, things are difficult and any success is dependent upon the interpretative skills of the listener. Words are difficult to make out as the tones are at a different vibration than we are used to hearing and even if the entity is well known to us, the message can get mixed up or be only partially understood, which is frustrating. Souls in transition seem to be closer to us and easier to understand. Those who have moved on to the next plane are much more difficult for us to comprehend. Judith had a confusing encounter with her father.

Judith's father was a clergyman who died when she was a teenager. She was close to him, and he ran interference between her and her mother with whom she had a challenging relationship. Judith's mother would have preferred to be the mother of sons, and not an attractive young daughter who gravitated towards centre stage. Some mothers, thankfully not all of them, don't yield the limelight easily.

Judith's dad was her hero. She always looked up to him, and he was protective of her. After he died, he dropped in to see her from time to time. Occasionally she dreamed of him. One night he appeared in her dreams with a warning. He was not his usual smiling self. On this occasion he was sombre and she knew from his demeanour that his message was important. He held up two fingers at her. The message she took from this was that he had come in peace to let her know of an impending death, and she had a nasty feeling that it was her own.

She woke up terrified. She told her astounded husband that her father told her that she was going to die soon. He didn't buy that at all. He argued with her stating that he was sure she had misinterpreted the message. He didn't believe that her father would do such a thing.

Soon after this, the world-renowned psychic Sylvia Browne appeared in a talkback television show, and Judith phoned in and, believe it or not, she got through to Sylvia on the air. She related her tale and her fears. Sylvia put her mind at rest. She held a similar view to Judith's husband. She told Judith that she was sure that a man who loved his daughter as he had done, would never scare her in this way. Judith relaxed somewhat and tried to set her worries aside.

That was in May. In June Judith's brother died and in July her mother did. In showing her two fingers, her father had been trying to warn her of two deaths. He was attempting to tell her he knew about them; that things were under control, and he would be there with her, just as he would be for her brother and mother. His intention was to forewarn her of the double tragedy, but sometimes despite the best intentions in the world, even ghosts deliver the message wrong, and you only understand in retrospect.

Synchronicity

Insight:

Synchronicity is not happenstance.

Synchronicity is a strange thing. It's when coincidence is just too unbelievable to be true. We all experience this in our lives and say, "Isn't that amazing?"

My daughter-in-law Ava arrived in from work and informed us that she had a near accident. We asked her what happened and she explained.

She was driving along Friend Street and came to a stop at the red light at Second Avenue. The light turned green, but for some inexplicable reason she didn't drive on. She simply sat there for a good ten seconds until impatient honks from frustrated motorists woke her out of her momentary daze and she turned the corner. She proceeded down Second Avenue and was alarmed to see a full sheet of plywood flying towards her at windshield height. For a time it flew horizontally and she didn't know what to do. She was confined to her lane of traffic with a high snow bank on her right. At the last possible moment the plywood dropped in front of her car, and then was picked up by the wind and tossed harmlessly over a snow bank. Had she turned the corner a few seconds earlier, it would certainly have hit her.

To me, her survival was an orchestrated event and one that is hard to dismiss. It's a wakeup call that life is unpredictable. It can be cut short at any time.

Synchronicity came into my life when my mother was dying. I looked after her for a month or so before she died. Each of us took turns in giving our mother one-on-one care and I had flown to New Zealand for my special time with her. Usually my mother was a wonderful patient. She never complained and was always grateful for whatever service we performed. One morning, however, she woke up at odds with herself. She had spent a restless night with a million questions about death and dying spinning through her mind—some theological and some medical—none of which I could answer. By this time I had lived out of New Zealand for close to 30 years and I had lost contact with people I would normally call upon for answers. I offered to make a few cold calls to local doctors and clergy, but mum wouldn't have it. She was only interested in opinions from certain people. She wasn't in the mood for platitudes.

My inability to assist left her frustrated and me feeling useless. I decided a change of scene might do us both good. I told her I was going to church and that I would be back as soon as possible. This was something I never did. None of us ever left mum alone, but this day I just felt I had to.

I had a word with the Man upstairs and said, "You created this situation. You deal with it; I can't. I'm going to Mass now; you take over." It was a spur of the moment decision and I had to run the half-mile distance. I was so late that I took a shortcut through the Anglican Bishop's residential grounds. Unfortunately, he was having breakfast with his wife in the front room at the time and so my trespass did not go unnoticed. When I eventually arrived at church, hot and bothered and out of breath, I slunk into a back row. A little voice in my head said, "Relax now. Don't worry."

The sermon that day took an unexpected theological turn. Usually we sit through the same-old, same-old sermons the world over, but this day was different. Every question my mother had raised on death and dying was answered. I was dumbfounded. I thanked God, and delayed a few extra minutes after Mass to request a copy of the sermon, which Father obligingly handed over. I then made my way home via the long route and not over the Bishop's front lawn.

When I arrived back in mum's room with theological answers in hand, I was surprised to find her sitting up in bed in a happy frame of mind. She told me that as I ran out the door, Mel had telephoned and was able to answer all of her technical medical questions on dying. They were chatting on the phone for the entire time that I was gone.

Mel is a nursing manager with 30 years' experience and my mother trusted her implicitly. In my anxiety I had forgotten all about her, but she had not forgotten about mum. Mel's timing was impeccable! So in just over an hour all of my mother's complex questions were answered to her satisfaction.

"The Home on the Coast Road" provided other examples of synchronicity. You have to wonder at the timing that allows the right person to be in exactly the right place at exactly the right time. In my view, synchronicity is not happenstance, but rather an orchestrated event, and a built-in factor of life as we know it.

It seems to me that when people remember to ask for help, the universe/ God moves in the most extraordinary ways to oblige—not always, but certainly often enough to be noticeable. At other times there appears to be a different game plan in play and, for whatever reason, things just don't work out as we would like. Life is endlessly surprising and never totally predictable. I believe the variables keep things interesting.

Life's Butterflies

I'm a people-watcher. Over the years I've watched and wondered about people's interactions and in the broader sense, relationships. Why do some people attract disaster and others not? Why are some more susceptible to bullying than others? In my life I've skated by, but I've been up close and personal with others who haven't been so lucky.

My father and I discussed this at some length, because like me, he was flummoxed by the fact that my mother could be so knowledgeable as to people's characters and yet attract the strangest people to her side. She could read anyone on sight when they had some involvement with one of us, but she was clueless when it came to herself. One of my sisters also has this selective blindness. By comparison, undesirables rarely approach me.

All of her life, my mother drew these people out of the woodwork. My father said that he had observed her people interactions carefully but could not pinpoint what she did wrong. I have been with her on several occasions when she's been accosted. Two of these took place in Toronto: once in the street when a strange person with a rat on his shoulder made a beeline for her, and once in an elevator when a scary individual tried to intimidate us. On both of these occasions I saw it coming. I tried to steer my mother away from rat-man, but my mother was strangely oblivious to the danger. She also insisted that we enter the elevator against my better judgment. I asked her to wait for the next one, but she said, "Don't be silly. This one is almost empty" and it was except for him.

After she had exposed both of us to danger twice inside of a week, I said to her, "When I say something off the wall to you, please follow my lead. It's because I've noticed something you haven't." And that's when I complained to my father. He commiserated with me. He had seen it all before.

Over the years, mum had more serious interactions—once in Washington DC when our home was broken into by a dangerous stalker, and once in London, England when a man with a foot fetish cornered her in a grocery store and assaulted her. She couldn't break free from him and had to scream for help.

And then there's my sister... My sister attracts both wonderful and awful people. My sister-in-law told me that when she and my sister were travelling together in Europe she watched a strange woman on the other side of the road fixate on Janna and make her way right to her and scream in her face. As a young girl, my sister was the sort to attract bullies and the rest of us spent our lives watching out for her and trying to protect her.

My mother never talked much about her childhood—just the odd story—but she did talk about bullies, and had a lifelong fear of the water after some kids rode a boat over the top of her while she was swimming. She said it was deliberate. It would be a horrifying experience not to be able to surface, especially for a child.

I have another friend who is an easy mark. She is frequently the target of embarrassing encounters with strangers—such as the time a fellow traveller on public transit found it necessary to disclose the intimate details of his personal sex life. It's like she hits the "talk" button and away they go. She is a shy woman, yet she attracts the most bizarre conversations. What could invite these interactions?

I was with her in a hockey arena once and noticed a peculiar individual on the other side of the building. I watched him hone in on my friend and then he made his way over to her. She had not noticed him, and was completely oblivious until he planted his face in front of hers. I watched the whole thing happen and was fascinated—what was he seeing? He was a whole arena away when he noticed her. What drew him? Although I was standing at my friend's side, I never warranted so much as a glance.

The simple answer, of course, would be that it is something in their auric fields—some attraction that people subliminally recognise and react to, but each of these women had a different personality and from what I can see, a different auric field. My mother was light and happy and her field was pink; my sister is more serious in nature and her field is blue; and my friend is usually intense and projects yellow. So apart from their auras being clear and bright, there is no obvious commonality and besides, if there were an auric clue, surely I could spot something—anything!

My father wondered about eye contact and then ruled it out. I, too, ruled it out.

One thing that they all had in common was a ready sense of humour with laughter never far away. Their faces were set in pleasant lines. But could people pick that up from across a street or an arena? Maybe—but it's a stretch. I think the missing link is body language. Another common feature placing these women at risk is that although they were all protective moms and switched on their sixth sense radar for their children, they were perhaps less vigilant for themselves and were more personally carefree and careless.

I'm also leaning towards the fact that these women were attractive in the finest sense of the word. People in general were drawn to them. In focusing on the unusual, dad and I neglected to note their overall popularity, humour, generosity of spirit, and innate trust of humanity. I think of them as life's butterflies, bright, light, beautiful, and not commonplace.

Whereas the average person would remove himself or herself straight away from a potentially dangerous situation or avoid it altogether, these women were kinder than that. They wouldn't avoid, or immediately detach and move on. They were trusting with a certain innocence of life. They would hear the individual out with the same courtesy reserved for a friend. This innate kindness and popularity comes with a risk. Popularity attracts jealousy, and jealousy can prompt bullying. But how do bullies know which people are susceptible? The answer must be in the body language. Attractive body language is open and relaxed. It is non-threatening and non-confrontational. Bullies would detect no impediment to their approach.

When we combine approachable body language with an attractive aura, and throw in trust and a lack of awareness as to one's personal surroundings, I think we have our key. Bullies and other fringe-dwellers survive by reading signs—facial expressions and body language. They are adept scene readers and are skilled in manipulation. They know how to twist a situation for their own ends, and how to prompt reactions of sympathy, empathy, guilt and fear.

Once again we have another of life's dilemmas—polarity. So, if we have shiny auras and fill our lives with love and laughter, we will draw all manner of people to us, including dangerous and undesirable ones; yet if we are down or maudlin, we'll draw nothing good and could see visitors from the dark side. The trick for surviving well in this life appears to be moderation: to be average and not outstanding; to be self-aware and vigilant; to aim for mediocrity in all things and take the middle road. Although the middle road is the road recommended by the Buddha, it doesn't sound too attractive to me and I can quite see why "butterflies" take the risk!

Time Warps

Insight:

Time is elastic.

My husband and I have a camp at the edge of the woods, sited between two lakes. In reality, it is a trailer, but we call it our camp. We spend most of our summer breaks there and have done so for many years. My husband, being highly social, visits friends, plays cards, and does the normal camp-type things. I am more solitary. I do join him for some card evenings but mostly I like to read and paint. One of my friends paints along with me.

Every Sunday my husband and I make the 20 minute run to the neighbouring township for church. It is a sweet little church. It was probably built in the 1950s but was recently modernised, and it has a lovely ambience, imprinted in part by the wonderful choir which makes your soul sing. It is always a joy to listen to.

While I am the type who is always ahead of schedule, my husband tends to run late. Getting anywhere on time is challenging for him. One Sunday we awoke late for church. We don't set alarm clocks at camp. We go into a much more relaxed headspace and tend to get up in tune with our body clocks rather than alarm clocks. So on this morning we had a choice to make. If we rushed, we could make it to church 10 minutes late, or we could stay home. We decided to go and to sneak into a back pew.

We did not speed that day for two reasons—(1) as a retired police officer, my husband does not relish breaking the law, and (2) the local police regularly patrol our route to town, so we would likely be caught if we did speed. That Sunday we knew we would be late; we accepted that fact, and drove on.

When we arrived at church we were stunned to find that we were five minutes early. We were both wearing our watches, and neither watch had stopped. Mass started on schedule. How did we make a 20-minute journey in so fast a time? It cannot be done. That was our first experience with time warps, and since then, we have experienced at least two more.

My sister told me she has had similar experiences in getting to work. She told me that she has covered huge distances in the space of a minute. In the normal course, this is impossible. However, her situation differs from ours in that she is conscious of trying to will time to slow. Neither my husband nor I consciously do this, although, of course, we don't want to be late either.

Scientists talk of a time-space continuum, but until we experienced these events, I did not realize how elastic the concept is. I now believe that time and space can bend at will. We just have to learn to master the technique.

Unidentified Flying Objects

The jury is still out on unidentified flying objects. I see two possibilities. One is that there are experimental sky-craft under secret development. The other is that there are indeed other civilizations out there, and some are more advanced than we are. There are arguments for both points of view, but I find one explanation more compelling than the other. As far as advanced sky-craft are concerned, to my knowledge, these must have been in development now for decades and yet never once reached rollout to the public. As for the theory about other civilizations—well, why not? We already acknowledge the complexity of our own world, could not a master creator have done this twice or more?

The first time I became interested in unidentified flying objects I was working as a flight attendant in New Zealand. On one of our layovers, our captain was noticeably upset. He told me that he was in the process of writing a book on UFO sightings in New Zealand, and someone had stolen all of his material. I asked why anyone would do such a thing and he suggested that there was probably a concern that his information could set off a mass panic. He told me then about some of his extraordinary sightings.

That was over 40 years ago. I will not attempt to provide those details now, just the gist of our conversation. He told me he was certain that the technology he saw was not yet invented by man. In those years, New Zealand was not a widely visited country and air travel would not be as hectic as it is today. We had one small national airline and one international one, and comparatively few overseas airlines had entrée to our airports. In other words, it was an open-sky situation over New Zealand.

I shuffled his information to the back of my mind and over the ensuing decades I read this report and that, and remained curious. I think I once saw a UFO in the twilight skies over our home in the 1970s. My neighbour and I watched some unusual antics above us, but the craft was either very high up or very small, and I could not swear to the fact that it was not a manmade craft. My husband, however, had a different experience, and so did our friends.

In the 70s there were a number of sightings reported in Ontario. In Mike's case, he was on duty one night with a fellow officer, Derek. They had parked the cruiser on the side of the highway awaiting the arrival of other officers to complete a mail run. They were stationary, facing east at the junction of Georgian Road and the highway. To the north, they caught sight of an unusual craft. It appeared to be no more than 60 metres above the ground and was a rectangular box type structure with a series of white and coloured lights protruding out parallel from the side of the craft, and aimed downwards like spotlights. It was nighttime and the lights were extremely bright.

What caught their attention was the hoverability and the apparent lack of a propulsion mechanism on the craft. The cruiser windows were open, yet there was dead silence all around them with no engine sounds of any sort. They watched fascinated as the craft floated horizontally, slowly and deliberately across the highway, moving west to east, and disappeared behind the trees. They started their car and attempted to drive to a better vantage point but were unsuccessful. The craft was already out of sight. Mike tells me that although he and Derek observed the craft for a couple of seconds, it was nonetheless a definitive close-up observation. Neither of them had any doubt about what they saw and they phoned the information back to dispatch.

There were other sightings that night by other witnesses, but the official word came down that they were looking at a weather balloon or other space debris. That may do for public consumption but it simply wasn't the case. This was a deliberate and controlled movement across the night sky.

Our friends also experienced a close encounter. We have known this couple, whom I'll rename Jack and Jenna, for 36 years. They are solid citizens. He was a principal and she was a teacher. They were out one evening when they noticed an unusual craft over their heads. Their description of the craft is similar to my husband's. Jenna said they felt terrified and unprotected out in the open, so they ran back home and hid in the basement. Jenna glanced back as she ran, and said that the craft was slowly following them—pacing them.

They made a pact that day never to discuss the event in public. These things open people to ridicule and the fallout could affect careers. However, Jenna was so traumatised that she had to talk about it to someone and so she told me, and I reassured her that she was not alone. I told her about my husband's encounter. Later she told me of another sighting in a neighbouring community.

Unidentified flying objects are just that—unidentified. Maybe it's time that we worked out precisely what these craft are and where they come from.

If in my small world I have met five credible people who have seen UFO's, how many do you know? And why do people still feel they can't speak up? It's time we all started talking about what we're seeing.

Time-Tracks

Insight:

Regression—A way to explore hidden lives.

Are we on a circular track in life? Do we die, and then relive to learn new experiences? I have always thought so. I believed that as a small child. I believed it as a young teenager when saying so out loud caused a great commotion in our religion class at school. The nuns immediately sent for a Doctor of Divinity to set their wayward student on the right path. That day he told all of us that while such beliefs are not currently in vogue in our church, they certainly have been in the past, and may be again.

I believe in the circle route as, to my way of thinking, it is the only thing that makes life fair. How else does one explain early deaths, and pain filled or difficult lives? I hold to the underlying tenets of karma and reincarnation, and there are many religions that share this view.

My friend Anna belongs to a non-Christian religion with ties back to the ancient Vedas. This religion also believes in karma and reincarnation, as well as soul travel to other planes. Anna is a medical intuitive and was a nursing professor before she retired. I met her at one of our alternative medicine seminars and she was extraordinary. She could see not only all levels of aura, but also the physical organs inside the body. She could read disease and foresee dying. It was a talent she didn't talk about except in select circles. She didn't want the attention.

Before she left town to take up a post overseas, I asked her to read my time-track. She was reluctant to do this as it is not something that her religion advocates. They don't like to trivialise their beliefs or create parlour games from them. I am respectful of other religions and so, eventually, I was able to convince her that I am interested in reincarnation and was interested in my time-track from that aspect. I wanted to know about my previous lives. In the end, she was persuaded and she read some of mine for me.

She told me that my husband and I have been together for a number of incarnations, and more often than not, not very happy ones. She indicated that we were making yet another attempt to get it right. I believed we had a sort of soul recognition when we met. We married despite being from different countries and cultures, and holding dissimilar politics and beliefs. Our paths just kept crossing and I got sick of saying goodbye to him. I couldn't argue with fate.

Anna told me that I've always been left of centre in my beliefs and a bit of a mystic, and that this has caused me problems in the past, and had even caused my death. She told me that once upon a time I was a strict and unpopular Mother Superior in a Convent and in a more recent incarnation, I was a nurse. I've also apparently experienced a number of violent deaths—one when I had my foot caught in an anchor rope and was dragged to the ocean bottom and drowned; another when I died in chains. She told me a number of other details which I won't get into, but some of this stuff resonated with me. It felt true.

Although I love the ocean and cruising is my idea of bliss, there is one size of boat that I cannot stand being on. One year I went sailing on a Flying Dutchman, which is a substantial yacht. As luck would have it, we chose a poor day for sailing and became becalmed in a pea-soup fog with ships going in and out of the harbour all around us. I panicked so badly that I actually jumped overboard and swam in. This is a dangerous thing to do, and not something I would normally attempt. I am not usually this fearful but on this day, on this yacht, I was. The anchor story hit home with me. I suspect I was on a boat of this size when I drowned.

The chains story also resonated. Anna told me that she could still see the chain-memory in my aura and she pulled at the memory visuals to tug them free. I felt intense pain down my spine as she worked, yet she never physically touched me. These are the residual cell memories that people talk about. I had never before experienced them and it was only in retrospect that I was able to make sense of the idea. That day Anna removed other psychic trauma memories by teasing them out of my aura with her hands, and I felt much lighter and better when she had finished.

So what are cell memories? Well, the jury is still out on that. Some think that the memories of our past lives are recorded in our cells and auric fields. Others think that the memories of our forebears are genetically passed on. I personally find both explanations credible, and do not believe that the acceptance of one theory precludes the other, however, I would redefine the terminology. I would call the past lives scenario, soul memories, and the genetically passed on ones, cell memories.[2]

Recently I had the opportunity to attend a conference with the celebrated Dr. Weiss, a psychiatrist with credentials from Yale and Columbia. He led all of us through a past life regression, and I was hoping to learn more about the lives that Anna had seen for me. When we started on this venture, we did so with the caution from Dr. Weiss that not everyone would be successful on their first attempt to regress. Sometimes it takes a bit longer to get with the program.

We started off with a relaxation meditation and then regressed in age until we finally ended up pre-womb in front of a closed door. I had no trouble in regressing this far. Now, we were instructed to open the door and look into a previous life. As I approached the door, I heard clearly in my head: "Don't open it." I thought, "Yes, I will. Everyone else is and I want to see too." So I did. I found myself lying on my back on the ground looking up at a darkening sky. I was on the desert flats somewhere—Nevada perhaps—and there was the barest outline of mountaintops in the distance. I didn't recognize their shape from this lifetime but they were nonetheless familiar to me. The sky was arresting with pinks and blues easing into purple with the approaching dusk. I was confused. I didn't know where I was or why I was lying down, but I understood that for some reason I couldn't move. I kept asking, 'Where am I?' and 'What's happening?' Then four beings appeared before me—light beings—and one of them said, "You've been shot." I didn't feel pain, but I did understand that I was dead. I was not frightened by them or by my experience. I merely wanted answers. Then I found myself back in the present.

I compared my experiences with those of the people around me. One of them asked me a question I had not considered. She said, "Were you male or female?" I realized that I knew I was male. I also recognized that I was not bad. So, who was I? Where was I? When did this happen? And why was I shot? Someone suggested that we should look at our feet during the regression, as shoes can provide a time-line and location, but I didn't do this.

I attempted regression again the following year, but this time my experience was strange and I found myself going into the future, or at least that's where I think I was. I saw architecture that I have never before seen in any country, in any of my travels. I understood that I was a teacher of sorts. On this occasion I could not see my feet as I was seated in a vehicle.

---

2   See also "Evidence from the Past" in Part 2.

My friend's experience was more confirming than mine. Some years before she had a regression with another practitioner. At that time she saw herself as a young woman in a village in Central or South America. She knew the location by the nature of the structures around her. Interestingly enough she also saw me there, so we apparently do keep the same friends from one lifetime to the next. Her new regression with Dr. Weiss brought her back to the very same village, but at a different stage in her life. There was continuity for her. That incarnation must have been important for her, a defining one, whereas for me it was a case of strange and stranger!

I can't wait to experience more. I feel like I am watching a serial play out in front of me, with many chapters left unread. I bought Dr. Weiss's CD[15] on regression and I will continue to explore these frontiers on my own. He told us the effect is cumulative and that we will see more, the more we do it. I will be interested to see if any of my next regressions match what my friends saw for me.

Auras

Insight:

You notice a lot more, when you "see" with soft eyes.

For many years now I have been able to see auras. I was not able to recognise these at first, as I did not appreciate that they are subtle energy fields, delicate in nature, and in constant motion rather than static. I also did not appreciate that everything has an aura whether living or inanimate. I saw without seeing, so to speak. I am not able to visualize all auric fields around a person, only the first three or four. Gifted psychics can usually see eleven, twelve, or even more. I can, however, feel them for 6 to 9 metres beyond the skin boundary. Most students in my classes can be taught to see and feel auras, which leads me to believe that it is an innate human ability.

I believe that auras are closely tied to the chakra systems, surrounding and layering the body for a variable distance. Like the major chakras, these auric fields run seven to a series. Each series is holographic and a finer version of the one before. The series repeat and link us in oneness with our world. I came to this conclusion after reviewing many of the theories that form the basis of our alternative healing arts and realizing that their foundations do not necessarily conflict but could, in fact, be congruent. Initially I foresaw only two seven-field series, however, I am now persuaded that there are more.

We are energy beings who vibrate to certain tonal frequencies. I tend to vibrate to the frequency that registers between blue and green—a clear shade of turquoise. The tonal sound of that vibration is between F and G on the musical scale. When I first learned of this, it came as no surprise. The key colour in my kitchen and wardrobe is turquoise. Many of my friends, as well as my sister Rosie, also register as turquoise through Kirlian photography.

My husband does not share my vibration. He is a balance of red, blue and yellow. I was always aware of his blue and yellow vibration, but the red was hidden from me until it was captured in auric photography.

It was particularly interesting to me that when he was photographed, his third eye opened and was recorded. The photographer had never before seen this captured on film, and neither had I. It seems that when Mike was faced with an unfamiliar situation (auric photography), he activated his third eye. This is probably a typical reaction for police officers, and other frontline personnel, when faced with something unusual.

I practice my aura reading in church. That is probably not the best way for a good Catholic girl to spend her time in church, but nonetheless that's what I do. My subjects are fixed in their seats and I have the opportunity to see an array of auras at the same time against the same backdrop. Sometimes I see the most extraordinary things. One Sunday I observed a huge shaft of light entering the priest's crown chakra. It was the purest white. He was immersed in what he was doing and receiving the most powerful energy to complete his task. I say powerful because white actually contains all colours. His energy source that day was impressive.

At other times, in other places, I see different things. Sometimes people are accompanied by one or two spirit individuals, and sometimes these individuals appear in the colours of healing (green) or intuition (indigo) or love (pink), and sometimes they appear black, dark, and murky. When you know the people they are attached to, it's never a surprise as to who accompanies them.

Some people believe they have spirit guides, whereas others believe that angels accompany them. Perhaps we have whatever we ask for and perhaps we have both. I believe I do.

Angelic forms show up in different ways in our auric fields and can be captured on film. Sometimes they appear as person-type shapes and sometimes as coloured energy orbs. These are good entities.

There are also their mirror opposites. The dark beings are never good company. They lower the vibrational "tone" surrounding an individual. Should we slip into negative emotions such as despair, we leave ourselves vulnerable to these entities. We need to protect ourselves. As we saw in "The Medium," the psychic was able to fend off an attack once she realized what was happening to her. We all have the same ability. But in order to do this, we must first recognize the dangers of negative emotions.

Regardless of the state we may find ourselves in—whether a high or low vibrational situation—it need never be permanent. We can alter our vibrational level up or down. Sometimes this is inadvertent, but it can also be deliberate. When I am well and happy my aura is a clear even colour. If I am sick or tired, my aura is weak and blotchy. In this state I become vulnerable and so I take the time to "feel better." Cups of tea, happy movies, family time—any number of things, restore my equilibrium. There is no need to allow my aura to weaken.

I once had my aura photographed when I was in a difficult work situation. I knew it was overwhelming for me, and so I protected myself with meditation. Nonetheless, I was flabbergasted to see that my working conditions had prompted a total aura change from clear turquoise to clear indigo. In other words, my whole body had gone into high alert and "protective" mode. Indigo is a higher vibration than turquoise. My awareness prompted my body to make the necessary adjustment to help me cope. It is reassuring to know we have this capability but it was still shocking to see the extent of the change in my field.

This is why I appreciate Kirlian photography. It captures the inner workings of our beings, and lets us know how we are managing. If an aura is murky, we can correct it. If it is stressed, we can change it. If we have moved into a state of high alert, it is time to change jobs.

I believe that with meditation we can go inwards and "tune" our vibrations to our normal personal best. We can also achieve this through prayer, which reaches outwards for help. If neither method suits us, there are always other ways of accentuating the positive—time with friends and family, and fun and laughter. Any and all of these methods work. When we are vibrating at the correct level for us, which differs between individuals, we will not attract the less desirable entities into our personal sacred space. That is to say, our auric space... but, unfortunately, that is not the whole picture.

We have less control over other spaces, which are subject to other influences. Some beings have a deep historic attraction to a location, and sometimes they will not leave. Of course, not all ghosts are bad. Some don't know they are dead; some don't recognize the way to the light; and some just can't bear to leave their familiar things. These are the benign entities, but the others, the evil ones, are a law unto themselves.

Benign ghosts can usually be persuaded to move on. We see these types of entities in "Mel's Ghost" and "The Tudor Brick House." The evil ones do not intend to go anywhere. They want to control their environment and everyone and everything in it. People are rarely comfortable sharing space with them. The vibrational differences between entity beings and human beings make co-existence uncomfortable for them and for us, and that, I believe, is the reason they attack. If they can hurt and frighten us, we will move to a state of anxiety or stress. Unless we remember to protect ourselves, our auras will weaken, and this is a more comfortable emotional state for them to be around. They don't like happiness and will do their best to disrupt and sabotage it.

In the final analysis, we can only be responsible for our own being. When evil entities attach to places, we can attempt to bless or smudge them away according to our various beliefs or, alternatively, take our leave of the place. In my view, we should never choose to co-exist with dark entities. At best, it's joyless and, at worst, it's dangerous.

Negativity

Insight:

Negativity—a real crippler.

One of the most destructive forces that I have come across is negativity. I don't think I fully appreciated the dangers of this until I started to write my stories and think about things in a more expanded context. Prior to this, I just knew that this happened or that happened, but I didn't take the time to put all the pieces all together.

My first conscious exposure to negative energy happened approximately twenty years ago when I attended a new age conference. It was a well-attended event and I was seated near the back of the hall. Just behind me were some acquaintances, one of whom was a medical intuitive.

I later learned from a witness to the event, that our presenter had had a heated argument with her spouse earlier in the day, and certainly by the time she took the podium that evening, she was upset. At the time, I noted her disposition in passing, as one does, but I was actually more interested in learning what she had to teach me, than in wondering about her frame of mind. At question time, however, my question annoyed her and she became angry, and I found myself suddenly feeling ill, and my discomfort lasted for days. I finally telephoned the medical intuitive and asked her what she saw. She told me then that the presenter at the conference had psychically punched me.

You might wonder how this attack was possible. We now know that energy follows thought/awareness. If negative energy is directed at someone else, they feel it. Just as we feel and bask in the warmth of love, we shrivel and suffer in response to hate, rage and other negative emotions. Once I realized the nature of my illness, I was able to re-centre and rebalance and I was fine.

The presenter that day allowed her temper to get the better of her, and with her ability to focus and direct energy, she either wilfully or inadvertently attacked. It doesn't really matter which way it happened, because the net effect is the same. I did not see it coming and was caught off guard. I doubt that the presenter actually intended to inflict pain. I think it more likely that she learned how to manipulate energy without learning how to control her emotions, and so in her hands, energy became like a loose cannon.

More recently, the same thing happened again, however, this time I recognised the cause of my discomfort, and re-centred and rebalanced.

Directed energy follows where attention goes. It has a very broad application and directed energy may have physical, emotional and psychic impacts.

I attended a most interesting class some years ago with a Qigong Master who gave us a demonstration of the power of energy. The energy itself was neither good nor bad, merely directed. This Master had learned his art from the Buddhist Monks in China and he was an amazing man. When I met him, he was in his 70s, but he had the physical stamina of a much younger person. On this particular day, he wanted to demonstrate energy applications in the hands of a Master.

There were approximately 60 students in the class. The Qigong Master had us line up, and focus our whole attention on our right arm and hand, which we were told to hold above our heads for approximately five seconds while he directed his attention to each of us in turn. The exercise was to pit our untrained minds and wills against his. We were to hold our arms steady and he would attempt to visibly knock them back with his mind from a distance of some 6 metres. His intent was to throw a psychic ball from the palm of his hand to ours. I really tried to hold my arm steady that day, as I am sure did the rest of the class, but one after the other we received a forceful impact which knocked our hands backwards. None of us was able to maintain our stance, except for one solitary person. Our Qigong Master was surprised at his resilience and enquired what discipline this individual practiced. It turned out that he was a Tai Chi Master. That day he pitted the force of his trained mind against that of the Qigong Master and the class saw a demonstration of directed energy sent and blocked.

I have seen other examples of directed and blocked energy. When I was younger I worked with an unpleasant individual. I was learning about energy shields at the time and so I put one in place around me. It is simple to put a shield in place. You just imagine it. In my mind I gave myself a Plexiglas shield. In due course, the woman came up to me and, as was her wont, was unspeakably rude. She then suddenly looked stricken and burst into tears. I couldn't help but wonder if there was a correlation between my shield and her tears, and so the next day I again put my shield in place, and tested it out. Once again, she approached me, and then inexplicably collapsed in tears. There was no other explanation for this that I could see. She was perfectly fine when she approached me and I said nothing to her. I realized then that whatever negativity she had directed at me, hit my shield and rebounded on her with full force and effect. The energy had to go somewhere, and the most direct route was back again. It did not have an impact on me at all. Needless to say, I don't put that sort of shield up any more. It was never my intention to hurt anyone.

Directed negativity is powerful. Don't ever underestimate it because it can cause real discomfort. Fortunately, the remedy is simple. Recognise, re-centre and rebalance.

Angry people affect their surroundings and those around them. If you must be in their orbit, it is always wise to set your boundaries so that nothing negative enters your space. This is easy to do. Imagine yourself surrounded and cushioned by a wonderful light—your choice of which one. Had the medium done this, ("The Medium") she would not have suffered the psychic attack that nearly killed her. Pink or blue will usually defuse a bad situation. Blue is a good colour for tense meetings. It calms things down. You can also put up a shield, but one where the energy passes harmlessly over the top and dissipates.

If negative energy and psychic injury all sound a little far-fetched, consider our language for a moment. We do have vocabulary for it—ill wishing, and the more severe version, cursing. In some cultures negative energy is actively and deliberately engaged, and cursing still persists in parts of the world today.

I find myself reminded repeatedly of the dangers of negativity. These emotions not only flood our bodies with the wrong sorts of chemicals, which can make us ill or dangerously strong, but they make our physical beings and auras attractive to the dark side. They imprint our surroundings, our jewellery, and our clothes. It is important to be careful about what we read, watch, say, and listen to, and to monitor our reactions. We are, after all, what we feel, think and do. We owe it to ourselves and everyone around us to raise the tone a little.

And, again, negativity has its polar opposite. I have been in places where there is an overpowering sense of goodness. Most of us have probably been in places of a higher vibration and instinctively recognize them. Some old churches have this; as do places in nature. These high spots appear to be places where higher thoughts have imprinted a positive energy memory. I found myself unexpectedly moved to tears at the crypt of the newly canonized Australian

Saint, Mary MacKillop. This was not what I was expecting. I was merely accompanying my sister to church but the positive energy off that tomb and in that church completely overwhelmed me. Similarly, most of us have probably been exposed to at least one higher being in our life. Some see the Dalai Lama this way or perhaps the Pope. For me it is the woman with the pure white aura in "Afterwards." Quite simply, I felt her goodness.

The Good and the Not-Good

My journey through psychic experiences left me feeling a bit pistol-whipped. While I never doubted the existence of God, or that God is good, I did not know what to make of the rest of it. What is evil? What are evil entities and why do they exist? Is there a heaven or hell, and what does it all mean anyway? Do we not proceed to an afterlife at death? There are clearly other dimensions out there that we can see and experience—what are they? They are too real to negate. What do they mean? What can we expect when we die?

It was strange to me that as a Christian person I did not have a clearer concept of evil. Our religion focuses on good, which is all well and fine but I do not believe we can ever understand good without a clear understanding of the other. There is no point in understanding half a story. I know I recognize evil when I see it. We all do. It sends shivers up your spine. Your flesh creeps. Fear and horror and loathing set in. Some people can even smell it. There is a stench. (See the "Home on the Coast Road.") But I still did not know where it fit in the scheme of things. Was evil the polar opposite of good? Or was it the absence of good? I did not know how to define it. You may ask why it matters. It matters because if we don't understand it, we won't understand the power of it. If evil stands in opposition to God/Creator/Source, then it is powerful. If it is merely the absence of good, it is weaker—the negative, the inverse. I wrestled with these concepts and finally contacted a dear mentor, a clergyman who understands my experiences and can speak my language. I now believe I understand.

The Creator/the All holds all existence in place—the good and the bad. And all of existence has free will. To choose the good/the of-God, is to be in harmony, in sync, and at one with the Creator and the All. To choose the not-good is to be in dissonance with the All. The good is a higher harmonic vibration. The not-good is a lower discordant vibration.

This same pattern holds true for all planes of existence, including the plane of the afterlife—the one we can occasionally see—where spirits range from angels to demons. There are probably many other planes of existence that remain hidden from us. Existence is fractal just as life on earth is fractal.

On earth, we recognize good people—the Mother Teresa types. There is a universal recognition of goodness and good places. We also recognize the not-good people and not-so-good places. In our own lives, we are somewhere on the spectrum between these extremes, each of us holding a uniquely different vibration.

What Elena and I did not appreciate is that the same patterning of existence holds true for the spiritual plane. Spirits can choose to turn away from good/God and make something else the centre of their world, but they always have the choice to upgrade their status. Thus, this is the reason we see a spectrum of ghosts, as well as a spectrum of guides and angels. There are angels and there are demons. We literally have the good, the bad and the evil with every possible category between, and some of us see them.

The good news is, that on every level of existence there is choice. Just because we die and move to the spirit world, does not mean we have run out of options. We always have free will. We can trade up on every level—which is not to say that it would be easy. We define ourselves. In order to upgrade, we would need to redefine ourselves, and that takes work. Nonetheless, we can be persuaded to choose the light. (See "Diane's Encounter.") This happened in many of our stories where the entities were encouraged to go into the light. Encourage is an interesting word. To encourage is to "give courage" to move on. Ministers and some mediums do this work. Sometimes entities need a little help, a signpost to show them the way. These are the "lost" souls.

We saw some afterlife choices in "Martha's Jump" and also in "Diane's Neath Death Experience." Martha received an invitation to come up and approach her Source. She felt she could not but was encouraged to try—to trust her Source. She did and found a peace that was life altering. Diane didn't know where she was, but she did know that she didn't want to meet anything from the dark side. She chose God. She could have chosen or not chosen. She always had options. Both Martha and Diane looked outwards for help. They trusted there was something good beyond themselves.

Evil is what its name implies—life inverted on itself (l-i-v-e and e-v-i-l). It is when the focus of our attention is consumed inwards. We feel no empathy, no sympathy, no interest, no love for anything or anyone outside of ourselves. It is total self-interest. We cannot recognize a God of love; we can only see ourselves, our desires, our wishes, our satisfaction. It is a self-absorption beyond description. We will attack or kill anyone or anything that interferes with us and our self-satisfaction. That is evil. How do we get there? By one not-good decision after another. Each choice of not-good desensitizes us further to the good. Thus, the pathway to evil is a pathway of choice, one desensitized step at a time.

We are not born evil. Christianity tells us we are flawed with original sin. The Eastern way of looking at this is we have karmic inheritance. We have karmic lessons to learn. We have soul memory. (See "Time Tracks" and "Screaming in the Night" in the story "Evidence from the Past.") We become anti-life through not-good behaviours and choices. Evil happens when we choose to make another not-good thing the centre of our world: power, greed, lust, etc. We can always choose to reverse the process. That is what free will is all about.

Hell, in my view, is disharmony with Source. We cannot be at one with God as we are discordant. We will choose the void rather than life. There, our emotional feeling is reduced to one of negativity. There is no joy, no bliss, no satisfaction, no peace. I don't believe there are fires of hell but I do believe that there are torments of the soul, cravings that can't be satisfied, burning desires that can never resolve. A disharmony of existence.

So, that is evil and hell. What about heaven? I believe that heaven is the total harmony of one with Source. We go into the light, into the Good, and into the bliss. We arrive. We are home. We are at-oneness. Our senses are satiated; complete.

So again, we come back to energy. We have the choice to tone-up or down. But now what concerns me are the dangers of desensitization. These creep up on us in everyday life. With over-exposure to some things, we can become immune to the horrors of killing, and to the sights of famine and starvation. With over-exposure, we risk the loss of our senses of empathy and sympathy, and of caring and compassion. We risk becoming un-shockable and unfeeling. We lose our innate sense of aversion. Consider the extent and nature of our visual exposure. This can be overwhelming and what does it do to the young? My concern is that we can unwittingly slip into an unhealthy outlook.

Perhaps it is time to focus on the heart-warming, the joyful, the inspirational—but not exclusively. There must always be room for the shocking—indeed it is necessary to bring reality to light—but these things must be kept within the tension of balance. We need to understand the whole. It serves no purpose to have either a blinkered view, or an overwhelmingly blinding one. As in all things, there must be balance in life. We need the ability to recognize the good, the bad and the evil. We also need time to rest our minds between these exposures and experiences, and to process our thoughts.

So, What Now?

Insight:

We have received an invitation from our creator to participate in creation.

In writing this collection, many of our stories challenged my belief system, and all in all that is a good thing. In particular, I had difficulty coming to terms with bilocation. I grew up on stories of the saints, and believed that the bilocations of individuals such as Padre Pio[16] lay firmly in the miracle category, something beyond normal human capability. I did not know what to do with bilocations when they happened in my own back yard.

The conclusion I came to is that it all comes down to energy. The difference between a miracle worker and the mirror opposite is their energy vibration. The miracle worker functions with a higher vibration (positive energy). While most of us fall within a certain mid-vibrational range, it is clearly possible for individuals to be at the extreme ends of the spectrum.

What I did not initially appreciate is that both negative and positive energy tap into creation. I had presumed that creation was always a positive thing. Not so!

Many years ago I attended a lecture on the occult presented by a Jesuit priest at the local University. At that lecture Father talked about mysticism and supernatural phenomena. He informed us that there have been instances where people have manifested lesser beings. These beings were seen by others who interacted with them. He stated that humans could only generate sub-human beings. In this, I believe he is mistaken. I believe we can generate sub-human lower selves and different selves.

What are the lesser beings Father referred to? I believe that these are the gargoyle/troll type creatures and amorphous masses that turned up in our collection in "Cassie's Stories" and "The Home on the Coast Road." They are beings of negative energy and they can persist (or subsist) for hundreds of years. In addition to these creatures, psychometry and other disciplines show us that negative energy itself can imprint locations and things for years after the originator's death. "Judith's Ring" and other stories illustrate this point.

However, neither Cate nor Dave generated a lesser being in "Flying High." While Dave's story remains unproven, there can be no doubt about Cate's. There were many witnesses to her bilocation. If an ordinary person in the ordinary course of life can split off holographic fully functioning selves, why can't others? I am now persuaded that they can.

Saints and miracle workers are persons with a high vibration of positive energy. They, too, are reputed to generate different selves. A search on Wikipedia lists many saints who have bilocated. In order to be recognized as a saint, these individuals would have been rigorously investigated by the Catholic Church.

So how we do explain this? In my view, it is all about energy. It appears that we humans have the ability to generate other "selves." Those with positive energy can reintegrate, whereas those with lower negative energy—being more dissociative—would be less likely to do so. Negative selves will linger on even after the death of their originator, impacting everything and everyone in their shared space. Thus, it appears likely that there is a spectrum of self possibilities.

I must confess when I first heard some of the stories about saints bilocating and levitating, I thought: oh, sure! But after you hear a number of somewhat similar stories, and some of them from people you trust, you have to ask yourself, but what if it's true? What does that mean?

The conclusion that I have come to is that we humans have received a creator-given invitation to participate fully in our lives, and more importantly in creation. We can generate positive thoughts and positive aspects of ourselves, or negative thoughts and negative aspects. Whatever we deign to do, we will have an impact on our surroundings. We cannot help but do so, yet how we choose to do so, is up to us.

I have had one further thought. My explorations into energy work have given me a new level of understanding about my religion. Christian Churches, such as the Catholic Church, have mysteries. One example would be the transubstantiation (turning bread and wine into the body and blood of Christ) and another would be miracles. Now that I understand the concept of changing/raising energy vibrations, these things make perfect sense. The priest raises the vibration of the bread and wine to Christ's unique vibrational level. Likewise, the miracle worker raises his own vibration to facilitate a desired result.

Bilocation has also forced me to re-examine my beliefs about the Trinity, or three persons in God. If humans can generate selves, then we should not limit God. I am now persuaded by the endless possibilities of God. The creator is the All, so forget the Trinity. Think infinity.

In life, there are always shades of grey. We have polarity as well as everything in between. Life is more than black and white. The trick is to recognize the huge range of possibility and not narrow our view. For me, energy vibration is the key to so much. We are energy, as is our planet and our universe, and energy vibrations dictate life as we know it. Understanding that we have options should prompt us to raise our vibration levels.

Science tells us that energy follows thought and awareness. Therefore, we have it within our power to change ourselves and our surroundings, as well as our reactions to situations. It takes time and practice to change one's vibrational level, but in essence, all that is required to start the process is a shift in attitude—which is well within our ability. The easiest way is through meditation (of the type which accesses the deep subconscious); another is through prayer. These both have a cumulative effect. The more we do it, the easier it becomes and the more effective the result.

It is important not only for ourselves but for everyone around us, that our vibrations be at our personal best. We now know that we directly affect each other, our surroundings and our things. Collectively, we have an effect upon our world.

HeartMath now reports a correlation between the human heart and our earth. Collective emotion has been, and continues to be, recorded around the world. Through Gregg Braden's "Fractal Time" we understand that:

> "In the words of HeartMath researchers, the relationship between the human heart and Earth's magnetic field suggests that 'strong collective emotion has a measureable impact on the earth's geomagnetic field.'" (Braden 195)[3]

In other words, HeartMath scientists believe that the attitude that humankind holds in its heart directly influences our earth. So our well-being is not only important to us personally, but to humanity, our world, and everything

---

3   To contact Gregg Braden, please see his website: www.greggbraden.com

in it. For things to function at their best, we must be at one with our universe. That is—collectively—all of us. The health of our world depends on it. Our stories tell us that our interactions are not confined to this plane of existence. There are connections to all planes, and possibly to all worlds.

As our subtitle states, this is a collection of stories of people in everyday life. I have provided my explanations (which remain subject to change), and you may have different ones. I find it interesting when ideologies and proofs converge.

**Picture depicting the 7 major chakras within the body
and the first 5 (of 7) auric fields of energy surrounding the body.**

Part Two
By
Elena J. Michaels

Bedside Visit

Insight:

The deep bond of love continues by those who have died.

While growing up, some children seem to need more medical attention than others and my daughter Jenny was one of them. Prior to the age of 20, Jenny had already been hospitalized on two occasions for pneumonia, once for seven days from a significant infection when her wisdom teeth broke through, and twice for surgery as a result of injuries to her knee that she sustained while riding and testing a new horse.

Hospitalizations are hard on Jenny. She is very much a homebody and loves her own bed, so each time she stayed in hospital, she surrounded herself with familiar items from home and as many stuffed animals as she could smuggle in.

During one of her more serious stays, I was sitting on a chair at the foot of her hospital bed as she lay sleeping when something totally unexpected happened. Jenny at this particular time was seriously ill from an infection that rapidly spread through her mouth and into her throat. She had trouble breathing, let alone eating, and there was a very real concern that her infection might prove to be drug resistant and move to other parts of her body. She was heavily sedated, with tubes everywhere. In addition to heavy-duty antibiotics, she had a feeding tube to nourish her young, dehydrating body. Fortunately, after four days of intensive drug therapy, her infection started to respond.

It was on the third day that the event occurred. I had been with her constantly. As she lay resting, I kept watch at the foot of her bed. At this exact time I was flipping through a magazine and sipping a coffee. Then I felt an odd and strange sensation. The atmosphere changed. And when I looked up, much to my amazement, I saw her deceased aunt and uncle—Jenny's beloved Tante and Zio. Both appeared at the head of her bed, and both seemed vibrant and healthy.

They had a look of love and compassion, and were gazing at Jenny, so seriously ill in bed. Then they turned their attention to me. They both smiled softly but said nothing, yet I heard their message clearly, "Don't worry; she will be okay." They both communicated with me, but not in the normal, verbal sense. It was more telepathic. I heard it in my head. I looked at both of them and said thank you. I glanced at my daughter, and when I looked back, they were gone, just as fast as they appeared.

I was confused. I had been sleep deprived for days and in a very fraught state with worry, yet I was sure that I had seen them. They were as large as life. I shook my head. Did I, or didn't I?

I felt their presence linger, and noted that a soothing calm had come over Jenny. She was resting more peacefully. As I went back to sipping my coffee, I questioned and second-guessed what I had seen. Was it really Zio and Tante transcending the veil of the spiritual world to visit a niece that they both dearly loved? I made a decision at that time not to tell anyone, for who would believe what I saw? At this time my former husband and I were already separated so I kept this experience to myself, not even telling my daughter. In fact, as my daughter recovered in hospital, I wrote this "visit" off to my exhaustion.

To give you some idea of the close relationship between Tante, Zio and my daughter, I need to explain how this came about. My former husband was the youngest of five children in a tight-knit Italian family. He was a menopause baby, and his siblings were old enough to be his parents, the oldest one being more than twenty-five years his senior. So Tante and Zio were like surrogate grandparents to Jenny. My own parents were hundreds of kilometres away, and my in-laws, who were wonderful people, were too elderly to be "active" grandparents, so Tante and Zio assumed that role. They were a very loving couple. They had five children of their own and were committed parents. However, both Tante and Zio died within two years of each other before Jenny turned 17.

Their deaths were protracted. When Tante became gravely ill, she was hospitalized in a large city 400 kilometres away from us to be close to one of her daughters. Before she died, there were a series of synchronistic events that brought Jenny to her bedside—a visit that was important to both of them.

Jenny studied politics at high school, and her political-science studies brought her on a field trip to the Parliament buildings. The students were there to observe politicians in action. However, when they arrived at their destination, they were not permitted to enter the building. There had been a fire alarm some time earlier, and the students were told that this would delay their entry by several hours.

Jenny took advantage of this downtime to see her aunt who was hospitalized nearby. It took a bit of arranging, but her teacher willingly assisted with the process. Little did any of us know but this would be the last time that Jenny would see her Tante, as she died about a month later. Just prior to her death, however, she made it known to all of her adult children, relatives and friends, that Jenny's visit was incredibly special to her. She dearly loved her. Later, at her aunt's funeral, Jenny felt privileged when she was asked to do a reading in honour of her beloved aunt. Zio, who was also very close to Jenny, died shortly after.

When Jenny herself came home from hospital, she was still not well enough to go to school and could not be left alone. As I was working at the time, she stayed at her father's office during the day, and at night she returned to stay with me. She was still too weak to do very much and spent most of the time sleeping, watching television, reading or simply resting.

On one of those first few days home from hospital, she fell into a deep sleep on the couch in her father's office. When she awoke, her eyes were drawn to the end table beside the couch. On the table she noticed a small card, just like the kind that comes with flowers when they are delivered. It was a small get well card, and when she read it, she saw that it was from her Zio and Tante. She was confused. How was this possible? They were dead! This card, however, was the one that they had sent to her along with a teddy bear when she was ill in hospital with pneumonia at the age of four! The card said: "To our dear little Jenny...get well...love from Zio and Tante." Jenny immediately called to her dad, and questioned him about how the card came to be on the end table. He simply shook his head. He had no idea at all. He did not bring this card to his office... and neither did anyone else.

When my daughter relayed the story to me, I felt a tingling sensation throughout my body and felt tears welling up in my eyes. I immediately thought about Jenny's bedside visitors. I knew at that moment, that it was really her Zio and Tante who had come to visit her while she lay ill in hospital. I quietly thanked them again as they had given me the sign that I needed to affirm what I saw. I did not tell my daughter the secret story of her bedside visitors until several years later, and now, even to this day, she still has that little get well card sitting beside her bed. Love really does transcend all planes of existence.

Chocolate Delight

Insight:

Occasionally we receive information or premonitions through dreams or other means of an event that has not yet happened but does.

When I was in my late teens, I moved away from home to attend university in a community about 200 kilometres away. While I went home on occasional weekends throughout the school year, like most students I returned home every summer to work. Once I completed my undergraduate degrees, I was swept away by the love in my life, a young Italian man named Anthony, and moved to a community more than 600 kilometres away so that I could be with him every day. He and I eventually married and had two beautiful children, but as some marriages go, we parted ways 23 years after taking our vows.

Like many relationships, this one started from most peculiar and synchronistic circumstances. I was in my first year of university and I did not know my husband-to-be, who was in his third year in business at the same university and living off campus at the time. Like many first year students, I felt a nervous sense of anxiety that comes with finally being on your own with no parents to guide you or should I say, nag you with their rules. I enjoyed every part of this newfound freedom. While I was vigilant about attending classes, completing required assignments and remaining academically on top of my studies, I also took advantage of many of the campus activities as a way to get to know others, develop new friendships, date various young men, and expand my horizons.

It was at one of these campus events early in my first year that I met Anthony's nephew who was also a first year student. He took a real interest in wanting to get to know me better. He was a pleasant and charming young man, and got up the courage to ask me if I would like to join him and some of his friends to attend a promotional karate demonstration on campus that evening. He boasted about his Italian uncle, a third degree black belt in karate, who was part of this exhibition and would be displaying his skills alongside his Sensei (karate master).

Karate was extremely popular at the time and had been sensationalized by many Hollywood movies about Bruce Lee, Chuck Norris and the like. I agreed to go along with him and his friends, but much to his surprise and long time regret, this became his first and his last outing with me. His uncle and I connected so well, that we exchanged phone numbers and began to talk to each other frequently throughout the following days and soon after began to casually date. I had several other young male suitors on campus who had been courting me as well. I needed to decide who I would commit to, and I chose Anthony.

We dated throughout my entire university career, and once I graduated, I moved to his home town in a medium-sized community in Ontario, further away from my family but closer to him. It was both a difficult and exciting time, as I was beginning the next phase of my young adult life. It was wonderful having a very small apartment of my own, and living in the same community as my boyfriend and his family, yet difficult not having easy access to my family that was a significant distance away.

Over the next four years, I only saw my parents and siblings a few times a year due to career, job and family commitments and responsibilities on everyone's part. This was coupled with the fact that, at that time, most families like mine would not drive distances such as these unless they were on vacation, or there was a special occasion. Additionally, one almost never travelled at Christmas given the blizzards that can manifest in the blink of an eye, making it treacherous and dangerous to drive. It was on one of these special occasions, Easter to be exact, that my boyfriend and I decided to take his parents with us and make the long trek to southern Ontario to visit my family. Everyone was there, my mom, dad, three sisters and brother along with their friends or partners, as well as my boyfriend and his parents.

While both sets of parents spent a lot of time together talking, like many siblings, we were giddy throughout the weekend, trying to cram catching up on each other's lives into one short weekend. We ate too much, drank a lot, and chatted endlessly until the early morning hours. On the second evening together, we retired late as usual, but while I slept, I had an unusual dream. I had a dream that I would be receiving a diamond ring from my boyfriend. As young couples, we flirted with the idea of marriage, but both of us were very diligent about ensuring that we had established careers and could support setting up a home with no debt before we would consider a life together. As our talks inched us closer and closer to that point, thoughts of a permanent commitment were still off in the distance.

However, this dream told me otherwise. As I drifted into a deep sleep, I clearly dreamt that I received my diamond in an unconventional way. My boyfriend, who was not quite visible in my dream, proudly handed me a chocolate Easter egg, and my diamond was actually encapsulated inside the hollow chocolate egg. How appropriate that we were celebrating Easter this very weekend.

Once I got out of bed on Easter morning, I simply had to tell my sisters about my dream. As exciting as it was, my excitement was tempered as it was that, only a dream. As sisters do, we delighted in the story, and mused at the prospect of marriage. We poured our morning coffee, but needed to join the hustle and bustle in and out of the kitchen, as preparations began for the turkey and all of the fixings for our mid-afternoon feast. Given the number of people that are at home for special occasions such as these, my mother in her usual domestic yet hostess-like style, had set up a long table throughout our living room the evening before, so that we could all sit together to eat. The table was beautifully decorated and adorned with the best of china plates, silver cutlery, and crystal stemware. Anyone who has hosted large dinner parties certainly understands the significant timing and undertaking it takes to feed a hungry crowd of 20 people.

Although I had woken to this dream, which felt wonderful to me at the time, I set it aside in my mind, and joined the others in getting everything ready. Standing in the kitchen peeling potatoes, I looked up towards the living room where the table had been set, and ever so gently, I felt this strange pull to go up and explore. In fact, I was so drawn that I walked up the few short steps to the raised living room and went right to a chair that had a beautifully wrapped Easter egg from Laura Secord, a well-known chocolatier, positioned on the seat.

This package had my name on it with no identification as to the sender. The egg which was under wraps and inside a box, was exactly as I had envisioned in my dream. I couldn't resist. I quietly tore off the packaging and pulled out what appeared to be a normal chocolate Easter egg, with little to make it stand apart from any other chocolate egg other than it was from Laura Secord.

I was standing there, with egg in hand, when my boyfriend woke up. He was entering the kitchen to pour a coffee and saw what I was doing. He looked at me in amazement and grinned as I proceeded to pull off pieces of chocolate as I just knew there was a beautiful prize waiting inside. By now, everyone was watching but only my sisters knew of my dream.

It was as though a carefully skilled surgeon had meticulously taken a piece of the chocolate, placed the diamond in its velvety case, back inside and melded the chocolate back onto the egg. To the untrained eye, it looked like a normal chocolate Easter egg, with no break in the mould, no crack in the seam, but I knew otherwise.

Inside was a delicately wrapped case that protected a glorious diamond ring. It was beautiful and while the emotion of the moment began to swell in all of us, my boyfriend was standing in complete and utter surprise looking at me and saying, "How did you know? Did someone from the store tell you?" My sisters could no longer contain themselves and yelled, "She dreamt about it last night!"

Needless to say, everyone was dumbfounded as I recounted my dream and no one was in a greater state of surprise than my boyfriend, now fiancé. While my sisters corroborated my story, over the years, he repeatedly asked me how I knew, and to this day, I don't think he ever believed for a moment that I had a premonition of this event.

This may be uncomfortable or hard for some to believe, especially for those who see time as a linear event, but I have learned that time is not linear. The past, present and future all blend with each other and the plot, or rather the story of our life has already been masterfully written prior to our birth into this earthly world.

Over the years, this event, this dream, this premonition continues to be a significant reminder to me that there is much more than what the naked eye can see. The rational mind tends to look for proof and dismiss what it can't physically see or touch. To me, there is no doubt in my mind, that there is far more to us as human beings, and to this universe, than what science can explain. How could I possibly see a future event that had not yet unfolded? And how could I describe it in meticulous detail without having somehow opened that door to what the future is meant to bring?

I believe that in life, there are certain predetermined milestones that we need to go through, but how we navigate them is a matter of will. In this case, this "surprise" engagement (which wasn't a surprise) and eventual marriage (and later divorce) were all milestones that I believe were predetermined in my life.

Divine Intervention at Play

Insight:

Angels come into our lives to protect or warn us of danger and/or to help us when we need them most.

Several years ago, a few of my friends and I attended a community workshop that hosted a well-known speaker known as the "Angel Lady." Emma, the Angel Lady is an unassuming and humble woman, but has experienced first-hand many interactions with angelic beings. She wasn't always able to feel, communicate or see angels, but this changed when her young son was dying.

While there are always skeptics in such a workshop, the subject matter fascinated most of us. We sincerely wanted to learn more about how we too could connect with our angel support system, if there actually is one. I am not saying I am a skeptic, but I am like many who want to see more tangible evidence of the spiritual world. This includes angelic celestial beings.

Even though I had already had some interesting spiritual experiences of my own such as premonitions, synchronistic events and some ghost encounters (all positive, mind you), I had never quite felt protected or overseen by divine beings. While I think skepticism is a good thing, this workshop pushed me to look at other events in my life and how they may have been influenced by things we never actually see, at least on the earthly plane. After this workshop, I have to say that I have come to see things in a different light.

During the workshop, Emma asked everyone to participate in two meditations. The first was to consider a significant event in our life that made us question whether or not divine intervention might have been at play. The second was to connect directly with the angel that is around you most.

There are many theories about angels. One that seems to be most prominent, is that unlike spirit guides, angels have never had an earthbound experience.

Spirit guides on the other hand have had at least one, possibly many earthly lives and, as a result, have experienced what it feels like to be human.

As we were led into the first meditation, like most meditations, Emma asked us to breathe slowly, relax our entire body and allow whatever thoughts we were having about possible interactions with angels to simply come in. It takes me a while to move into a meditation and like many, my mind filled with thoughts. What should I make for dinner? Do I have to take my children anywhere tonight? How will the roads be when I drive home? Many of these kinds of thoughts and others just seem to pour in until I can settle my mind for a bit. For me, moving into this relaxed, meditative state is not always easy.

During this workshop, it did take me a bit of time, but I finally moved into a meditative state, and once I did, two distinct events popped into my head. I really hadn't thought about these in the context of specific angelic interventions before. Once they came to mind during this meditation however, I saw them in a different light.

Both of these experiences were related to near-collisions with the potential of serious injury or accidental death to me or my family. I am not sure what it is about my angels but they appear to be super-vigilant when I'm driving. I don't think there is anything wrong with my driving. In fact, I believe I am a good driver winter and summer, but I am glad that I know now that I have angels watching over and protecting me. It was Emma's workshop that put these events right into my head during the meditation and shed new light on what really happened.

Going the Wrong Way

In one of the stories, I was taking my daughter who was around ten or eleven years of age to visit my sister at her camp about six hours away. It was an exceptionally hot summer day and I was on an unfamiliar stretch of road.

We had just left a medium-sized community after picking up snacks, and a coffee for me, and began travelling along a four-lane divided highway. It was a scenic route much like it is in many parts of central and northern Ontario, adorned with beautiful rock outcrops, towering pine and cedar trees, and crystal clear lakes. The divided highway was such that you could not see the two lanes on either side of the median, going north or south.

The roads were clear, and the traffic was very light with occasional vehicles that I passed. I was heading southbound and moving along a long stretch of highway, just having passed a vehicle on my right. There was a black pickup truck about 300 metres ahead of me in the other lane and we were both travelling at a consistent and similar speed, about 100 kilometres an hour.

As we were driving along, we came to a very long hill that I could not yet see over. The driver in the pickup truck who was just slightly ahead of me neared the top of the hill first, and continued at his rate of speed. As he reached the crest of the hill, he opened his window and he waved me over.

My first fleeting thought was that there was construction or a slow moving vehicle up ahead and that maybe I should move over. It felt like a long lingering thought. In that same split second however, my truck unexpectedly swerved over into the right hand lane but not by my hand. I almost felt like I was moving in slow motion, but in reality it was just a second or two. The moment I was thrust into the other lane, a car went flying by me at a high rate of speed going the wrong way! If I had crested the hill, in my lane, our vehicles would have hit head-on. At the rate of speed we were each travelling, in opposite directions, it is quite likely that all of us would have been killed.

I was shaking and trembling, tightly gripping the wheel. I then saw the light-haired man that flagged me over, just ahead, stopped on the side of the road. He was waiting to see if I was okay or, in my view, to pick up the pieces of what would have been a horrific accident. I pulled up beside him and he asked how I was. I said I didn't know what happened and thanked him for flagging me over. "You must have an angel on your side" he said, as he didn't think I could possibly have moved over fast enough, and all he could do was wait and watch. It was literally a matter of a few seconds from the time he reached the crest of the hill, flagged me over, I was thrust over and the car flew by.

Needless to say I was now shaking and the driver of the vehicle that came at me head-on just kept on going. We don't know how that driver got onto the highway going the wrong way, as there was no exit or entrance ramp for quite a distance. He must have driven for some time not realizing he was going the wrong way...or maybe he did. The driver in the pickup truck called the police right away to report the incident. However, we never found out if the other driver was ever stopped, or realized that he was on the wrong side of the road and in the wrong set of lanes.

The pickup truck driver made sure I was okay and I thanked him repeatedly. He was humble and kept saying, what happened was almost impossible to imagine, but that it wasn't my turn to die today. We each went our separate ways as I still had a long way to go with my daughter. During this meditation, I felt like I relived the entire experience again, but from a very, very different perspective; an angelic one. Was this man in the pickup truck an angel? Or did angels intervene to move me over, on the hot summer day, to avoid sure death?

Late One Night

As if one story wasn't enough, another one popped into my mind just as quickly. Again, it was about a near collision.

My mother was visiting from out of town. One evening during her visit, we decided to go out to play at a small casino about a half an hour away from my home. We played the majority of the evening, and while I don't remember if we won or lost, we certainly won on our way home.

It was already dark and quite late when we decided to leave. We had just left the casino, and were travelling at the posted speed limit of 80 kilometres, not daring to go over as the road is frequented by patrolling police. We were coming up to a signalized intersection, where two main highways intersect and the light in my direction was green. On the other side of the highway, a car was facing towards me and was stopped at the lights with his or her left-hand signal indicator on. They appeared to be waiting for me to drive through as I had the right of way. However, just before I entered the intersection at 80 kilometres an hour, the car began to pull across in front of me to make a turn. All I could think of at that very moment was: we are going to hit. I knew I needed to turn my truck hard to the left to minimize the impact, but there was going to be one. It is amazing what goes through your mind in a matter of a second or two, and like my other story, everything again felt like slow motion...but I was waiting for that crashing sound.

I could see my mother and she was bracing for impact. As I veered to the left, all I could think about was ensuring that she did not get hurt. I was intent on trying to get over far enough so that the impact would be confined to the back passenger side. I could not possibly get over far enough to avoid the collision, and I could not turn too sharply or too fast for fear of rolling my jeep. Again, it was in that split second that my mother and I literally felt my vehicle picked up by some force and thrust out of harm's way. We travelled much further to the left than was humanly possible.

We pulled through the intersection and stopped on the shoulder. I sat there in awe looking at my mom and saying, "What just happened? How did we not get hit?" She was still clenching the dash and looked at me in disbelief, and said she didn't know. By rights, we should have been in the middle of a serious accident. We both knew it. We both felt that the car had been pushed aside but not by my hand or my driving skills. It was something else.

While I would like to take credit for this magnificent defensive driving, I knew it wasn't me. Emma's workshop and meditation showed me what I already knew...that I was moved by the hand of an angelic being, and that divine timing, or divine intervention—whatever you want to call it—was at play here. My mother felt it and so did I.

Stairs

Insight:

Each of us has one or more spirit guides who have previously lived on earth, and are here to help us in this lifetime.

How many times have you ever run down a set of stairs and slipped, or almost fallen and thought—I should slow down? I have done that myself—usually when I am in a hurry. My mind is somewhere else. My hands are too full of stuff that I am carrying and I don't want to make another trip up or down.

Although some stories have focused on the role of divine intervention, this story is about a potentially serious fall on a set of stairs, and about another kind of divine helper from the other side called a spirit guide.

As mentioned earlier, as I understand it, an angel has never had an earthly life and lived in a human body, even though they sometimes appear in human form. A spirit guide however may have lived one or more human lives and is a spirit that is committed to helping you in this life. It may be someone that you shared a past life with who has offered to help you in this one. Sometimes additional spirit guides come in to help you at specific points in your life. For example, a spirit guide may be someone you were close to who has already died in this lifetime. In any event, spirit guides are not to be confused with angels.

This story is about my mother who believes that her mother's spirit is around to help and to guide her at critical times. Her mother, or my grandmother was a victim of WWII, but the circumstances surrounding her death are unclear. Shortly before the war broke out, however, she predicted her own demise. She put cards out to read her future as she quite often did, and began to weep. My mom who was almost a teen at the time, asked her what was wrong, and she told her that soon they would be apart, and through her tears, told my mother that they would never see each other again.

My mother, her siblings and my grandmother lived in Latvia when the war broke out. Her two brothers were both killed at different times at the onset of the war. One was in his late teens and the other one had just turned twenty. My mother and her sister, who were in their early teens, escaped as Russia bombed and invaded their city. Both fled but were later captured by German soldiers as they crossed the German front. They were held in a German prison camp for the remainder of the war, but were released once the war ended, and then chose to immigrate to Australia.

My grandmother however was captured by Russian soldiers at the time of the invasion of their city. When the war ended, although my mother tried to find her mother, she was informed that she had died in a Russian prison camp hospital. A few years later however, several nuns located my mom to tell her that her mother was still alive but close to death. As my mother understands it, she was the victim of medical experimentation and while she lived to see the end of the war, she remained a prisoner in a facility where horrendous experiments were done on human subjects. Although my mom wanted desperately to see her, the nuns had used an underground network to get the information to her, but would be killed if the network was uncovered and exposed. My grandmother died shortly after.

My mother's background is important to understand as it helps to underscore the special bond between my mom and hers. My mother believes that her own mother is her spirit guide and that she comes in times of life threatening illness, desperation, or in this story, potentially serious injury.

Fast forward 40 years. One day when no one was home, my mom was busy vacuuming and cleaning the house. She took a great deal of pride in her home and it was always clean and well looked after.

On this occasion, she had been working very hard and once she was done, decided to carry the cumbersome vacuum down the stairs into the basement where it was stored. She started to make the trek down with the vacuum and hose in her right arm while trying to hold the railing with her left hand. Suddenly, she lost her footing. The vacuum flew out of her arms. She tried to grip the railing, but flipped on a step, and her body bounced all the way to the bottom. She was just like a rag doll. As she landed, her head crashed against the concrete floor and she could not move. She was completely incapacitated, and knew she was badly injured.

Suddenly, she began to feel a warmth slowly surrounding and holding her. She does not know how much time passed, but she felt herself physically lifted and brought to her feet by no volition of her own. She stood there shaking, fearful of moving, not knowing the extent of her injuries or what had just happened. She then got the sense of her mother's spirit and she was once again enwrapped in love and warmth. As suddenly as she felt the familiar presence, it left.

As she was standing there, she slowly tested her limbs and discovered that despite her serious fall, she was able to move. The vacuum, however, was broken into pieces all over the floor. She made her way up the stairs and sat down. All she could think of was that her mother had intervened and somehow healed her.

My mom did not break a bone, sustain a concussion or even a bump, and there was not a bruise to be found (unlike a similar tumble that I had down the stairs several years ago). Her body felt perfectly fine, but a different kind of shock began to set in. While she was acutely aware of the serious potential for injury, she was overcome by the reality that her mother's spirit had transcended the spiritual veil to help her in a time of great need.

She knows that her mother loves her and continues to watch out for her. She misses her dearly and often talks of her longing to see her once again. I know she will one day. My grandmother will undoubtedly be there with open arms, full of love—the kind of love that continues to transcend the veil between the human and the spiritual worlds; the world of our spirit guides.

Evidence from the Past

Insight:

*Our cells carry the memory of all of our past lives & some believe
that our cells carry the trauma of our family history throughout time.*

There are many theories about the cycle of life and death and if indeed we live more than one life. The following are a collection of stories that may or may not convince you of eternal life...an eternal life where our soul continues to live on, even though our physical body, the shell that houses our soul, dies. Although scientists rationalize that once the physical body dies we are dead and gone, never to exist again, that same scientific lens also tells us that we are made up of pure energy that can't be destroyed—in other words, energy never dies.

Taking this a step further, this would then mean that since we are energy, we too never die. While it doesn't make sense to many, the theory of reincarnation offers one perspective—perhaps the key to understanding what happens to us when our physical body eventually stops living. Here are a few stories that challenge the view that we only live once.

Screaming in the Night

My son Jason was born a jovial happy baby who was easy to care for from the moment of birth, unlike his older sister who was colicky for over a year. Even as a baby, it would take very little to make him smile and his belly laugh could fill a room. Both of my children were alert babies, walked at an early age, and spoke full sentences by the time they were two. When Jason was about two, my former husband and I endured a strange set of experiences. These experiences lasted almost six weeks and all occurred in the middle of the night.

It was like clockwork. Every evening, Jason would be put to bed around 8:00 p.m. and after a brief playtime he would nod off to sleep. While he went to bed with ease, often climbing into his own crib, he was actually a very restless sleeper and still is to this day. Truth be told, he was restless shortly after he was conceived, often moving in the womb in quite a dramatic fashion numerous times throughout my pregnancy.

However, shortly after he turned two years of age, every night around 2:00 a.m. Jason would wake up screaming. It wasn't a whimper, a cry or a gesture for attention, but a full-blown scream. Each night I would go into his room and try to soothe him to no avail. It would last for one to two hours and it was impossible to calm him down. Holding him close, rocking him gently and speaking softly did nothing. As others needed their sleep, it was my habit to take him downstairs into our recreation room, well away from the rest of the family.

Although he did not appear to be in any pain, I brought him to our family doctor several times during the course of these six weeks. Our family doctor explained to me that Jason was experiencing "night terrors." He told me not to worry, that they would go away in a few weeks. He also told me that various babies have this experience and there is no medical explanation for them, or again, any need to worry. They would go away on their own and wouldn't cause any medical problems that doctors were aware of.

I had not heard of night terrors before, but as I co-wrote this book, I came across another group of people who also share this condition. These are victims of Post Traumatic Stress Disorder or PTSD for short. A friend of mine (a Captain in the military who has completed several tours of duty), is experiencing PTSD. One of his symptoms is night terrors which he talks about on his blog.

I researched PTSD a bit further and found that anyone who has been traumatized (single event or repeated) can experience PTSD though not everyone reacts the same. Certain triggers seem to cause it to manifest as a full blown disorder in some and not in others. I think the connection to trauma is a significant one, and as you will see in my story about Jason, I came to learn that he was experiencing or reliving trauma but it was not from this lifetime.

You can well imagine how difficult it was to comprehend what was happening to Jason, and that according to medical experts there was nothing wrong. However, I noticed a very distinct pattern with Jason. When he would wake up at night and begin to scream, as mentioned, nothing I did could soothe him. You have to remember, during the daytime, he was a very affectionate baby and always ready for a cuddle, but when he was experiencing a night terror, he was not the same child. It was as though he was someone else, and I was not there. His eyes would be wide-open and they would completely dilate and be fixated, but not on me. In fact, I felt like he was looking right through me and was focused on something or someone else.

It was terrifying to me as a parent, to have my own son not know who I was and to be unable to comfort him. A number of times, I offhandedly said that it felt like he was "possessed." I knew nothing of spiritual issues at the time. My only knowledge was through my Catholic upbringing. There was a God who was good and a devil that was evil. We had one life to get it right and if we blew it by committing mortal (grave) sins and did not ask for forgiveness before we died, we would be doomed to an eternity in hell. There's very little in between. So you can well imagine when we were going through this experience, (with no medical explanation) how much our minds wandered. It was so frightening that my husband and I avoided the subject because we didn't know what was happening and were scared to think the worst.

As the weeks wore on, Jason would eventually settle himself in my arms after about an hour of screaming. When he did, it was almost as though he would collapse from exhaustion and fall immediately into a deep sleep. After about the fourth week and several visits to the doctor, I discovered that I could almost shock him out of his screaming state by putting a cold popsicle into his mouth for a moment. It was as if the cold stimulus on his lips and in his mouth would provide the necessary impetus to stop whatever he was experiencing. As soon as I did this, he would collapse into my arms and fall into an instantaneous deep sleep.

As quickly as the night terrors began, they stopped, just like my doctor and the medical books predicted. The cause, however, nagged me for many years. How could this be? As time went on, I put this question aside, until I began to open my mind to spiritual issues that were triggered by a number of synchronistic events in my life in my mid-40s. I read a great deal at this time, especially books of a spiritual nature and those of the paranormal. I cannot explain this, but as I was reading a book by Sylvia Browne, a world renowned psychic, I read a section in her book entitled "A Psychic's Guide to Our World and Beyond—The Other Side and Back" on cell memory and past lives. All of a sudden, I was brought back to memories of my son and his night terrors. Could this be the explanation?

Death in Another Life

If you have not heard of cell memory, my understanding is that each and every one of the cells in our body memorizes or has a memory of everything that we have ever experienced in this life as well as all of our past lives. Cell memory supports theories of reincarnation. As we evolve spiritually with each life, we grow through various stages, and are presented with a variety of experiences (both good and bad). We plan our life experiences with other spiritual beings before we come into each life, to help us grow and complete our tasks for the current lifetime.

When I read this section on cell memory I asked myself whether or not this might hold some key to understanding what happened to my young son some ten years earlier. I turned a few more pages and I got my answer. Sylvia Browne explained that children, up until the age of about ten, continue to be connected to the spiritual world, since they only left it a short while before to return to earth for another life experience. As they grow, we adults thwart their understanding of what they see in our world. We tend to negate the spiritual realm.

As children are so connected to the spiritual realm from the time they are born, they often remember part of their most recent past life, both the good and the bad. One of the things they remember most, as it is so fresh in their minds, is how they died in that life. This memory, along with other experiences from each lifetime, becomes stored in each of our cells—much like a computer stores information that can be retrieved at any time.

As logic would hold, if that death was traumatic, in all likelihood the memory of that trauma might continue into our current life. Following this thinking, Browne described night terrors to a tee! She stated that they are a carryover from a previous life, and that our cells continue to hold that memory, actually the memory of a traumatic death.

While this may not make sense to many, it made perfect sense to me...that my young infant son, who screamed incessantly in the night for a number of weeks without any apparent medical or physical condition, was still experiencing a carryover or memory of a traumatic death in a previous life.

The possibility of karmic implications and that we may have experienced past lives may hold the key to many questions we currently have. For example: why children die young; or why someone we love develops a terminal illness and dies before their time; or why some people seem to experience one trauma after another; or why certain acts of nature (often equated with an act of God) wipe out an entire coastline populated with innocent people. The list of questions we have is endless.

It is suggested that cell memory, or the memory of a previous life that is somehow imprinted in our cells, may also play a role in unwarranted fears, such as fear of heights, spiders, water and other such objects or situations. Additionally, the onset of those fears might manifest at a specific time in our life or at a specific age without any apparent reason. This would make sense. If we drowned when we were twenty, a fear of water may not develop until we are twenty once again in this life.

When I was in my mid-forties, I developed an unwarranted fear of going down the stairs and if anyone saw me, I would be hanging onto a railing for dear life. Previous to this, I would often run up and down a set of stairs with ease, but all of a sudden, I began to feel as though I was going to fall down the stairs and be seriously injured or even die. I could not, for the life of me, understand why I was so uncomfortable or felt the need to hang on so tightly.

It was not until I began to read about cell memory that I not only uncovered what I thought might have been the reasons for my son's night terrors, but also the reason for my own unwarranted fear about stairs.

In this same section of the book by Sylvia Browne, she discusses how cell memory impacts on fears that have no foundation in our current life. We can eliminate these fears by meditating and asking that they be removed as they don't belong in this lifetime.

I tried this meditation for about three weeks, each and every day. To my amazement, it actually worked. To this day, I no longer fear stairs. It took time and commitment to address this fear. Some psychologists say that these types of changes are due to the power of suggestion. All I can say is that meditation to release this stored memory worked.

Afterthought ~

What this small collection of stories has shown me is that cell memories can carry over into this lifetime in the form of phobias and fears. Addressing cell memory-based fears can have a dramatic and positive impact on your life, your beliefs and your health. It can mean the difference between falling ill, based on a past life experience, to living a life in this lifetime free of the history of the past.

Additionally, we are now learning that there are other aspects to this huge puzzle... and that is the case of historic trauma.

Historic Trauma

Recently there has been greater attention paid to the subject of historic trauma. Currently, most of the literature focuses on population groups or cultures such as North American Indians, Holocaust survivors and others who were the victims of mass genocide, or groups that experienced collective trauma. In most cases, historic trauma is defined as trauma that has been experienced over the life span and across generations, that is manifesting in individuals in their current lifetime.

Cell biologist Dr. Bruce Lipton states that:

> "we are learning organisms that can incorporate life experiences into our genomes and pass them on to our offspring, who will then incorporate them into their life experiences into the genome to further human evolution."[17]

As a result, we pass on both good and bad experiences, traits and qualities that carry over generations.

In speaking to a psychiatrist colleague, he said that experts in the field are now seeing trauma that occurred in previous generations as a significant life experience for second and third generation children. These children never directly experienced the trauma in question but are now displaying symptoms of it. Experts are perplexed by the cause. He said that historic trauma is now being identified as a possible source of current trauma. This is the subject of a new emerging field of study called epigenetics.

According to a recent BBC story "Ghosts in Your Genes" it is believed:

> "genes have a 'memory.' That the lives of your grandparents, the air that they breathed, the food they ate and even the things they saw can directly affect you, decades later, despite you never experiencing these things yourself."[18]

The good news according to this article is that it need not be a life sentence through successive generations. It can be remedied.

While most of the focus has been on large, collective groups as in the case of intergenerational trauma, the same principle is now being applied to individuals. So, in essence, not only do your cells remember your past lives, but the lives and circumstances that affected your family, generations back. These experiences can set up a trigger that alters your genes to respond to your life and your environment in a certain way. It certainly calls into question what impacts on child development as it is a much deeper question than simply nature versus nurture. It may be the result of something that is embedded in our cells throughout time.

I mention historic trauma and although it is related to our own past lives, it is more than that. It is related to the lives of others in our lives and may hold the key to understanding some of the repeated challenges that we face.

The idea of releasing some of these effects from my own life recently came to the forefront. Throughout my life I have been faced with recurrent challenges. I would get close to some desired goal, to the point where I can almost touch and taste it and then I'm thwarted—just like that. I even tried the various practices as discussed in Dr. Wayne's Dyer's "Power of Intention—Learning to Co-create Your World Your Way" but nothing seemed to work. I have now come to understand that it is quite possible that the issues in my life are much deeper than that, and possibly historical—imprinted in my cells and soul from my past and the history of my family.

Although this book is not about my personal journey, I wanted to share this with you as I did see several non-traditional therapists who specialize in this area. When I described my life circumstances, and my family's generational history, they independently came to the same conclusion: that historic trauma is impacting my life today. While I still don't know if what they each did worked, they took me through a number of exercises, one of which we share in the conclusion of this book. (Postscript ~ Convergence).

Afterthought ~

In going back to the idea of past lives and the influence that they have on each and every one of us today, we are now beginning to expand our thinking even further. It is now believed that even more aspects of our past, not only our own, but of the family that we were born into, creates the trigger that impacts on our genes. This in turn alters our emotional, physical and spiritual health, well-being and responses in this lifetime.

Could this hold the key to understanding some forms of mental illness such as PTSD and other conditions? Given the limited success that we have seen in the field to treat such illnesses, is it possible that we may be missing other potentially significant and contributing factors—that of historic trauma or the carryover of past life cell and soul memory, particularly for those with heightened sensitivity? Having worked in the addictions and mental health field for most of my career, I believe that these factors are worthy of far greater research, consideration and attention.

Uncovering Past Lives ~ Reincarnation

Insight:

We have all lived multiple lives in the past. Each one is meant to teach us or others, important lessons. If we don't learn these lessons, they carry over into the next life.

While there are countless stories on reincarnation, the following three stories have led to my belief that we have all lived past lives. Two are related to people that I know in this lifetime and the other involves someone I met at a spiritual conference where past lives were explored.

Spiritual Mentor

The first is a story about an overwhelming familiarity that I had with someone that I barely knew. To this day, this person still does not know this as I have not divulged any of it to him (as he likely would have thought I was crazy) but from the time I met him I could not shake the feeling that I "knew" him, but not from this life. So much about him was familiar to me and all I could say was that I felt very "connected" to him and that this familiarity had a profound effect on me. It was not a sexual or physical attraction in the conventional sense; just a certainty that I knew him.

As noted, this feeling was overwhelmingly strong and I felt that I had actually shared not one, but a number of previous lives with him in various capacities; one as brother and sister, one as mother and son, and one where he was a spiritual mentor of some sort to me. Again, the idea of reincarnation was a newer one to me but I could not shake this feeling of knowing him from before.

It became so strong that I wanted to find out more and whether or not we had actually shared one or more past lives. Then the opportunity to find out more presented itself. I heard of a woman who lived close by who was skilled in conducting past life regressions, so I made an appointment.

This is what happened during the regression. First I was asked to lie in a comfortable position on a bed. The therapist whom I will call Diane, sat in a chair next to me. Diane advised me that it generally takes about an hour and a half for one regression, but that she would not stop the process if it went longer. She also said that as I was being brought through the regression, if I cried, she would not offer me anything like a tissue or a glass of water, or stop the regression (if it was too painful or frightening) unless I specifically asked her to.

She also advised me that some regressions can be traumatic, especially so if the person being regressed had been involved in a serious situation like a violent death. The realization or confirmation that you were the perpetrator (as opposed to the victim) of a violent act is often even more traumatic. Not to minimize victimization, she added that most of us don't want to believe that we could ever be so cruel as to hurt or kill someone else, as that realization can be devastating. It takes a skilled clinician to work through such trauma from the past in a current life.

To start the regression, we began the process with a common meditation. It included relaxation techniques of tightening and then releasing muscles in my body from toe to head, trying to release any thoughts and focusing on the rhythm of my breathing, both in and out.

As my body and mind began to relax, I was guided through the process of going down a set of stairs and at the bottom of the stairs I was offered a choice of three doors to go through. The therapist constantly asked me to let her know what I was seeing.

The door I chose, led me to a beautiful sandy ocean beach where I began to walk. It was early morning, and after describing the beach, the time of day and the cloud coverage, I was asked to continue walking. As I did, I noticed a boat in the distance that was approaching the shore and once I got closer, it pulled in and anchored just offshore. I was asked to describe the boat and if I wanted to get on this boat or wait for another one. I chose to get on this one.

At first this craft felt like a large motorized speedboat, but as we clipped along the waterway, I suddenly saw the captain who was steering the boat transform into a young man. The boat also changed from a speedboat into a gondola. We went for a long, long ride along a canal of some sort. I felt that I was in some place like Venice but not the Venice that we know. This one lacked the many houses along the canal banks. Incidentally, in this lifetime, I have never been to Venice.

Slowly, the gondola came to a stop to drop me off. I half expected to be in Venice or one of the Mediterranean countries, but this was not the case. I was asked to get off the boat and to look down at my feet to see what I was wearing, and much to my surprise, I saw leather sandals on my feet. When I looked up, I was in a small native village in the middle of a tropical rainforest. In the distance was a large set of mountains with a cascading stream. This was not at all what I was expecting to see.

As the regression continued, I was asked to describe in detail, what I was wearing, what my hair looked like, what gender I was and my age. I am not sure what tribe I was from, but my skin was dark and my hair was long and braided. I was in my late teens or early 20s. I was wearing a leather wrap and a beaded top.

As I began to walk, I saw small campfires all around, children playing, women carrying water or cooking and men sharpening their arrows. Everyone in the village was happy to see me and it seemed that I had been away for some time. In the distance, a native man began walking towards me and invited me to join him at his fire and enjoy a warm herbal tisane.

I need to say that during the regression it felt like a movie was playing out, that a parallel world was unfolding around the third eye (area slightly above and between your eyes). Everything felt just as real as it does in this world and while I was very conscious of my surroundings and that I was lying on a bed in someone's office, I was also experiencing the life within the regression and could be prompted to jump to important and key events in that life.

What unfolded during the regression surprised me even further. The man who invited me to his fire was older than me and a healer for his own and surrounding villages. He was, however, the last person that villagers would go to see, as his medicine was unconventional. His role was similar to a shaman. He was treated with great reverence, but also great fear.

I learned that I admired his abilities as a healer and spent every waking hour trying to learn what he would teach me. He died at around 40 years of age which was fairly typical for that time, and I was both lost and devastated by his death.

As he was dying, I was visualizing the story in my mind's eye as if I was there—as if I was really there. I was weeping over him as he drew his last breath. As I was recounting his death scene to the therapist, spontaneous tears began to roll down my cheeks, this time in the therapist's room. It was the gentle flow of tears, as I could feel the sadness I was feeling at that moment a long time ago when he died. He taught me so much about life, about being a healer and ultimately about death. He told me I needed to believe that I would see him again.

I took over his role as a healer and grew to be an old and respected elder in the village. I died many years later and was glad when I died as I knew I would see him again. In fact, he welcomed me on the other side.

The man, this healer, my mentor, was the man that I knew in this life. He did not look exactly the same as he does in this life, but his energy is the same. It was so clear to me that it was him, and I now understand why he had so much influence on me in this lifetime. He taught me so many things in the past that I have brought into the future—which is now.

Just before the regression ended, the therapist took me to the time right after my death and into the space and place between lives. It is believed by many mystics that this is the place where we recover from our last life. Here we replenish our soul and our energy, and decide with a large council of loving spiritual beings, what new things we would like to learn in the next life, or what we still need to learn that will carry over from the past life.

When she asked me to look around the room I was in and describe who I saw, I saw this man from this past life, and much to my amazement, my good friend and co-author of this book. Marion was there with a big smile, helping me chart out my next life, in other words this one.

Just prior to coming out of the semi-hypnotic state I was in, the therapist asked me what I had learned from that life. The message that I received was that I needed to learn to accept the gifts that I have and to not be afraid of them. I can understand this so clearly. In this life, my pursuit of spiritual issues has not always been an easy one, yet I have always felt a calling towards spirituality even though it conflicts with some religious ideologies. Incidentally, the person that taught me the most in this previous life is a very committed Born Again Christian who would not likely endorse this kind of thinking. Ironic, isn't it?

Same Past Life; Different Regression ~ Prolonged Grief

My co-author and I have had many lively discussions about what we believe, some of which are written in this book. We have also attended several conferences together that have been sponsored by Hay House—one of the world's largest publishing houses of spiritual books. These conferences are both overwhelming and amazing in that you have access to many exceptionally gifted and talented psychics, mediums, healers, scientists and others, many of whom are published and well-read authors. Thousands attend these events, each with their own purpose, their own needs and their own reasons for being there.

One of the most exceptional presentations we attended was by Dr. Brian Weiss (psychiatrist). He accidentally stumbled onto past life regressions with a patient he refers to as Catherine. Catherine came to see him as she was suffering from anxiety, fear, insomnia, and panic attacks. As part of his normal therapy regimen, Dr. Weiss used a blend of medication combined with other treatments including an exploration of her childhood experiences. Catherine's problems were persistent and did not improve with these traditional methods. As a result Dr. Weiss decided to use hypnosis, but the unexpected happened. In a hypnotic state, Catherine began to talk about another life, not the current one she was living. Over the course of several sessions, the same thing happened each time and more past lives came to the surface. Catherine could recall them with impeccable detail and then spoke of the time between lives. It was during one of those sessions that she informed Dr. Weiss that his son, who had previously died, and other deceased family members were with her. Catherine provided details about his son's death that only a few family members knew.[19]

This started a significant shift in Dr. Weiss's career as he realized that her story and the countless stories of other individuals that he has since regressed, all illustrate one thing—that some of us *[perhaps all of us?]* have lived before and that under hypnosis, we can often recall with great accuracy and clarity, stories of past lives. Each past life is as clear as if it were being lived today and usually has some profound implication or message for what is happening in this lifetime. It could be an unexplained fear, the onset of a physical and/or a mental illness, emotional pain and suffering, problems in relationships, etc.

Going back to the regression at the spiritual conference, in his very soft and gentle way, Dr. Weiss was able to help the large audience I was in, move into a deep meditation. He initially asked everyone to find a comfortable spot and proceeded with various relaxation strategies. Once we were in a relaxed state, he asked everyone to go back to their birth and move backwards from there. He gently took us through the birth canal to a set of doors, and asked us to select a door.

The door selected was a matter of personal choice. When you opened the door and walked through, it usually took you to your most relevant past life. This is similar to the process that the other therapist used with me a few years earlier.

Several months prior to Dr. Weiss's regression, I had been in discussions with a man whom I really liked. It began as a professional relationship and evolved into a personal friendship. We enjoyed each other's company and I believed that our friendship could deepen into courtship, however that never happened.

This man lost his wife many years earlier and had never resolved his grief. For whatever reason, he chose not to allow himself to become involved in another deep relationship ever again. He continues to carry the pain of losing his young wife so early in their marriage. Although I could not fully understand why he would not or could not move on so many years later, I had to accept that it was his choice to make.

Interestingly, I hadn't really thought about him for some time, and certainly not as I went into the meditation and this regression. I truly expected my regression to take me to another time, another world, another place. However, as I went through the door and was asked to look at my feet, just like the previous regression, I quietly said, "Not again!" I was wearing the same sandals, the same clothing and was in the same village, but this time, I was viewing my own death.

If you remember back to my other regression, I lived to be an elderly, respected shamanistic village woman. I never married and never had children. As a result, there was no family to bury me when I died. But here he was. The man from my current life who buried his wife years back in this lifetime, was slowly and gently burying me, placing stone upon stone, and quietly sobbing. He was all alone as he knelt beside me.

As I came to understand, he was one of the younger men in the village who always had enormous respect for me. From a distance, he would often observe me working. This watching was not at all in the stalking sense, but watching with interest and great admiration. Similar to his current life, he was a quiet, well respected man. He was married and had his own children, but he always felt a special admiration and affinity for me...and here he was burying me stone by stone.

It became so painfully clear to me why he could not date me. In the past he had buried me and in this life he had buried his beloved wife. He could not bear these memoires. He decided not to enter into any relationship that could again put him in harm's way or deep grief. Just like in my previous regression, this past life played out like a movie and the tears began to roll down my cheeks.

At this time, Dr. Weiss moved everyone into the present and the meditation and regression was over, but not for me. By now I was sobbing and my friends came over to soothe me not understanding what had just happened. Once I explained who was there in my regression and what transpired, my friends embraced me. They too understood the meaning behind this regression and why the man who I thought would date me, never could. It made perfect sense.

Afterthought ~

In both of these regressions I was brought to the same place and to the same time, but under different circumstances. Both were connected to two people that I know in this current life who have had a significant impact on me but for very different reasons, and in very different ways.

I should say that it is also believed that our souls travel with the same group of people or rather souls throughout time. In each life however, we manifest in various ways and often take on different roles and relationships. It could be mother to son, sister to sister, teacher to student, or strangers that collide with each other; same souls, different times, different reasons for being.

One thing that is clear is that these relationships, these circumstances over eons, are meant to help each of us grow through the lessons that we have agreed to learn. It is also believed that if we don't learn these lessons, they will be repeated in another life. If this is the case, isn't it better to resolve whatever you need to in this life, particularly those painful lessons, so that you don't have to repeat them?

Incidentally, while the man in my first story and first regression is now, in this lifetime, zealous in his religious convictions, the man in my second story, although raised Catholic is now atheist.

There are times that I have stepped back from these two regressions to look at a much larger question which is why was I placed between two individuals in this lifetime with completely polarized views about God. I think I now know the answer. It was to push me and to push me hard into really exploring, understanding and internalizing what I truly believe, some of which is reflected throughout this book.

Lost in This Life

While the two previous stories are about past life regressions that I have experienced firsthand, I would be remiss in not sharing a story about a past life that someone else had experienced.

My good friend and co-author and I were at the spiritual conference that I discussed earlier and we went to a session with a highly energetic healer whom I will call Melanie. Melanie, or Mel as she was known, was very engaging and she liked to be very interactive with her audience.

I have learned over the last few years of attending this conference that where you sit has a lot to do with you and the group that you gravitate towards in this lifetime. In other words, like-minded people, or people with similar life experiences, tend to sit in the same area as they often share the same vibration. I thought this was quite absurd when I first heard it, but it is actually true.

Over the last few years, one psychic medium in particular always asks his audience about some pertinent aspect of their lives. For example, he will ask how many people have lost a child and it seems that most of those individuals are sitting in the same area although they do not know each other.

I mention this because as I came into the room for the session with Mel, I sat in several places and kept moving about the room until I finally settled in a comfortable spot. A nice looking woman, who I will call Angela, sat in front of me. She appeared to be somewhere in her late 30s or early 40s, however it was hard to tell as she looked exhausted by life. Angela turned around to introduce herself to me before my friends sat down. She said she felt drawn to sitting near me as she thought I had something important to tell her. For the life of me, I had no idea what that was, but I was okay with that. After all, it was a spiritual conference and it draws many people from many walks of life for many different reasons.

Mel asked us to divide ourselves into groups of five or six people and the woman in front of me instinctively pulled her chair around into the group that was forming around me. We did several fun exercises about first impressions, which we were asked to share with each other, and surprisingly they were quite accurate.

In the next exercise, the entire small group was to close their eyes and focus on one individual in the group at a time for a few minutes to look at one of their past lives. This time is was Angela's turn.

As I closed my eyes, I was immediately brought to a time in the 16th or 17th century (I think) and I saw Angela in a beautiful long ball gown dancing with a tall and handsome British soldier of rank; I think he was a Captain. They were so very much in love with each other. I could see it in their eyes and the energy between them was powerful and warm. The gala was being held as the Captain and others were sailing the next morning to go west to explore new lands. Angela and the Captain were in their early 20s and were to be married once he returned.

What I saw next was Angela as an older woman in that life, weeping and in deep grief. The love of her life never returned and she did not know if he had died or simply left her. At that time in history there was no communication to know what had happened, but to her, he simply vanished and it destroyed her life. She never married and her heart was filled with pain and grief until she died.

We began to relay our stories to Angela, one by one. It was now my turn. I explained what I saw and she began to weep almost inconsolably. She said she knew that she had to sit with me as I had a very important message for her and this regression pointed directly to it.

Apparently in her current life she has not been able to enter into any relationships with a man since her early 20s and would sabotage the relationship before it even got started. The kicker was that her childhood boyfriend, whom she was very much in love with, allegedly committed suicide just before they were to get married and she has been at a loss ever since. He was using drugs at the time and she did not know if he intentionally killed himself or if he accidentally died from a drug overdose. The parallels between her past life and her current life experiences were astounding.

Through her tears, she looked as dumbfounded as I did and I gently said, "It is time to let go of the pain of the past and move on." She said she didn't know how and my friend and I directed her to a healer at the conference. She left thanking me, and hugging me, but upset by what had just happened. We never saw her for the remainder of the conference. I only hope that somehow, someway, she was able to find someone to help her to release the pain from the past and the present so that she could once again move on in her life with thoughts of the future.

This experience taught me so many things. Most of all it taught me that we go through multiple lives to deal with challenges that we have accepted before we are born into the next life. If those challenges are not dealt with, they keep coming back until they are.

Ghostly Real Estate

Insight:

*Negative and positive energy can be imprinted
on material items such as houses.*

Negative energies can contaminate individual homes and affect whole towns. There are some towns or sections of towns or roadways that feel like energy voids that suck the life out of everyone and everything in it. If you are relocating, for your own comfort, you should do some research ahead of time to find out about the history of the community, and most importantly, about the house that you are buying—especially those who lived and died in it.

Both my good friend Diane and I are single parents who live in a community far away from extended family. Although we have been on our own for different lengths of time, we have both talked about a longing to find a way to be closer to family. There is nothing like getting together with a sister, a brother, a mother or another family member to share a few laughs, have dinner, go golfing or just spend a weekend together without a long drive to get there and back. There are days I envy those who have family around them to share, to help, to have fun with, though there are other days that I remember an old saying that my father had, "After three days, company smells like old fish." With that in mind, both of us recognized that we still needed our individual independence and thought living somewhere between family members, or rather a short drive away, would be ideal.

To make such a change, would require a lot of effort, including the need to determine an employer's flexibility to accommodate a move and a community that would suit our individual needs. As anyone knows, uprooting where you have lived, and in my case for over 30 years, is significant.

It had been a very long time since I explored communities in this area. My visits usually consisted of one stop—directly to where I am staying and once there, staying put until I leave. Going back home was no different.

On one occasion, we both needed to be at the same meeting and decided to drive down together a few days ahead of time to check out the real estate in a town where Diane would consider living if the opportunity to move presented itself. The town was quaint with boutiques, artisans and gift shops, and beautiful homes and gardens along the waterfront. During the summer months, the town overflowed with visitors coming to shop and attend the live, world-renowned theatre.

Diane had already connected with a real estate agent who scheduled us to visit six homes that day. We spent the day touring various properties, and were quite disappointed by what we saw in our price range.

As we went through each home however, we both commented on the energy you could feel in each house. In one place we felt extreme sadness and knew that it had been owned by an elderly couple, and that one partner had died. A small memorial tucked away in the basement in her honour confirmed our suspicion; in fact we felt that everything in the home was left as it was when she died. The agent told us the elderly man who had never gotten over his wife's death, died shortly after her. He entered a long term care facility as he could not care for himself and could not bear to live in the home without her.

Another home felt like there had been a great deal of anger and fighting and that a couple had separated, and again we were right. It was amazing how both of us would feel the energy in each home and once we compared notes (or rather our impressions and feelings), we felt similar things. Each time, the real estate agent confirmed our suspicions.

As we pieced our thoughts together, we agreed that neither of us would consider, even in a desperate situation, moving into one of the homes that we toured. We bid the agent good bye, exchanged business cards and thanked her for her time. As we finished up, we drove to Diane's son's home for dinner, but on the way, we saw a beautiful old two-storey stone house with a sign on the front lawn which said: For Sale by the Owner.

We were both impressed with the look of the home which appeared to be turn-of-the-century and had been renovated into a duplex. Diane excitedly called the number listed on the sign and spoke with the owner. The house had been turned into rental property and the owner and his wife occupied the second floor which was their apartment. She explained to him that we were only in town for one night and he agreed to have us come and look at the house later that evening.

After dinner, Diane, her son and I drove over to the stone house which was within walking distance of downtown. It was an ideal location for Diane as she could be close to family and to the downtown core which offered plenty of entertainment, along with the shopping, boutiques and restaurants that she wanted. This house also offered the added benefit of a rental unit to help supplement the mortgage needed to purchase the home.

The stone exterior was solid in appearance and it was clear that someone had taken time and effort to maintain a small beautiful garden. In fact there was no lawn to cut as all had been converted to front and backyard gardens and a lovely trellis adorned with ivy encompassed the backyard. This was ideal for Diane as she did not want a large outdoor area (which is my preference), and the garden was readymade.

We knocked at the front door and an elderly man with a gravelly voice appeared. He was tall, thin, and not very personable. It was clear from the moment we entered, how the house had been divided as there was a door on the right closing off the apartment on the main floor and a long beautiful dark oak staircase leading to the next floor and the upstairs apartment. I saw that there were shoes neatly placed at the base of the staircase and instinctively asked if he would like us to take our shoes off and he very firmly said, "Yes." We all removed our shoes but as I looked up the ascending staircase, I became fixated on a picture that was on the wall right at the entry, somewhat behind, but not quite under the staircase. I did not immediately notice it when we entered the foyer of the home, but now this picture was noticing me!

It was the picture of an older stout woman with a stern look. She had short dark hair, dark clothes and a bit of lace at her collar. She looked to be of European heritage and I felt she was somehow related to the man. There wasn't much pleasant about her but I felt this woman staring right at me and watching my every move. I wondered if anyone else felt it. Although I did not ask, no one else reacted with the hesitation that I did.

We entered the very sterile upstairs apartment. There were few personal items other than some simply placed furniture to indicate that anyone lived there. Everything was impeccably clean, and nothing was out of place.

The wife sat in a rocking chair in the corner of the living room, and while she said hello, she never got up to greet us. She was extremely quiet and almost had a fearful, ill look about her, but as I engaged in a conversation with her, she seemed relieved. Apparently she was the person who tended to the garden and was modest about the work she had done. It was clear that she was intimidated and cautious about speaking, and her husband certainly kept an ear to what was being said. I also felt someone else was listening and watching—the woman in the picture. I sensed her energy and presence in every room I entered and felt her staring at me as if to assess who I was and what I wanted.

As I walked through every room in the two bedroom apartment, I felt her following me. I did not see her in the visible sense, but I certainly could feel her energy. It wasn't an overly creepy feeling. The man who owned the building and lived upstairs had that hands down, but she was just watching every move I made and everywhere I went.

None of us could put a finger on our impressions in that apartment. Even the kitchen, which in most homes has some appliances or other things on the counter, had nothing. It was completely bare. Every room was the same—an emptiness, a starkness and a sterility. The owner continued the tour and once done inside, took us downstairs and showed us the backyard in which it was evident that his wife took a great deal of pride.

He offered to take us into the basement. The basement was similar to a lot of basements in that community where the parging was peeling off the old concrete foundation. The concrete floor was damp and there was evidence of previous flooding. In fact, there were two sump pumps which helped keep the water out in the spring. The basement was full of hardware supplies such as tools, nails, and other equipment, but once again, this woman from the picture was following us, or rather me, through this maze-like basement.

As I turned one corner in the basement I felt she was right in front of me. At that very moment, I could hear my friend Diane beginning to breathe heavily, almost hyperventilating. I turned to her to ask her if she was okay, as she was making a beeline for the basement door to get outside. She quietly, but firmly said, "No." I followed right behind her and asked what had happened. She said she had seen a shadowy figure and that something brushed against her.

Diane was still struggling for breath. I asked her what it looked like, and she said "I don't know, I did not want to look directly at it, but it was there all right." We continued our very brief conversation as I knew the homeowner and Diane's son would be out shortly. I simply said to her, that I, too, had felt the presence of a female ghost since our arrival and that she had been watching and following me everywhere we went. Diane, almost yelling said, "Who? Who?" and I said, "The old woman in the picture in the front foyer."

We never went back into the house. We politely said, "Good-bye" to the owner and told him we would let him know if we were interested in purchasing the home. By now, both Diane and I knew that would never be the case. As we left, I looked back at the house and could sense the old woman looking from the upstairs window. I sensed no emotion; she was just watching and her eyes were boring into me.

When we got to the safety of my jeep that had been parked across the road in front of the house, we couldn't stop talking. Diane's breathing had settled down, and her son looked at us as though we had gone mad, as he had not felt or seen anything, anywhere, in or about the house. We compared notes and Diane wanted to know everything I felt, and especially what this woman looked like, as neither she, nor her son, remembered the picture on the wall.

I described her appearance and what I felt as we toured the apartment. It was hard to describe; just a strong feeling and impression of her energy. We chatted for a long time about this and the impressions we all had about the sterility of the home, the quietness of the man's wife and the discomfort we felt with the man and his mannerisms. How the old woman in the picture was related, I still don't know, but I knew she was. One thing I did know for sure, however, was that neither of us wanted to go back into that home, and neither of us had any interest in purchasing it. In fact, for me, I have no interest in purchasing anything in that town at all. I was uncomfortable with the old history of the town, the mustiness of every damp basement, the energy from each home, and the ghost in the stone house. I am certain this town has many more stories to tell, but I am not interested in personalizing those stories by the home that I live in.

An Uplifting Experience

Insight:

We can change the nature of matter.

For all of my teenage years, I lived out in the country between a large urban centre and a small rural town. While life was very busy, it was very different than how teens spend most of their time today. We did not have computers, the internet, cell phones, cable television and all of those luxuries and conveniences that we now feel are essential. Most families cooked from scratch, seldom ate at restaurants and spent most of their time with inexpensive indoor and outdoor recreational activities and hobbies. Parents did not drive their children to ten different places each week for dance lessons, hockey practice, music class or gymnastics. There was no time or money to indulge in some of these extracurricular activities that many think are critical to the development of their child's well-being today.

Instead, most girls my age had chores at home, helped with the cooking and babysat the younger children in the household. We were allowed to go to Girl Guides, belong to 4H clubs and babysit to earn spending money for clothes, but most of these activities were intended to help us grow into upstanding community citizens, caring mothers and dutiful spouses. We could participate in school sports only if there was an after-school bus (or a late bus as it was called), but most of the time we just took a bat, a ball and a glove and played baseball at the nearby field until dark. We were never bored, and there was always something to do.

To experience a bit of independence, we were allowed to go on hikes for hours upon end, and camp out in the woods that often surrounded the land owned by farmers in the area. Parents did not worry what their children were up to so long as they were home on time, with homework done, and weren't in

233

any sort of trouble in school or in the community. Times were very different and although crimes against children occurred, they were not as prevalent or public as they seem to be now. In other words, most parents felt reasonably safe to let their children go off on their own for extended periods of time during the day or the evening, without too much worry.

Although one of my younger sisters (who is quite close in age to me) did not hang out with the same friends that I did, as teens, we still belonged to the same clubs, participated in the same sports and often went camping together as a group. We had a couple of favourite camping spots: one where we would pitch several tents by a river bank and have large bonfires, and another was a cabin in the woods near a farmer's field some 15 kilometres away. While we enjoyed both, our activities at each location varied.

I don't know how this got started, or whose idea it was, but as kids, we were all quite fascinated by various aspects of the paranormal. At the time however, anything to do with ghosts or spirit communication through séances, Ouija Boards and other activities was considered dabbling in the occult and viewed in a very negative light. Most people preferred not to talk about it at all for fear of negative repercussions from the church and ultimately from God. As a result, much of it was done in secrecy with a select group of like-minded or curious individuals. It intrigued many, including us.

Over the period of several years during many of our camping adventures, we stumbled across a peculiar activity which I will call levitation. It was not really levitation in the conventional sense where you are able to raise an object (inanimate or live) with your mind but that is what I will call it for this story. During this time, there was also a popular television series called "Bewitched" where a friendly witch became the wife of a military man. In this television comedy, the witch, named Samantha was unaccustomed to human ways. According to the story, she could twitch her nose and in the blink of an eye, could levitate objects, clean the house, or make things appear or disappear.

In our case, it was none of these things but rather the ability to raise a person by being physically connected to them. All we needed to do was touch the person and repeat a brief but effective chant. I have no idea how or why it worked, but it did.

Here is how it went. One person would lay flat on their back; everyone else would surround them. We came to learn that two people could do this as effectively as three, four or five. It really didn't matter. As the person lay down, we would all bend over and put two fingers from each hand slightly under the sides of the person lying flat. If there were enough of us, we would have one person at the head, one on each side and one at their feet. All of us had our eyes closed, but I don't think it was necessary. I think more of that was for effect and to get us in the mood.

In most cases, the person leading the chant for this session would be situated at the head. They would begin by saying, "You're falling down a deep dark hole" and everyone, one by one, would slowly whisper the same words right after one another. We would go around the circle several times with no pauses in between and then one more time around with the last few words. I don't recall all of the words to each phrase of the chant, but in essence we began with, "You're falling down a deep dark hole"...to "You're going faster and faster and faster"...to "You're dead." It was all done systematically, around the circle with the quiet intent of lifting the person.

Once the chant was done, we would silently count to three in our heads, and then simply and miraculously, lift the person who was now as light as a feather. They felt almost non-existent and weightless. We could easily hold that person high above our heads—but remember, we only had two fingers on each hand under them and there was no effort of any kind exerted to lift them or to hold them high.

The moment someone giggled or lost their concentration, the person would become heavy and begin to drop like a lead balloon. We all knew this would happen, and as a group of giggling teens, anticipated that we would have to accommodate for the change in weight once we started giggling. There were times that we were able to hold that position, with the person lying flat but up in the air, for at least a minute or two.

Endless hours were spent as we each took turns chanting or lying still, waiting to be lifted. It was very exciting at the time. None of us ever feared this activity or this levitation, or tried to understand why or how we were able to do this with such ease. We just could.

We never told anyone about our levitation game, and never really talked openly about the implications of what we were doing. We were just a group of teens having fun on one of our many weekend camping trips. I think in the back of our minds, we all wondered how we could do this amazing feat, and if we were crossing a line into the spiritual world of the occult.

It is many, many years since I have done this, and over the last few years I have begun to question what actually happened and how we could do what we did. I lean towards believing that somehow our chant would put us into a semi-meditative state and that the connection/belief amongst us created a link or the synergy needed to accomplish this feat. It was not possible for one person to do the chant and lift someone else. At least two people were always required to do the lifting.

Was it the energy flowing amongst us that created a connection allowing us to lift someone with complete ease? Did we alter the nature of energy by the words that we used? Was it the deep meditative state that we put ourselves into? Did it have anything to do with believing we could do this? How did we change the molecular weight of matter? Or was it far more spiritual (light or dark) in the sense that we were calling upon something not of this world for help?

I also questioned if the death chant we used had any embedded power. Could we have been causing or facilitating an out-of-body experience, and could the person that was being lifted possibly die and not return?

I now think back to that time and I am glad that nothing sinister or tragic ever happened. It was all in good fun and we would spend hours playing this game—but was it a game? Or was it something more? And would I try it again, knowing what I know now? Probably not!

Afterthought ~

If chanting can change the weight of matter, could chanting also provide an explanation for the perplexing questions surrounding the construction of the pyramids?

Out of the Mouths of Babes

Insight:

Children sometimes remember aspects of their most recent past life and the wisdom that came with that life—it is we as adults who teach them to forget.

As discussed in "Evidence from the Past," it is believed that children up to the age of 10 have the innate ability to both communicate with spirits and see them, and that many remember some aspects of their previous lives. It is also believed that by the time a child turns ten, this ability and the memories of the spirit world disappear because many of us, in Western society, have taught children not to believe in anything spiritual beyond what conventional religion teaches us. This, of course, includes past lives and reincarnation.

Over the years, several stories have been relayed to me by parents about their children who have told them unusual tales or have behaved in ways that are difficult to understand or describe. Three intriguing stories come from others and one from my son.

The "Other" Mother

In the first story, Maria, the mother of a four year old girl was visiting one afternoon. It was a beautiful sunny summer day so we sat on my back deck enjoying some iced tea. Her daughter Vanessa was busy playing about in the yard as any little four year old child would do. After kicking a ball around for a while, Vanessa became bored and came onto the deck to pet one of my cats who purred with contentment. As we watched the two of them on the deck, Maria turned to me and said that she had not told anyone this story, not even her husband, but that she was very worried about her daughter.

To put it into context, Maria is a devout Catholic, but her daughter had been telling her stories and talking about things not of this world. The main theme of Vanessa's stories were related directly to Maria—that Maria was much nicer than her "other" mother. Vanessa would go on at length about how her other mother was very mean and that she liked Maria much better.

This was a story that repeated itself far too often and usually in the middle of intensive play. I have heard that rote activities, like driving and similar activities that are done on a regular basis such as play, could bring about an almost meditative-like state which opens the way for spirit communication, intuition and premonitions. There are many stories of children who talk to an invisible friend during play. Is this the creation of an overactive imagination, or are they really seeing something that we as adults don't see or have closed our minds off from seeing? This could explain why Vanessa was remembering some distinct features about another mother, possibly from a previous life.

According to Maria, the words simply came out of Vanessa's mouth as a matter of fact. On some occasions, Vanessa would also divulge more detailed information about her "other" mother, including some aspects of her clothing and her demeanour. For fear of feeding into Vanessa's stories, or what Maria thought may be fantasies, Maria would change the subject and ignore any references that had been made to another mother.

My friend looked at me and asked me if I thought that there was something wrong with Vanessa or if there was something evil, in the sense of possession that she should worry about. She had even considered going to the priest to discuss her concerns. Maria was somewhat aware of my expanded spiritual interest and exploration, so I carefully considered my response.

Knowing Maria's religious convictions, I subtly touched on the subject of past lives by saying that some people think that we have all lived past lives, and that sometimes children, while they are young, still have memories of these lives. I simply put it out there for her to consider, and added that it would be interesting to ask Vanessa more about her "other" mother in a very non-threatening way. Unfortunately, Maria would have nothing to do with it. She said she couldn't possibly do that for fear of feeding into an already worrisome behaviour and that it was contrary to her belief system. She said her husband would also be extremely upset at the thought of exploring such a dangerous fantasy.

I realized that Maria was stuck in her perception of religion and spirituality. She was unwilling to consider another perspective. I respected her position and gently moved onto another subject and we finished our iced tea.

How Did She Know?

The second story was relayed to me by an acquaintance of mine, Suzanne. Her brother Bill has a child named Sherri. Bill came to Suzanne after a most unusual experience with his daughter.

One warm fall day after shopping in the city, Bill and Sherri were returning to their home in the country. Sherri was living with her father, and she and her dad had driven that route many times. On this occasion, Sherri's father was deep in thought about the recent death of his own elderly uncle who had been ill for a long time.

While he drove, he mulled over a few things in his mind. They passed a small country cemetery near their home. This cemetery included the remains of various members of Bill's family, but this is not something that Sherri would know or even be aware of given her tender young age of four. Bill had not spoken to Sherri about his uncle's death as it is hard enough for an adult to understand the finality of death, but even more difficult to explain this to a child.

As they drove past the cemetery, the most unusual thing happened. Sherri began to talk about the cemetery, who was buried there, how they were related to the family and when they had died. Bill was taken aback but said very little as Sherri relayed her most impressive stock of information. Much like in the story about Maria and Vanessa, Bill thought it was best not to say too much. He made a mental note of the names that she conveyed, their relationship to the family and the approximate year of their death.

Later that night, he began wondering about what he had heard and what she had said. He decided to return to the cemetery a few days later to look at the tombstones and the information that was inscribed. Much to his amazement, little Sherri knew far more than he anticipated and she had recited with impeccable accuracy the names of those who had died and the year of their death.

Although he never told anyone except his sister Suzanne, he did ask his mother questions about who was buried in that cemetery and how they were related. His astonishment grew to disbelief when everything she said was consistent with little Sherri's information.

Sherri never mentioned anything more about those who were buried in the family cemetery by the road, and Bill never asked anything further. To this day, Bill thinks she has no recollection of the event, or the most unusual yet accurate information that she conveyed on that warm summer day.

Afterthought ~

What happened in both of these stories? Several things are possible. In the case of Maria and Vanessa, it appears that the memory or rather the cell memory of Vanessa's previous life transcended into this one. To Vanessa, the memory of her previous mother was still fresh and had not been forgotten.

In the case of Sherri, did she tap into a data bank of information that she could access and relay to her father? Or was she herself one of the family members who had died over a century before and was now living a new life? She seemed to know far too much detail about the people and their deaths. This would not be standard knowledge for a 4 year old.

Angel Protection

In the third short story, a young boy named Terry was sitting beside me in church one Sunday. I knew his family very well, and he always enjoyed being around me. Although I was not much of a churchgoer, as I had lost some of my belief in religion as a whole, I would go to the Catholic Mass with my children on most Sundays, just to provide a spiritual backdrop for their lives. Unfortunately however, my children often became rather bored with the sermon, so I would bring them some paper to draw on and a book or two for them to read.

On this occasion, four year old Terry sat to my left, while my six year old son sat to my right. Terry, like my son was a bit bored and somewhat restless. I gave him some paper and he proceeded to draw a picture of his house. Above it, he drew a picture of what appeared to be an angel. When I asked him about the figure above his house and how he came up with this idea, he said that he saw the angel over his house every night. I asked him to describe the angel and while I half expected a storybook version, he proceeded to describe this androgynous entity with incredible and credible detail.

He said the angel wasn't a boy or a girl, and that it had a beautiful white glow around it from head to toe. He said the angel wasn't a person, but came from God to watch over Terry and his family. The gown the angel wore was white and flowing and the hair was golden in colour. According to this four year old, he would see the angel every night and knew it was always there. I asked him if it was a story he had heard from his mother or his father, but he said, "No." In fact he said he had never told anyone at all, including his parents. He just saw this angel each and every night, and felt that this celestial being was watching over his house and everyone who lived there.

Over the next year, Terry's family would visit on occasion and each time he played and drew pictures, he drew an angel looking over his house, so it did not appear to be a onetime vision. I didn't pry too much, but as Terry grew older, things changed. I had not seen him for several years as his family had moved away, but when I saw Terry I once again asked him how the angel that watched over and guarded his house was doing. Terry looked at me as if to say, I don't know what you are talking about. I never pressed the matter any further, but I remember with great clarity the beautiful pictures that he drew of the angel that protected his home.

Heavenly Look

My son Jason has always been an inquisitive child and even as a young adult, still loves to sit by me for hours talking about very complex subjects such as the cycles of nature, the spirit world, and the psychology of people. On one such occasion when he was about seven years old, I was reading a book in my favourite spot and he tucked in beside me and asked me what I was reading. At the time, I was reading Sylvia Browne's book "A Psychic's Guide to Our World and Beyond—The Other Side and Back." I told him the story was about a woman who was able to see things like angels and ghosts and this part was about her visits to heaven. My son asked me what heaven was like and rather than answer him, I thought I would turn the question over to him. I asked him what he thought. Well, I did not expect the answer that I received.

His answer was so detailed that it made me feel as though he really knew and had actually visited or witnessed heaven, and even more profoundly had remembered! He described heaven as a place of great beauty and colour, unlike anything that we have seen before. He said if you can imagine the brightest of colours that we have here on earth, they are even brighter in heaven, so much that we don't have words to describe them. He went on to say that everyone moves about almost like they are floating, and while no one talks—as they communicate through thought—once you think of something it actually happens. For example if you want to live in a large elaborate home in the mountains or in a seaside cottage on the beach, you could in the blink of an eye, or rather the blink of a thought. He also went on to say that everyone gets along and that there is no anger, no hatred, no meanness like we experience here, only love. He added that there were angels everywhere but that they were different from us. Last, he also said that heaven had crystal-like structures of great beauty, kind of like castles, and old but incredible buildings with lots of pillars everywhere. These words were his, not mine.

I will never forget the detail of his description. It shouldn't have surprised me though. As noted in the other stories, children remember or see things that we don't or that we have forgotten. Interestingly I asked him several years later, much like I did with Terry, about his story and he does not remember this incredible description—this glimpse into heaven that he gave me.

What is even more interesting is that authors such as Browne and various other people who have gone through near-death experiences describe heaven in strikingly similar ways. Incredible beauty, indescribable colour, communication by thought, magnificent structures, and heavenly beings that emanate pure love and light.

Some also believe that heaven is not somewhere up in the sky and in the stars, but rather right here in another higher vibrating dimension. This is a dimension that we are not very good at connecting with given our vibration, our limited being and our reliance on our mind to rationalize every thought and everything that we see around us. Some think that gravitational pull has no effect in this dimension. This makes sense, as many who report sightings say that the ghosts appear to float several feet off the ground.

Afterthought ~

In each of these stories, something miraculous has happened. Both children who told stories of a past life or past relatives now deceased, accessed information from some place other than here—where else would this information have come from if it wasn't from the past, from heaven, from a spiritual being, or from another life? Did they receive it through divine means or did they experience a connection into a place where information about the past flows freely to the present and the future and vice versa; where time knows no boundaries? Or was it the result of cell memories from a past life that they were still able to access?

In Terry's story, how could he so clearly and distinctly see an angel when no one else could, and with Jason, his description of heaven matches those of many others who claim to have visited heaven and remembered its grandiose and indescribable beauty.

In these stories, all four children were under the age of ten. They were able to see spirits, heaven, their past, or a past life. Whatever their experience was, each story provides us with an incredible glimpse into another world as portrayed and conveyed out of the mouths of babes.

Roadside Angel

Insight:

Angels can appear when you least expect them,
but usually when you need them most.

It was a hot summer day, not unlike most summer days in this part of the country. I was in the early throes of separation from my husband of 23 years and running away for a few days with my two young teens to take solace, and visit my family over 600 kilometres away.

As with any long trip I take, especially by car, I generally conduct a thorough check of my vehicle well before leaving. This of course includes checking the tires to make sure they are sound and have the appropriate amount of air, ensuring that the radiator fluid and reserve antifreeze levels are full, all belts that drive the motor are tight and not cracked, and that my windshield fluid is topped up.

The trip to my parents is a long one, and at that time, for approximately one half of the northern leg of this journey, the road consisted of a two lane highway with few rest stops, gas stations or washrooms along the route. Even though this northern section is more remote, it is naturally landscaped with beautiful pine trees, colourful rock outcrops and glistening crystal clear lakes, rivers and waterfalls. The population in this part of the province is sparse by comparison to its southern counterpart, but in the summertime, the population triples as cottagers arrive to enjoy the peace and serenity of the area.

My truck checked out and everything, by all counts, seemed perfectly fine with the exception of the stress that I was feeling. I always went well prepared for these long road trips. I made sure that I was equipped with water, extra food, blankets, pillows, bug repellent, a working flashlight, and depending on the season, extra supplies to weather any storm that I might encounter winter, summer, fall or spring.

Anyone from the north and experienced in travelling this route, knows they need to be prepared as the highway can be shut down at a moment's notice due extreme weather, or collisions with other vehicles, or large animals such as moose, deer or bear. Periodically, if someone has died en route, the highway can be closed for hours upon hours. So, again, it is customary to be well prepared.

There are no alternative routes around some sections of highway and one of the main stopping points along route is about two hours away from my home. It is frequented by many travellers needing to use washroom facilities, pick up coffee or fast food, or simply gas up their vehicle, boat or snowmobile depending on the season. Like many others, we always stopped at this location, and today was no different.

My children and I parked close to the coffee shop building and we all went inside for our quick break before getting back on the road again. We made our purchases and as I came out, arms filled with coffee, bagels and treats, I noticed a darker green van parked beside my truck on the passenger side. A man was standing between our vehicles. "Nothing unusual," I thought but as I got closer to my vehicle, the man asked me if the truck was mine.

My first thought was that perhaps he had hit my truck with his van and my second was more instinctive, to be careful as I was not sure who he was, or why he was asking. He did not make me feel uncomfortable in any way, but all of my life I have been taught to be cautious about strangers approaching me.

The well-groomed man looked to be in his early 40s. He then proceeded to explain why he had asked me about my vehicle. He had been inside the coffee shop with his wife (who I believe was sitting on the passenger side of their van), when he had a strange intuition. As he was about to get into the driver's seat, he felt compelled to check the front passenger tire of my truck. He said his wife thought he was crazy, as there was no apparent reason why he should do so.

From the outside, the tire looked perfectly fine, and in fact was a top of the line, fairly new, all-season radial tire with little indication of wear and tear. He felt compelled to run his hand over my tire and continued on to explore even the inside wall of the tire—the side connected to the drive train. He was shocked by what he found. The steel belt on the inside wall of the tire had torn through and shards of steel were already protruding. A blow out was imminent.

Despite his wife's discomfort, he felt he could not leave. He himself was visibly shaken. He could not believe the information he had received, or the action he had taken. He told me that it was almost as if he was pushed to move his hand further and further over the tire in search of the problem.

Once the significance of the problem became apparent to him, he explained that he needed to wait until I came out. Undoubtedly he could see my disbelief.

As I knelt down to check for myself, he held the top of my hand, pulled it over the tire and suggested that I gingerly run my hand on the inside to see and feel what he was talking about. He cautioned me to do so carefully, as he feared I would be cut by the pieces of steel that were already poking through.

As he gently spoke to me, he must have sensed my continued scepticism. I knew I had a problem but, initially, I did not want to recognize the severity of it. He asked me how far I was going, and when I explained that I still had another four hours of driving on major highways, he urged me to have my tire changed immediately. In fact he almost begged me, at a minimum, to get off the highway and go into a small neighbouring town to have my spare tire put on. He waited until I promised to do so. By now I appreciated the gravity of the situation, and the risks to my children and me if I did not take immediate action.

He got into his vehicle and waited until I got into mine. I half thought he might follow me to see if I pulled off towards the small town about 15 kilometres up the road, but when I looked back in my mirror I could not see where he and his wife had gone. I then began to question what had just happened, as he seemed to just disappear, but trusted that I needed to have my tire changed.

I drove carefully into this small town. I did not expect much to be open on a Sunday morning except for perhaps some of the larger retail stores. A large hardware/tire store chain was open and I drove in asking for their help to change the tire. When they looked at my spare, they quickly informed me that I could not drive on it for any long distances, and certainly not at a higher rate of speed. It was one of those very small temporary spares suitable for slow driving for a short distance. Since I intended to travel for another four hours one way, and then return, I asked them to replace my tire with a suitable new one.

Unfortunately, they did not carry the type of tire I needed and I sat there, almost in tears, wondering what to do next. A kind service technician came up to me, and after overhearing my plight, told me that a small family owned tire store was located just up the road. While he doubted that they would be open on a Sunday, it was worth a try. This left me with another dilemma. If they weren't open and it was the only place around to get outfitted with the right tire, we might be stranded for the night.

I prepared my children for this possibility, and as I drove down the road, much to my surprise, this little tire shop was open. I later found out that they open for a few hours each Sunday morning specifically to help tourists who need new tires for their vehicles or their trailers.

I explained my situation to the older gentleman who owned the shop and he went over to check my tire. He was somewhat sceptical as even to the trained eye, when he looked at my vehicle from the front and from the side, absolutely nothing was apparent. However, when I related my story to him, which I quite honestly think he did not believe, he ran his hand on the inside of my tire, and was just as shocked as I was initially by the protruding steel. He could not explain or understand what had happened to my tire until he put my vehicle up on the hoist.

Apparently, the lower ball joint, although it had been recently replaced, was damaged. As a result, the tire, as it rotated, leaned in towards my vehicle as I was driving, so only the inside tread was touching as I drove. That part of the tire was so worn it was ready to blow out.

He was sympathetic to my needs and asked his son to stay on to replace the ball joint and change the tire as the store was about to close. The older man then phoned the hardware/tire store that I had been at but an hour earlier, asking them to deliver a ball joint for my truck, as he did not have any in stock. He then proceeded to look for a tire to match the ones I already had on. As luck would have it, after what seemed like forever while he was checking, he had only one matching tire in stock. It was exactly the same brand, kind and size that I needed. It had just come in the previous day on special order for the local police department, but he decided the urgency rested with me, and that he could order another tire for them the following business day. Was this just chance, a strange coincidence or synchronicity at play?

For a proprietor of a very small shop, his generosity was huge. He gave me a significant discount on the tire, charged me cost for the ball joint, and next to nothing for the labour. I paid for the work ahead of time so that he and his wife could leave while the shop closed for the day, and his son continued to work on my vehicle. As I stood there, I noticed many handwritten letters of thanks to this man for his kindness and the help that he has afforded tourists along the way and over the years. The letters were from all over Canada and the United States. It was apparent that this man cared for the people he has helped and that many were appreciative of his generosity.

My children and I walked to a garden centre nearby. I purchased a beautiful hanging basket of brightly coloured flowers and asked his son to give the flowers to his parents as now they were gone for the day. His son also showed me the tire that he had removed from my vehicle. When he hit it lightly, the tire exploded, tearing a large gaping hole in the side wall of the tire. It was shocking to see how close we came to having a blow out that day. This scenario would surely have altered or possibly even taken our lives.

The entire experience took the span of about five hours, but in those five hours, I was privileged to encounter many wonderful people that day; people who helped and accommodated the needs that I had in those few desperate hours.

I have since recounted this story many times to friends and family. I still to this day, can recall the shy nature of the man who stood by my truck and felt so compelled to check my tire for no other reason than feeling a tremendous urgency to do so. Had he not done this, surely my tire would have blown out at a high rate of speed and in all likelihood, neither my children nor I would be here today to tell the story of this roadside angel.

In my view there is no logical explanation. I have come to believe that some sort of divine being or divine intervention was at play. In point of fact, I never saw this man's wife, but once I assured him that I would get the tire changed, both he and his alleged wife vanished. There are many stories of angels who appear in human form, help when they are needed most, then disappear. I continue to ask myself the question—who was he?

This along with the many synchronicities and helpful people that came into my life for those five brief hours was overwhelming. I feel most grateful to each and every one of them, and especially the roadside angel, as his actions protected my children and me from danger.

Synchronicity in Dying

Insight:

Sometimes things spin out of control in our lives, but when you look back, you will see the unfolding synchronicity of a story with many lessons to be learned.

While varying views exist on death, and whether or not there is life after death, one thing inevitable in all of our lives is that we will die. Ironically, it is an inescapable part of life. Although we try to prolong life through exercise, healthy diet, medications, medical interventions and other measures, I believe when it is your time to die, it is your time and nothing you do can change destiny.

My father is a case in point. Approximately five years before he died, he developed a number of serious health problems, some that were never completely diagnosed. The onset was rather gradual, but he developed congestive heart failure which robbed him of his strength, his stamina and his ability to walk with ease. As time went on, his legs grew more and more painful and he often related his pain to walking on shards of broken glass. One can only imagine how difficult it was for him as he was an avid outdoorsman, an excellent craftsman, and a strong, hard working man who eventually became dependent on someone else for his most basic needs.

As his strength diminished and his pain increased, my mom took on the responsibility of looking after their home and became his primary caregiver. It was not a simple role as he was a very stubborn and proud man and despite how ill or incapacitated he was, he would keep trying to do things on his own. No one could blame him, but his body would simply not cooperate.

Many times, he injured himself by falling down the stairs, falling out of bed or slipping outside, even when he was asked to wait for someone to give him a hand. On one occasion, he would not wait inside a hospital lobby after a medical appointment and as he lifted himself out of a wheelchair and tried to step outside, he fell and broke his hip. He ended up going right back into hospital again. This was one of those times when we thought he would never survive the surgery to replace his frail hip, but he did. The stories of his stubbornness are endless and the strain and stress that he caused for everyone, especially my mother, was extreme.

Given the range of health problems he was experiencing, including a number of mini-strokes, he was hospitalized on numerous occasions. On one of those occasions, when surgeons were going to operate on his heart, they admittedly, by accident, overmedicated him which caused temporary psychosis. As a result of the medical error, he became so agitated and confused that the doctors refused to operate and decided that he was no longer an eligible candidate for surgery. During this period he experienced a number of hallucinations, many related to seeing dead relatives and friends, some of whom told him that he had still more to do on this earth before he could die.

On one of those occasions, just as I came to visit, he was screaming in his hospital room. I calmed him down and asked him why he was screaming. He related a story of being placed in a glass box from which he could not escape. He said he was speaking to my deceased mother and father-in-law, not vocally, but through their minds interacting with his. They asked him the following mathematical question: "What is two plus two?" and like most of us he said, "Four." He was advised that he was wrong and that the answer is five. He was also told that not everything is as logical as it seems or as he believes and that he was not always right. In his typical style he vehemently argued that they were wrong and that he was right. After much arguing he conceded and eventually learned that the lesson he was to take away from this experience was that he could not escape (the glass box) until he agreed that he could be wrong. This was an important lesson for my father who was extremely inflexible.

Over a four year period, there were many experiences like this with him and it was not only my father who suffered through his failing health, but also my mother. Then, the moment of synchronicity or in this case the inevitable truth came. It all happened very, very fast.

For some reason, I had a strong impulse to call my mom one day from work, only to find that she had been very ill and had not told anyone. Even though she said she was all right, I felt an urgency to get her help. I called all of my siblings who lived much closer to her than me, and the only one that was available was my sister Vicky. Although she did not get along very well with either mom or dad at the time, I pleaded with her to drive to their home several hours away, which she did that afternoon.

My mom was hospitalized and operated on that night. We found out that if she had waited any longer, even a few hours, she would have died. So my intuition was right; the situation was grave.

Now we were faced with the dilemma of what to do with our dad. No one was able to move in to care for him and mom would not be able to look after him either, at least not until she was fully recovered. My mom would have rejected the idea of placing him in a nursing home, but we had little choice.

When we called the agency that looks after placing elderly people, we were told that it could take months to place him, however, once they visited and saw his condition, a spot miraculously appeared in a brand new facility just 30 kilometres away. He could move in within the week. We were relieved to say the least and it seemed like this was yet another critical synchronistic piece.

During the entire unfolding of this chain of events, I was only able to help by long distance. In fact, the day that my mom went to hospital, I became seriously ill with a flu that left me weak and unable to eat or move—very unusual for me. This flu took hold of me like none I have ever had. However, even if I had felt well enough to go to see my parents, I would not have been able to do so. We were experiencing horrible weather and in fact the highway that I would need to take to my parents' home community (600 kilometres away) had been repeatedly closed due to extreme blizzard conditions, and all flights had been cancelled. As hard as it was for me to wait at a distance, I could only take this as a sign that I was not meant to be there to provide the care or make the decisions that needed to be made. Often, these defaulted to me when I was around. All I could do was help by phone.

Vicky agreed to stay and help, but just a few days before my dad was to move, he became violently ill with the flu. Vicky took over and looked after all of his needs. He was a seriously sick man. Vicky and my dad had never been particularly close, but in those few days, they developed a strong friendship and bond after many lost years. Each learned to respect the other. Several days later, my dad was well enough to move.

All of this happened within the span of five days, but it did not end there. My father settled into the nursing home very well. He was placed in a large single room that overlooked a huge field where a new housing development was being built. As an architect, he was delighted at the prospect of being able to watch this new development grow.

After a few days, I too began to feel better and decided to make the trek to see my parents. The roads were still treacherous but passable. When I got to the nursing home with another sister, Cheryl, I was stunned to see the condition of my dad. Apparently, just before I arrived, he had suffered a massive stroke that left him partially paralyzed.

The nursing home said they would continue to care for him unless his condition turned critical, so after a few days, I returned to my home to be with my children. My dad remained stable for a few days, but then took another turn for the worse and was hospitalized.

Meanwhile, my mom who was still extremely ill in hospital, became increasingly agitated and despite her doctor's wishes, asked to be discharged so she could see her husband as he lay in a hospital bed 80 kilometres away from hers. That day, the weather once again turned blizzard-like, but Cheryl, who does not normally rely on her intuition, felt it necessary to take mom directly to the hospital. They managed to spend a few hours with dad and while he did not wake from his comatose state, my mom thought he gently squeezed her hand as she spoke to him through her tears. The nursing staff said it was a matter of days before he would die, but that he was still strong and that my mom should go home to rest and come back the next day. However, the next day the storm continued, and although mom had planned to go back to the hospital shortly after dinner, they called to say that my dad had unexpectedly passed away. The weather was so extreme, that even the funeral home would not go out to get him.

From two weeks to the day, my mother almost died, underwent emergency surgery, was forced to give up the difficult caregiver role that she had assumed for five years, and my father was placed in a nursing home, suffered a massive stroke, was hospitalized and then died.

While we all grieved the loss of my father, I could not help but feel that the events were so synchronistic in their unfolding, that only divine intervention and destiny could have dealt this deck. I could not see it in any other light. The divine timing and care they received dovetailed in such a way that it could be managed. The divine domino effect!

During the visitation, my siblings and I were asked to have a picture taken with my father's dead body in his open casket. None of us were keen to do this, but it was traditional in his European homeland to send pictures of the deceased relative—morbid to us, but tradition to them.

I stood at the side of the coffin with my three sisters and brother. We were giggling, somewhat for comic relief I guess, when one of my sisters said we should be a little quieter. I said, "Don't worry, if dad wants us to be quiet, he will tell us" and that he did. The moment those words were out of my mouth, a large picture of him flew off of its stand, fell to the floor, and much to our shock and surprise did not break. I proceeded to say, "Sorry dad" and we all just grinned with a bit of trepidation.

After the funeral and my return home, I deeply pondered the synchronicity of the last few weeks. As mentioned, I could still not believe how everything, even though tragic and sad, flowed together so quickly. I was not so sad for myself or my father as I truly believed his time had come. His illness had already robbed him of any quality of life. He was no longer in any pain and his death, in my view, was a blessing in disguise.

Later that night I prayed for my mom to continue to get better, and for my dad to find peace. As I slept, he came to me in a dream. In his typical high-risk style, I saw a cedar strip boat swerving through the water headed directly for me on the shore. The boat crashed right beside me, and my dad crawled out from under the hull, looking terrific. He appeared to be in his 30s. Some spiritual writers say that we all appear to be in our 30s in heaven, and often we don't recognize loved ones who are visiting if we did not know how they looked at that time. It was unmistakable to me, however, it was definitely him! He smiled at me and said, "I am doing great" and then he was gone. I truly felt he had come to visit me that night and just wanted to confirm what I already knew—that everything happens for a reason and despite our sadness about his physical death, that he was doing well in his new spiritual life.

The Man in the Room

Insights:

Do lost entities miss or crave human and physical contact/touch? Do they do things to get attention? Are they attached to people, places and/or things?

As part of my former job, I was required to travel in and out of communities in Ontario at different times throughout the year. While the location and purpose was never the same, it often required overnight stays at various hotels throughout the province.

On one occasion, I was travelling to a meeting in a medium-sized community about four hours away and needed to stay for one night. Most of the hotels that I have stayed at have been of decent quality and aesthetics, ranging from five-star, to mediocre, to nondescript. The hotel I stayed at this time was somewhere in between: clean, and reasonable in price and quality. I had stayed there once before, so there was some familiarity with the premises.

The meeting that day had been complex with diverging views by participants with significantly different mandates. I always feel both energized and exhausted by meetings such as these where there are some ideological and philosophical differences of opinion but there is room to find common-ground and sometimes even consensus. This was one of those meetings that required a great deal of effort to both listen and to be heard, though progress had been made.

After the meeting, I took some downtime and went for a short walk as the early winter weather had taken a turn for the worse. It was snowing and blowing and the roads were turning into treacherous skating rinks. I returned to the hotel for a quiet dinner by myself, and then went to my room to catch-up on my emails, do some work on my computer, read for a bit and then retire for the night. I was exhausted by the time I settled into bed. As a matter of routine, I seem to have difficulty sleeping the first night in any hotel and this night was not any different. I tossed and turned for some time, unsure of what time I had actually fallen asleep.

The details are still somewhat fuzzy to me, but I felt I was in a deep sleep, when I began to feel the presence of someone in my room. Part of me felt like I was dreaming, but part of me knew I was awake. A bit fearful to open my eyes, I slowly did, and was startled by the image of a man standing at the foot of my bed in my almost dark room.

He was not frightening in the sense of being an evil spirit, but rather an ordinary man standing at the end of my bed, looking at me. He was wearing clothing from what I believed was circa the 60s with a shirt, dark pants and a semi-colourful argyle sweater. His hair was light and almost brush-cut in style. He was clean shaven, had a rounded face and was not too tall, maybe just under six feet. I felt he was in his early to mid-50s.

He stared at me for what felt like a long time but which I am sure was only a few seconds. I lay in my bed slowly forcing myself to sit up but stared at him the entire time. He approached me very slowly and reached out to hug me.

I was frozen and could not move, and I distinctly remember yelling, "Leave me alone. Get out of here" several times. My voice felt raspy and I felt like I was speaking in slow motion. Although I felt I was yelling, I am not sure if anything actually came out of my mouth that was audible. At first he continued to move toward me and I could feel him trying to embrace me, in fact I could feel his touch. Then after yelling several times and pushing him away he was gone, he disappeared...just as fast as he appeared.

I turned on the light trying to make sense of what just happened and still shaking from the experience. I looked at the clock and it was around 3:00 a.m. and there was no one in my room now. My door was still bolted as I had left it, my window was still sealed shut, and everything remained untouched, exactly like it was when I went to bed.

I know that sometimes we have lucid dreams that feel real, but this one was different. I did not know the man that appeared in my room, but I could certainly see him as clearly as I see everyone on a normal day. I also felt his energy and his effort to embrace me, and my struggle to push him away and ward him off by yelling. I still feel it today, just like it was today and when I close my eyes, I still have his image imprinted on my brain.

As tired as I was, I could not go back to sleep. The experience felt so real and I was afraid that if I turned off the light, he would appear again. I believe

I must have dozed off with the light on, but I was exhausted when it was time to get ready to head off to breakfast and my next meeting, before my long drive home.

I debated that morning whether I should ask the person on the main desk of the hotel if someone had ever seen a spirit in the hotel before or if there had been a death in the hotel years earlier, but I didn't for fear of them thinking I was crazy. As strong as my curiosity was, I never had the courage to ask.

When I returned to my home community, I did a bit of research about the area and the hotel, but never came across anything that would provide a clue as to who he was, what he wanted, where and when he died, or why he sought me out. Although I will make sure never to stay in that same room again, that memory is as vivid as the evening that I met the man in my room.

Trusting Your Gut

Insight:
*More often than not, our logical mind gets in
the way of listening to our intuition.*

I once asked a high-level police officer how much of his work is related to intuition or trusting his gut. He was a homicide detective for much of his policing career and is now in a senior executive position. His answer was somewhat unexpected but expected. He said that the work of a police officer is to follow the facts. But by the same token, quite often it is your gut that leads you to those facts in the first place.

I am still not very good at trusting my intuition, unlike my co-author Marion. She trusts her gut and her intuition at every turn and it is a skill that she has honed over the years. I still second-guess myself, although I have had a variety of experiences where that intuition has come into play, and you would think I would have learned to trust it by now, but I still don't one hundred percent.

From my perspective there is a very fine line between what we call intuition, mind-cross and even premonitions. But one fact that does remain is that the information that we get, comes from somewhere. Does it come from an inner knowing—meaning that it is information that is already inside of us that we ourselves are able to access and use? Is it a knowing that is given to us by an outside source such as spirit guides, angels or other entities that manifest at certain times? Or is it a knowing that comes from gaining access to information from other sources such as ancient records or our contract for this life? World-renowned psychic and author Sylvia Browne claims that she is able to access information about us from these sources.

The following is a collection of some of my experiences and the those of others. They might seem small and mundane as individual events, but when strung together, they paint a pattern that illustrates that we are able to receive information before an event and avoid a potentially tragic outcome. Often it is a fleeting moment of questioning, an insight that just comes to you, a picture of something in your mind or in your thoughts, or even a push, telling you to call someone or do something now. Trusting it is something else.

Bear-Wise

Interestingly, even as I write this collection of stories, I am constantly reminded of the power of intuition. I power walk almost every night. The distance varies, but it is anywhere from two to four kilometres. It is a great way to stay in shape, revitalize, rework the day's events or make plans. This night was no different.

I put on my jacket and just as I touched the doorknob to go out the front door, I got a strong message in my head not to go; that it is dangerous tonight. I thought, don't be silly, you're just going for a walk which you do every night.

It was fairly late and already dark, but I went anyway, not trusting the message that I had just received. I walked a short distance and turned to go up a hilly street, and part way up I heard a loud whisper, "Stop, there's a bear right beside you." I recognized the voice, and saw my friends Janet and Jim standing in their open garage. I stopped dead in my tracks and said, "Where?" "Beside you, by the van" Jim replied. I turned around immediately, and he cautioned me, "Don't run!"

Even though I know better than to run from a black bear, it was an instinctive move and I again slowed my pace to a fast walk, all the time watching behind me and saying, "Keep your eye on the bear for me and let me know if it is coming after me!"

I returned to the safety of my house. I wasn't shaking, just thankful that Janet and Jim were outside watching the pesky intruder. After all it wasn't the first time that I have come across a bear in my travels.

Although bears are not that uncommon in the area that I live, it is a sure sign that they are either going into or getting out of hibernation as food is scarce. As a result, they start making their way into residential areas and the smell of outdoor barbecues and garbage buffets eliminates their fear of humans. I knew better than to stick around, and while black bears generally don't attack humans, who wants to be that close to find out? Next time I hope I will trust my intuition which is almost never wrong...I just don't listen too well, or I second guess what I am hearing.

Message from Across the Miles

One cold winter day, my parents went out for a long walk through the snowy forest near their home in the country. Going for long walks and hikes with family members was somewhat of a tradition that I was raised with and still do today. It is a great way to feel invigorated and learn about nature—the various birds, trees, and the changing seasons, to name a few.

On this day, my mom and dad went out on their own and it was exceptionally difficult to navigate the terrain as there had been a heavy snowfall earlier that day. The snow was not packed down and in some cases was knee-deep, making the outing a bit more strenuous.

They were several kilometres from home when my mom had a premonition that there was a very important message that just came in for them at home. They needed to get back right away. My dad didn't argue, knowing that my mother's intuition was usually accurate. They trudged through the heavy snow and when they got back home, there was a message waiting for them. My mother's aunt, who she was very close to, had just died. While she had not been ill, she suffered a massive heart attack. The message my mother received was loud and clear. Unlike me, my mother listens to her messages and trusts her intuition all of the time.

Car Trouble

On my way to work one day, I kept getting this picture of car trouble. It wasn't like a serious accident, but it was going to be enough to warrant attention and it was also going to be inconvenient. I keep my truck in good working order and have it checked and serviced on a regular basis, so for the life of me, I couldn't figure out what it could be. Later that night, I received a call from my daughter who was stranded at the university after a night class. Her tire had gone flat and she needed roadside assistance as she and her boyfriend could not get the tire off no matter how hard they tried. Now I knew what the car trouble message was telling me. It wasn't about me; it was about someone close to me.

On another occasion, my daughter was returning to her school out of town. She was all packed to go. Something told me to go out and check her passenger-side tire and indeed it was dangerously low. She may have missed it completely as she was backed into the driveway and was not getting in on the passenger's side. It was over a 400 kilometre drive back to her school and this could have been extremely dangerous if she had a blowout or a flat on a remote stretch of highway.

Same daughter—another situation, again involving the same car! On this occasion, my daughter and her boyfriend were visiting for the weekend. They had been out to a movie earlier in the evening and were settled in for the night when I got this strong urging to look at their car, which I did, through the window. Everything looked fine. But I got another urging to look again, this time out the front door. Now I saw what I couldn't see from my window vantage point. The car's interior light had been left on.

Anyone who has ever had this experience knows that the battery would have been dead in the morning. The next day was a statutory holiday so this would have been inconvenient. It would have meant that my daughter and her boyfriend would have had to wait until the next shopping day to pick up a new battery.

Although charging her car battery might have been an option, her battery had already died and been recharged several times on previous occasions. In other words, it was no longer holding its charge and in all likelihood would need to be changed. If it had died this time, she would have also missed an important assignment deadline and one of her exam preparation classes.

Needless to say, I now check her car all of the time!

Mother-Child Connection

There is something about a connection between mother and child. There are untold numbers of stories where mothers seem to feel something about their child, something that needs attention. It could be a cry for help, a need for some love or a warning of something that is about to happen. My daughter Jenny, and my son Jason and I have that kind of connection. One of us thinks of the other and moments later the phone rings and it is not hard to guess who it is. This happens constantly.

I have also had countless experiences of times when I just knew something was wrong and that I needed to check on one of my children. There are so many, many stories of mothers just "knowing" something is wrong and that they need to call or to see their child, no matter what age. Perhaps this knowing starts with conception, and the natural, physical and emotional bond between mother and child continues to develop through gestation and birth. For some, this bond strengthens over a lifetime.

I found that quite often when my children were young and if they became sick, I was also very good at figuring out what was wrong, even though the doctors were unable to. On one such occasion, when Jenny was around four, she became very sick, high-fevered and lethargic. I brought her in to see my family doctor a number of times, and to several after-hour clinic physicians over the course of ten days. My family doctor insisted it was her asthma, and others said it was a flu. Despite my insistence that something else was wrong, they all dismissed my concerns.

After six visits in less than two weeks, Jenny was not any better and I felt a strong calling to take her into a particular clinic immediately. It was Easter Sunday and we were all dressed to go to a large family dinner. She was still not feeling well, and certainly not herself. I took her into the clinic and upon examining Jenny, the older doctor asked me to wait with her and left. He was back in several minutes and advised me that she was going to hospital and into an oxygen tent immediately. If I was unable to take her, an ambulance would.

Once at the hospital and after a series of tests, it was determined that she had an aggressive pneumonia and if I had waited even a few more hours, and not trusted my persistent intuition, she may not have survived. She was placed in an oxygen tent and started on a high dose of strong antibiotics. I was allowed to stay in my daughter's hospital room around the clock, but was not allowed to sleep in a bed. Instead, I could use a large chair to rest beside her. She began to improve slightly on Easter Monday, however, that night, the nurses came in and removed the oxygen tent and were in the process of completely changing her medications. I asked them what they were doing, and who changed the orders. Apparently it was our family doctor, the one who ignored the pneumonia from the outset. I insisted that they contact the on-call paediatrician who initially admitted her and told them to leave her on the course of medications that he had prescribed until morning. I asked the nurses to contact both doctors and ask them to be at the hospital the first thing the next day.

I did not need to say much to my family doctor as the on-call paediatrician certainly said enough—and it was loud enough for everyone on the hospital floor to hear. Apparently my family physician misread the chest x-ray. Needless to say I "fired" him on the spot.

I now know, however, that it was my gut and the connection between my daughter and me, the connection of a mother and child, that kept relentlessly pushing me for answers and ways to make sure that whatever was affecting my daughter was being treated the right way. Who knows what would have happened if I did not listen.

Just Knowing

It was a very warm fall afternoon and I was attending classes at the local university. I already had two undergraduate degrees but decided that I wanted to expand my academic knowledge and try a course in a new specialized master's program as a mature student.

Being a mature student is very different, at least for me. My level of commitment and effort far exceeded the commitment and effort I put in during my undergraduate years, so I was both excited and anxious about attending.

At the time I was married, and while I was heading off to class, my then-husband decided to go spend some time at his parent's home a few blocks away to tinker on his dune buggy. Actually it wasn't a dune buggy yet, it was an old Volkswagen beetle that was being cut down to become a dune buggy. He also loved to spend time with his elderly father and learn from his extensive knowledge of machinery, cars, and how things worked.

As it was my first night at class, I was eager to meet all of the students and the new professor. I made it to class on time and spent the next hour listening to his expectations as he reviewed the syllabus. We were let out early and rather than go for coffee with some of my new classmates, I had this urgent sense that I had to leave; that I should not go for coffee or return home. Instead, I should go straight to my in-laws' house.

I was a few kilometres from my in-laws' home where my husband was playing with his new toy, when I had the sense that something terrible had happened to him. I sped to his parents' home and I had barely pulled into the driveway when I jumped out of my vehicle and yelled, "Where is he? Is he okay?" His parents immediately surrounded me and were visibly shaken. They told me that there had been an explosion and that my husband had been burnt, but that they didn't know how badly. He had been taken to the hospital by ambulance.

I jumped back into my vehicle and drove to the hospital. As I got to the emergency department, they ushered me in to the room where he was lying. He was on a stretcher, shirt off, work pants on, and his face covered with a large towel. There were basins with ice water beside him and I had no idea what to expect, but I was told in my head that he would be okay.

Just then, the nurse entered the room to cool the towels again, and she told my husband that I was there. She removed the towel on his face to replace it with another. It was then I saw my husband's face.

I was so thankful when I saw him, as I did not know what to expect or how badly he had been burned. His face had streaks of charred burnt skin that radiated from his chin and fanned out all the way to his hairline which was also burnt, along with his eyebrows. Fortunately, the area around his eyes was untouched. We later learned from the doctor, that it was nothing short of a miracle that he was not severely burnt, disfigured, blind or dead.

Apparently Anthony made a decision to wear his goggles that day instead of a full-face shield which is normally worn while welding. He was using his welding torches to cut off a part of the dune buggy bumper. However, when he cut through the bumper, he hit a hydraulic shock and the hydraulic oil caused an explosion. The explosion knocked him backwards as the fiery impact first hit his chest and then flamed up onto his face. His clothes were on fire and the garage behind him was also on fire. In all of the panic, he tore off his coveralls but distinctly remembered that I had repeatedly told him: never put butter on a burn (which his mom had run inside to get). Instead he used cold water to cool his skin.

His elderly mother was in a complete state of distress as he yelled at her to call for an ambulance. Anthony grabbed the garden hose and ran cold water over his face and body. He also used the water hose to put out the fire on the doorframe of the garage.

The doctor told us that if he had worn a full-face shield, the flame would have gone under the shield and created a concentrated fireball. He would have suffered extensive deep burns to his eyes and face, and could have been blinded or killed.

Anthony remained in hospital for about a week. While his recovery took some time, we were thankful that the long-term effects of the burns were unnoticeable. His face suffered minimal scaring, and most of the hair on his eyebrows and head grew back.

Both Anthony and I experienced some sort of inner knowing. For some reason he made a decision to use his goggles that day which created a seal around his eyes rather than the more usual face shield. I also experienced an intuition that urged me to go directly to his parent's home because something terrible had happened to Anthony. I also knew before I saw his face at the hospital that he was going to be okay.

Dying Message

My father and mother-in-law were in their mid-60s when I met them. As mentioned in previous stories, my then-husband Anthony was the baby of an Italian family and there was quite a spread of ages between him and his closest siblings—almost 20 years. I always called my father-in-law Nono (Italian for grandfather) and my mother-in-law, Nona (Italian for grandmother) as I didn't quite feel right about calling them mom and dad as many do. I never knew my own grandparents because they lived in Europe behind the former Iron Curtain and most of them died around the time of World War II.

Nono and Nona were very much like what I envisioned grandparents to be. I was their youngest daughter-in-law and very much loved. Anthony and I spent a great deal of time with them even when we had our own children. Together, we often went to the family camp or had dinner on weekends. In their later years we helped them with their many needs up until the time they each died in a long term care facility. I had a very special bond with both of them and miss them a great deal.

Nona, who developed Alzheimer's disease in her late 80s, fell out of a hospital bed on one of her many stays, and died in her early 90s from complications due to a broken hip. Nono, who shared a room in the same long term care facility with Nona, died several years later in his mid 90s. He was a very vibrant, strong and proud man up until his death and did not want to be reliant on anyone.

It was early fall and I had this urging to go visit Nono in the nursing home. Anthony and I were already having problems in our marriage and while we each continued to visit Nono, just as other family members did, we often went at different times.

I had just visited Nono on the weekend, but mid-week, I was out in the community travelling from one meeting to the next, when I felt a strong pull to go up to the nursing home right away. I didn't usually do this and I thought about waiting until the evening, but I got the distinct message that I needed to go right away.

I was completely taken aback when I saw my father-in-law. On the weekend he was fine. He walked with me using his walker, and we went down to the dining room, had snacks and spent time chatting. However, this time when I went into his room, he was lying very still in his bed with his eyes wide open. He had the look of death. I was with my mother-in-law when her sister died and her eyes were dark, the pupils were completely dilated and there was a hollowness about her. Nono looked the same. To me it was like something was missing, like the light or spirit of Nono was already gone. He was in a comatose-like state, and unable to speak or move. When I entered his room, I felt like he was trying to move his head to look over at me. I am certain that he knew I was there.

I immediately called Anthony and suggested he come up to the nursing home right away as I thought his father was going to die at any moment. He called all of his siblings, and took our two children with him to see his dad. The priest at the nursing home came in to give The Sacrament of the Sick (Last Rites) as is traditional in the Roman Catholic faith.

Over the next day, all of Anthony's siblings, their spouses and some of the adult grandchildren came to the nursing home to stay with Nono. The staff, who is very compassionate during a time of death, moved my father-in-law into a large private room where family could gather and spend time with their loved one. Family members filled the room and hallway day and night. On some occasions there were up to 20 family members at a time. However, days passed and Nono was still alive, though the doctors said they did not know how or why. He remained in a comatose-like state and never spoke or acknowledged anyone's presence during the entire time.

In the hallway, one of Anthony's adult nephews approached me as he knew I was very interested in spiritual issues, and he asked me what I thought... why was Nono still hanging on? I had already asked my father-in-law this same question from my mind to his. The distinct message that I got was, "I want to be alone when I die."

I couched my answer to Anthony's nephew as other family members were in earshot and said, "I have read that sometimes people want to be alone when they die. It doesn't mean they don't love everyone who has come to visit, but that dying is a very private thing and maybe he wants to die alone." It appalled other family members that I would say such a thing. They dismissed what I had said and continued their vigil morning, noon and night. By the fourth day, everyone was becoming tired, so various shifts were set up so that Nono would not die alone. They felt it was their obligation for someone to be there when he took his last living breath.

On the fifth day, my brother-in-law and his wife offered to do the shift for the night. My sister-in-law left around 2:00 a.m. leaving my brother-in-law, Angelo all by himself with Nono. Around 4:00 a.m., Angelo went out of the room and down the hall to get a drink of water from a fountain. He said he was only gone one or two minutes at the most. When he got back, Nono was dead. He truly wanted to be alone when he died and he waited for a moment of privacy to cross over to the spiritual world.

I think death is a very personal thing and the wishes of those who are dying need to be honoured as much as possible. I am sure that every one of us will have our own wishes when it is our own time to cross over. While Anthony's family was well meaning and really loved and cared about Nono, no one could know what he wanted at that moment, but I heard it. That day, when I asked him the question, "Why are you still hanging on?" I clearly and distinctly felt the crossing of our minds and heard his dying wishes.

Afterthought ~

While each story in this chapter has many little twists and turns, the common feature that they all share is that there was some sort of knowing that something was going to happen or had just happened. Each story shows how important it is to trust your gut and what you are hearing, but intuition and mind-cross can be a tricky thing.

Many spiritual writers say that the reason we don't listen to our intuition or when our mind crosses with someone else's is because we let logic get in the way. While some eastern cultures are taught to trust and listen to their intuition, in western society we're taught to rely on logic. This causes us to second-guess much of what we hear. We have all done it. We ask ourselves—is what I am hearing true or real? Is it wishful thinking? Or is it just nonsense?

Sometimes the information does come from an outside source, or outside helpers such as angels, spirit guides or ghosts that plant the seed in our thoughts, but we have to remember that however it comes to us, there is a bountiful source of information available if only we will listen!

Twin Love

Insights:

Angelic help is but a prayer away. Love knows no boundaries.

For most families, pregnancy is a joyous occasion. For women, the anticipation, the trepidation and the excitement of a new child growing inside is difficult to describe. Sometimes, the changes can be so subtle that it is hard to know you are even pregnant. For others, the changes throughout the body may be gradual with the ever so slight growing of the belly, and yet others may experience a daunting and draining feeling accompanied by sheer exhaustion, sickness and shall I say expansion.

Katrina and her husband were happily married and already had two children. One child was close to five years of age, and the other was a three year old toddler. While children at these ages no longer need complete assistance with eating and dressing, any parent knows that they are also some of the busiest and active ages of exploration, growth and learning. So while children can do a lot on their own, they continue to require constant attention, supervision and guidance.

Katrina's mother had died years earlier and it was very hard, like it is for many new mothers, to raise children without the support of a mother close by. Some women have been fortunate to have the support of their mother during pregnancy and those early years, to provide relief and guidance, or just be around when needed. I know what that is like. My parents lived many kilometres away and were not available on a moment's notice. My in-laws were elderly and did not have the stamina or energy to deal with the demands of young babies and children, so I know all too well how hard that must have been for Katrina.

When news came that Katrina was pregnant, she and her husband were happy, but recognized the incredible added responsibilities and time that would be needed with a new baby. However, 16 weeks into Katrina's pregnancy, she found out that she was pregnant, not only with one child but with two! She and her husband were not only shocked but almost devastated by the new prospect of now having to care for and provide for two additional children with two young ones at home.

Having already gone through two pregnancies, Katrina was well aware of the changes that her body would go through but I don't believe that most women can anticipate how it must feel to be pregnant with twins. The accelerated growth of your body along with the changes and fluctuations in hormones would have been overwhelmingly exhausting. Katrina knew this so well and indeed she was exhausted by these changes and the additional demands of caring for two young children.

The pregnancy advanced as most pregnancies do. The appointments with medical specialists, along with the constant tests and monitoring to make sure everything was progressing in a healthy way became a matter of routine. However, by the last two months of gestation, Katrina found herself not only increasingly exhausted but unable to sleep.

Her inability to sleep was compounded by the size of her ever-growing belly. She was unable to sleep on her back given the extra weight of the two young babies growing inside of her. It was impossible to find a comfortable sleeping position. She tried everything. She tried putting a pillow between her legs, positioning her knees apart and other strategies but none of them seemed to work. She also kept her pain to herself, not wanting to disturb her husband as he slept. Every night was the same.

One night, as she lay in exhaustion, tossing and turning, a slow glow entered her room and at the foot of her bed she saw two entities. They appeared to be two girls in their teens. Katrina said that they were indescribably beautiful and that their hair swayed and moved like it does in the wind.

On the right, the beautiful entity's hair was auburn in colour and in a bob-shaped cut. The one on the left had long, dark and flowing hair. Katrina was not frightened by them at all, even when they reached over towards her legs. Curiously watching them, they moved about and positioned her legs to make her comfortable and shortly after, Katrina drifted off into a deep sound sleep, one of the best she had enjoyed in months.

At first she thought it was a sleep deprived dream and that her conscious/ semiconscious state had made her see things, but not so. For the next few weeks, these "angels" as Katrina called them, would come back every night. And every night, they would help reposition her legs to allow her to sleep.

She dared not tell anyone, for fear of what they might think, but one morning, she decided it was time to tell her husband about her nightly visitors. She described for him how these angels came to her aid every night, and moved her legs under the heavy weight of the ever-growing twins so that she could sleep. Her husband had always been a very supportive man and he was intent on hearing her story. He had no reason to disbelieve what she said, and was glad his exhausted wife had found a way to sleep.

Much to Katrina's dismay however, the day that she told her husband, the two beautiful entities never came back. She was so sad and longed to see them but she knew in her heart that something very special had happened. She tried to understand why they did not return, but she and husband thought that it may have been because they were no longer needed. Her husband had not been aware of his wife's extreme discomfort. Now he knew, and he was quite willing to take the place of those entities who had helped her every night.

Katrina also knew that her twins would be two beautiful daughters, who to this day she still calls her angels, but her story did not end here.

Most parents well understand the cycle of sleep deprivation and exhaustion that comes with newborns, but in Katrina and her husband's case, they had four children under five, two of them newborns.

She recalls that during those first six months, she felt like a machine. She and her husband rotated sleep schedules and at times she felt like she was almost asleep and awake at the same time. At one point, her exhaustion was so overwhelming she did not know how they were going to make it through.

It was on one of those nights, where she sat rocking one of her babies during feeding that another entity appeared. This time it was Katrina's mother who had died when Katrina was 25. Katrina's mother died before any of Katrina's children were born. In Katrina's mind, she had never seen her grandchildren. Her mother looked at her with great love and approval at seeing the latest arrivals and then slowly disappeared. Katrina couldn't believe her eyes and called to her to come back, but she didn't.

At that pivotal moment, Katrina knew everything would be okay. That life would develop a new sense of normalcy and that all was unfolding as it was meant to be under divine guidance and love.

Spirits of Children Helping Children

Insight:

Ghosts can take many forms and sometimes appear in a way so as to not frighten us.

My mother was born and raised in pre-World War II Latvia. She was the youngest child of a family of two older brothers (who both died in the war) and one older sister. Her father was a German Baron and both of his parents resided in Germany. Her mother on the other hand, was of Russian and Lithuanian decent. At the time however, her parent's marriage was considered rather scandalous as those from Germany and Russia/Lithuania did not mix, especially in marriage. As a result, her parents moved to Latvia where my mother was born, as this state of the (former) USSR was more neutral at the time.

Although her childhood memories are very sporadic, as my mom is almost 80 years of age, she does remember that as a child, she was extremely anaemic and often travelled to what were known as health spas or special farms in Germany to help strengthen her frail body. Her family also appeared to be rather well off and distinguished for the times as pictures show them donning expensive clothing and jewellery. She recalls that her aunts and uncles had all attended university and had various degrees, something that was considered a privilege in this society. So, in other words, she came from a very advantaged family.

Her father died when she was an infant, and her German grandparents decided to move to the old section of a medium-sized city in Latvia to be closer to their daughter-in-law and their grandchildren, who lived in the new section. My mother recalls her grandmother as being a very distinguished and well preserved woman for her age. She was rather short, stout and matronly, yet had a gentle way about her, especially with my mother. She was also extremely superstitious, a trait that my mom also adopted and continues today. My mom sees a black cat and she will travel for kilometres to be sure she does not cross its path. She has many other superstitions that she adheres to as well. That just seems to be what resonates with her.

Her grandfather on the other hand was completely different. He was a very tall, gentle and kind man, almost completely opposite to her grandmother. He always wore a three piece suit adorned with a beautifully chained gold pocket watch, and dearly loved his little granddaughter.

My mom had a very special bond with both of her grandparents and was allowed to travel on the tram from the new part of town to the old section which took close to an hour, and visit by herself whenever she liked. She recalls that most parents did not worry about their children travelling long distances such as this all alone, as there was little to fear and worry about, unlike today.

When visiting her grandparents, my mother remembers that she was allowed to read some old and precious books that were kept in a beautifully ornate trunk that was located in a special room. She would be allowed to read for hours on end sitting on a delicately decorated ottoman situated by a bay window looking out onto the street. Although she cannot remember the books that she read, she recalls that they were antiquated and beautifully bound with leather and gold embossed covers. She recalls that they were stories from long ago, kind of like fairy tales and that she was only allowed one book at a time as these books were rare and quite old and expensive.

On one occasion, she heard a most unusual story that was related to her by her own mother, about her grandmother's books. Several young men attempted to break into her grandparent's home, and her grandmother took out one of her books—actually a special book that was kept under lock and key. She cited a few words from the book to fend off the would-be thieves. My mother doesn't remember the actual words, but she remembers being told about the attempted break-in and robbery, and her grandmother's actions. The thieves ran as fast as they could and never came back. This special book was kept separate from other books that my mother was allowed to read. This one she was never allowed to touch, see or read. Was it a book of spells, or magic, or something else? We still don't know.

When my mom was around eight years of age, her grandmother became ill but it was not considered critical at the time. One day however, my mom felt a sense of urgency to go and visit her grandmother. She sought and received permission to go as her own mother was not expecting anything unusual to happen.

My mom took the long tram ride as a matter of routine, and got off at the stop as she always did. As she was walking up the road near her grandparents' home and looking ahead, there at the building on the corner where she usually turned, she spotted two children—a boy and a girl—peeking around the corner.

They were close to her age, but there was something very peculiar about these children. They were not upright, as if they were standing. Instead, they were completely sideways! She could not see the bottom half of them as there was no bottom half, and they had a translucent appearance.

These ghostly children did not frighten her; in fact they almost had a mischievous look to them. They reminded her of court jesters as they were behaving in a silly way as if trying to catch her attention.

I have read that sometimes children see friendlier looking ghosts which signal an impending death and that these ghosts often appear as children so as not to frighten them. As she cautiously approached the corner, looking for these two ghosts, they disappeared just as fast as they appeared and were nowhere to be found.

The moment my mother (who was a young child herself) saw these ghosts, she knew deep inside that her grandmother had just died. As she entered her grandparents' flat a few minutes later, her grandfather was quietly sobbing, and she went over to hug him. He told her that her grandmother had just died. Apparently, she had unexpectedly taken a turn for the worse. My mother said she already knew.

There are many unusual parts to my mother's recollection of this story. As she and I discussed this story, as we have done in the past, we couldn't help but feel that her grandmother was connected to the spiritual world in some way. Was she psychic? Was the book she read from a book of spells or magic? Or was she able to ask for spiritual help to provide protection when she needed it most? And who were the two ghosts? Were they former deceased relatives that came to my mother to prepare her for the death of her grandmother? And why did they appear as children?

It sounds like my great-grandmother was somewhat psychic, and my grandmother too. I never had the privilege of knowing or meeting any of my grandparents or great-grandparents as some died before and during the war, and others were held behind the "Iron Curtain" and not allowed to travel out of their country...and likewise, no one wanted to travel in for fear that they would never be allowed to leave. So as a result, much of my family history is still buried in that part of the world.

So while I can't verify any parts of this story, I have heard it retold by my mother many times, and the story has never changed. It is always the same and I trust that it's true. She was close to both of her grandparents, and her grandmother showed some unusual abilities. My mother had an urging to visit her ailing grandmother and saw the ghosts of two children that foretold that she was too late, and that her grandmother had already died.

Moving Energy

Insight:

Everything is made of energy. When we are injured or in pain, the energy flow is impeded, but it can be moved back into balance to start the healing process.

As my co-author explained in her short biography and several of her stories, she teaches Therapeutic Touch.™ I have taken level 1 & 2 with Marion and another instructor. When one first hears about energy work it sounds a little hard to believe, but like my co-author, I have had a number of experiences where I have used this form of energy work on injuries. This is a compilation of a few very short stories which have been particularly impactful for me and for others, just to illustrate the significance of our energy fields and how we can help put them back into balance.

Hot Time in the Summer

It was one of those beautiful summer days and too hot to cook inside. I decided that it would be a great day to barbecue. I lit my propane barbecue and while waiting for it to heat up, I went inside to prepare the steaks. Once I spiced them up, I went outside and began to cook.

As I was turning the meat on the grill, one piece started to fall. Instinctively I grabbed it and touched the hot grill with my left thumb and you could see the grill mark impression burnt into my skin.

As it was badly burned, I put ice cold water on it as recommended. I did that for about five minutes, but the pain did not go away and my thumb continued to throb. Who would think such a small burn would hurt so much?

I fluctuated between cooking and putting my left thumb in cold water and then stopped in my tracks. I sometimes don't remember to do a Therapeutic

Touch™ treatment but this day, I thought to myself, "Okay, I am going to give it a try." It is not that I don't believe in Therapeutic Touch,™ I do, but I haven't used it as often as my co-author, who uses it instinctively. I am not quite there yet.

I began to make the motion of pulling the burn out and away from my skin. I continued to do this and every once in awhile, I would smooth the skin down without ever touching it. I held the intention of helping the skin to heal and the burn to go away. Although Therapeutic Touch™ treatments do not need to be lengthy to be effective, I did do this for about half an hour.

As I moved my hand along the burnt area, it felt better and better. I stopped, had my dinner, and by the time I did the dishes the pain was almost gone. By morning, there was no evidence that I had ever sustained a burn.

Tree-Hugger

When I moved into my home almost a decade ago, I had a lot of work to do both inside and out. The previous owners had three small children and little time was spent decorating indoors or tending to the yard outside. There was a lot of painting required and there were no gardens or walkways of any kind. The deck was falling apart and dangerous to walk on.

With the help of my sisters, who visited on occasion, and my daughter, it took a couple of years to tear down and build a new deck, put in a small water pond and landscape the entire yard, front and back. Anyone who knows me, knows that I love to garden and be outdoors. I wanted to create a comfortable and serene living space to enjoy. My yard is also surrounded by tall and beautiful pines that provide the added privacy that I wanted to create a park-like atmosphere.

Several years ago, a disease began to strike the pine trees in the area that I lived, and one of the trees in my yard looked like it was going to die. This nasty infestation had already taken hold of other pines in the surrounding forest, and my horticulturist neighbour said that it was very difficult to get rid of. He sprayed all of the trees in his yard and mine with a solution to kill off the infestation, but nothing seemed to work. I was worried that summer and pondered what to do, when an idea struck me.

As mentioned many times throughout these stories, everything is made of energy, including humans, animals, plants and trees. It would stand to reason, that if you could help people by using treatments like Therapeutic Touch™ (energy work) you could apply the same principle and technique to other living things such as trees. I know of others who have used these treatments successfully so I thought I would give it a try.

I may have looked silly, but for the next three weeks, I would go over to the tree every evening, touch it and visualize it as a tall and healthy tree. Then, I would give it a treatment in my mind, holding the base of its trunk. Bit by bit, the tree that was dying, began to revitalize, and new growth appeared at the end of each branch. By the third week, there was no evidence of disease remaining. To top it all off, by fall, all of my trees produced a bumper crop of pinecones, the largest that I have ever seen in my yard.

I constantly need to remind myself that since all living things are connected, energy and other treatments have an extended benefit. To treat one tree was to treat all neighbouring trees. So this bumper crop should not have surprised me; the trees in my yard certainly showed me this. Every day I am thankful for and enjoy my beautiful yard and my beautiful healthy trees.

This particular event surprised my neighbour who had warned me that my tree and others may die. I never told him what I did, and he couldn't understand how the tree was restored to its natural, healthy self.

The Pesky Goat

As mentioned, I have found on many occasions that when I do energy work, others around me are somewhat sceptical of the treatment. They just don't believe or understand how it is possible to treat something without ever touching it. Even though my sisters have come to understand some of my thinking and my beliefs, they still have a hard time comprehending a number of things including energy work.

On this occasion I was out at the barn where my daughter rides with one of my sisters and her daughter. My daughter Jenny was grooming her horse in the barn and Barney the goat decided to wander in looking for attention.

He was a funny little goat that was rescued from another farm where he was treated badly, so when he arrived at this farm, he had quite an attitude. Anyone that has ever been around a goat knows where the saying, "Stubborn as a goat" came from. Barney was very aggressive with the horses and would even burrow and hide in their hay and jump at them when they came to eat. Needless to say, he was bitten and kicked by some of the horses until he learned to behave.

On this occasion, Barney came up to me and stood between me and the horse in crossties, looking for attention. He had a large welt on his back about the size of an egg. My daughter Jenny asked if I would give him a Therapeutic Touch™ treatment as she was worried that the welt would get worse. I proceeded like I always do. Much to everyone's amazement, when I moved my hand over Barney's back to shift and rebalance his energy, the area of the welt lifted up a few inches as my hand passed over it. I was surprised by the visual effect and continued with my treatment until I felt everything settle down. I then grounded the goat.

It astonished my sister and her daughter, but Barney was happy and his wound healed in a short time without incident.

Hiding the Pain

As mentioned in the story about Barney the goat, some of my family members, especially my sisters, are still somewhat sceptical about my beliefs and what I do. Even hearing these stories, they have a hard time being convinced. While they are interested and understand the theory that everything is energy, somehow it doesn't apply to them.

On another occasion when several of my sisters were visiting, they asked me to do a Therapeutic Touch™ treatment on them to show them what it felt like. Everyone feels energy differently and I tend to feel heat in my hands when there is an area that needs to be treated. Some say that they feel heat when my hands pass over certain areas, but I feel it is usually their own heat that is radiating to my hands and back to them.

One of my sisters sat in the chair while I proceeded to do the treatment. She told me that one of her shoulders was sore but when I asked, which one, she said, "You tell me."

I conducted a scan over her body and said it was her right shoulder and she said I was correct. "Whew," I thought. I continued over her body with a full scan just to see what else I could feel. I noticed something on her upper right leg. There was a lot of heat in the area. I asked her, "What's going on here?" She looked at me in disbelief.

As she stared at me, she took my hand and pressed it against a large lump. She had not told anyone about the lump and was amazed that I knew it was there. I continued the treatment and once I was finished, we talked about what just happened, but more importantly, what she should do.

She had ignored the lump hoping it would somehow magically go away. Unfortunately, it was only getting worse and more painful as time went on.

It took a while for her to go to see her doctor and I am sure the treatment and my nagging had something to do with it. After a number of tests, they determined that it was a femoral hernia and that she would require surgery to have it repaired.

I am happy to say that she recently had the surgery and all has gone well. Would she have acted if I had not felt the heat in that area? Or would she have waited until something more serious developed? I can't answer. I am just glad that I felt it, and that she followed through with getting it medically treated.

Afterthought ~

Again, each of these stories is about energy and moving energy in a way to initiate the healing process. Therapeutic Touch™ is now a recognized treatment in many hospitals. However it is a complementary medicine and should not be used as a substitute for medical attention. It is just one of the many tools that can be used in tandem with other medical treatments.

Negative Presence

Insight:

Everything is made of energy – people, things and entities can have positive or negative energy. Negative energy usually presents as cold and dark.

Throughout this book, my co-author Marion and I have touched on both positive and negative energies and how these might feel. If you look through your own life, you will probably see that at one time or another, you have experienced someone who made you feel uncomfortable right off the bat. It might have been a subtle feeling or it might have been strong, but in either case, you steered away.

As in the story "Ghostly Real Estate" my friend and I felt both positive and negative energy that continues to linger long after residents have moved out or died. Some believe that energy, positive or negative, actually becomes imprinted in certain locations. I distinctly recall the feeling I had when I purchased my own home. The moment that I walked in to look at the house, I felt positive and warm; it was a place that I could live and raise my children and I continue to live here to this day. It just feels good.

On the other hand, negative energy sends us in the other direction. It could be from an argument that just happened or fighting that has been going on for a very long time. Negative energy can be imprinted as noted above, or it can present in various forms: human form, something in the "air" or an entity that just swept in for a moment in time. Its presence is distinct. It feels cold and dark.

While most of my experiences have been with positive spiritual entities, my mother has had a couple of incidents over the years that have involved negative energies, both of which happened during the night. Here are those stories.

Working the Night Shift

My mother used to work the afternoon shift at a local hospital which made it easier for childcare. She would be home in the morning to get the children ready for school and would prepare what she could ahead of time for dinner that night.

As my older sister left home in her mid teens, I was the oldest of the siblings at home and often took over finishing dinner preparations and helping everyone get their homework started until my dad got home from work. This schedule seemed to work well for everyone, as the children had an adult at home for the majority of the time except for just after school when I took over.

Often, when my mother came home after 11:00 p.m., everyone was either getting into bed or already sleeping which gave her a bit of quiet time to catch up and do other things before the morning hours. She frequently read a book to relax as part of her downtime. She recognized, however, that once she started a book, she had a difficult time putting it down. She would become so immersed in the book that sometimes it would be two or three in the morning before she realized that the time had just flown by and that she better get some sleep before everyone got up to start their day.

One evening, she was relaxing with her feet up and enjoying a cup of coffee. She was engrossed in her romance novel and everything seemed perfect—the house was warm; everyone was sleeping; it was quiet; and the weather outside was calm. Then it happened.

Suddenly, she sensed an eerie feeling creeping through the house. She described it as a bad feeling and a bad energy. She said it started out quite subtly but became stronger and stronger, and filled the living room where she was reading. Her instinct, based on her religious upbringing, was to get a rosary, but that was in her bedroom and she did not want to wake my father or anyone else in the house.

She sat for what she said felt like a long time deciding what to do but it was probably just a few moments before she slowly made her way to the kitchen, all of the while saying, "What is this? Go away!" which she repeated a number of times. She went into the kitchen and all she could think of was taking two knives out and making a cross that she held in front of her.

She said she stood her ground and repeated, "Go away" all the while holding her makeshift cross. Again, she had no idea how much time had passed, but slowly, the negative energy lifted and was replaced once again by a warm, positive feeling. It left as quickly as it came.

This story still sticks out in her mind. She feels that some evil, negative presence entered her home and entered her space late into the night. She had no idea why this happened, but she felt that her actions helped dispel whatever or whoever it was.

Dark Visitor

My mother has two distinct stories of negative energy; the one above, and another that happened at a time when my father was travelling for work and she was home alone with the children. My dad didn't travel that often, but when he did, it was for one night stays as he preferred to be at home in the comfort of his own bed like most of us.

It was on one of these nights when my father was gone that my mother was sound asleep in her bed when she felt that someone or something was in the house. She opened her eyes, and there, in her doorway stood a tall figure looking right at her. The figure wore a black cape and a large brimmed dark hat. She could not make out the face of the figure but she felt it was a male energy as she referred to the entity as a "He."

She said he was tall and filled her entire doorway. She said it startled her more than frightened her, but just as soon as she saw him, he disappeared. By now she was completely wide-awake and she said that it was no dream. It was as real as you or me, and not something she imagined in a dreamlike state.

It was interesting that she did not feel frightened, but perhaps there wasn't time for this as the figure left so quickly. She was unable to sleep for the rest of the night, but as she retells the story, the image of this black caped figure is imprinted in her mind.

The story doesn't end here though. You can't imagine my surprise when my co-author, at dinner one evening a number of years ago, described a negative energy with striking similarities to the figure that was in the doorway of my mother's bedroom. What are the chances of that?

In her story "Ouija Board" Marion described a tall dark figure with a long black cape and a large brimmed black hat, only her figure carried an extremely negative energy. It was obvious that this entity in my mother's story woke her, but she never attributed a negative feel to this energy, though she knew it wasn't good. Was it because she did not have enough time to feel that negativity as it startled her and left so quickly? If she had not woken up, what could have happened? Fortunately we will never know, but whatever it was, it did not bring her any harm as it left the moment that she saw it.

Keeping a Watchful Eye

Insights:

Ghosts can remain earthbound for many reasons. Some are tied to a place, person or thing and don't want to leave or don't know how to leave. Some have important messages for those who are still living.

Over the last 10–15 years, there has been a greater acceptance of gay men and women. This is the story of a gay man named Tim whose spirit remained in his home after he died. It is believed that he stayed on the earthly plane to watch over his house and those who lived there.

Tim was a rather flamboyant man who lived in a large city and worked as a stylist for a major television network. He lived next door to his elderly mother and their houses were connected by a breezeway and their yards were joined by a large gate.

Tim died somewhere in his 50's, some suspect from HIV/AIDS although the circumstances surrounding his death are unknown. Shortly after his death, his nephew John moved into the house with his wife. The couple lived there for a few years. The house was tucked away into an older section of the city and had already been renovated a number of times and a large extension had been added to the back. When Tim's nephew put the house up for sale, Carol and her partner Anne, who had already been living in the neighbourhood, bought it right away.

According to Carol, as you walked into the house, the staircase, which had an older white railing, was on the right and the main living area was on the left. The living room, dining area and kitchen were all adjoined into one large open area. It was a cute little house and perfect for Carol and Anne and their two dogs.

Within the first few days of moving into the house, however, something very strange happened. On the evening in question, Carol and Anne were sitting on their couch facing the television. This meant that the staircase was on their left. They were watching a drama series with the two dogs tucked in near them. As they relaxed enjoying their show, both dogs suddenly began to growl and the hair on the back of their necks stood up. Carol and Anne, not knowing what was going on, watched their dogs as they bolted towards the staircase, and then momentarily froze in their tracks. As quickly as they did this, their growling subsided, the hair on their necks slowly dropped and everything seemed to go back to normal—but not for long.

All of a sudden, both Carol and her partner watched in horror as a male figure with a black hooded bomber type jacket ran up the stairs. The dogs once again began to bark fiercely and shot up the stairs after this ghostlike figure. Within a few minutes they came back down the stairs, both very timid and unsettled.

Carol and Ann were frightened by what they had just witnessed. Neither of them spoke for what felt like a long time, but as they started to talk, they were speaking in broken sentences and over each other. "Did you see…" said Carol just as her partner said "…the man running up the stairs?" They continued back and forth for some time, both feeling completely stunned by their ordeal. After a long discussion about the entity that ran up the stairs, they reluctantly went to bed for the night, still not knowing what to make of what they had just seen.

The following day, they joined their next door neighbours for dinner. They had known John and Cheryl for a few years already as they had met them on previous occasions and become good friends. Although Carol and Anne felt frightened by their experience from the evening before, they reluctantly decided to further explore the matter by asking John and Cheryl about the previous owners of the house.

As they were recounting their story, John left the room for a few minutes. He returned with a staff photograph from his workplace, which was actually the same large television network that Tim had worked for. He showed his neighbours the picture and asked them if they recognized anyone from the photo. It didn't take long. They both pointed to a man in the picture that was wearing the same black hooded jacket that the ghost in their new house was wearing!

While alive, Tim was a reddish faced man with curly hair and a moustache. As mentioned, he was rather flamboyant and it was not known whether everyone at work knew that he was gay, but he reflected the stereotype.

So, apparently the ghost was the ghost of Tim, the previous owner of the house that Carol and Anne had just purchased. However, while the mysterious identity of the ghost in the house had now been solved, the story of this ghost continues.

Several days later, Carol was up in her bedroom when her black lab jumped onto her bed. Once again his fur stood on end and he began to growl. It is well acknowledged that animals are far more sensitive to other vibrations and sounds than humans. As such, it is no surprise that the dog sensed the presence of the ghost before it manifested in front of Carol in her bedroom. He wore the same black hooded bomber jacket and while she could not make out his face, she felt a male presence and knew it was Tim.

Carol was terrified even though she now knew who he was. Seeing a ghost is not an everyday experience for most, including Carol, but she knew that Tim did not belong here. Shaking from what she was seeing, she mustered the courage to tell Tim to go to the light.

Often when ghosts become earthbound and have not left to enter the spiritual world, they either believe they are still alive and have not acknowledged their death or they are attached to something or someone and are unwilling to leave. It is always recommended that you encourage them to go to the light so that they can leave their earthbound ties and move on to the spiritual realm where they really should be. However, just like humans, not all ghosts comply with requests that are made and directions that are given.

Once Carol said this, the ghost of Tim disappeared. Neither she, nor Anne saw him again. Their lives returned to normal—as normal as could be, given this experience.

About a year later however, Carol and Anne decided to put their basement apartment up for rent again, as their tenant had just moved out. The apartment rented quickly as apartments were scarce in the city. Carol knew of someone looking for accommodation and decided to rent the apartment to one of her friends, a man named Chris.

Within two weeks of moving in, their new tenant Chris began asking Carol and Anne if they knew if someone had ever died in the house. Their previous tenant had never said anything to them, but here was Chris, describing a very detailed picture of someone he had been seeing in his apartment. Chris also asked if the previous owner was a gay male and if he wore a black bomber type jacket with a hood.

Indeed, Tim had returned, or perhaps he had just never left and had merely chosen not to manifest before Carol or Anne any longer. No one really knows for sure, but what was certain, was that Tim was once again making his presence known.

Carol brought Chris to the neighbour next door and asked to see the picture of the staff at the television network...the one that she and Anne had seen about a year before, and previously identified Tim from. Sure enough, just like Carol and Anne, Chris immediately pointed to Tim.

After they all returned to the house, Chris continued to see Tim on a regular basis for a long period even though Carol and Anne didn't. Chris then began to receive clear messages and guidance from Tim who was still "living" in the house, but again was only manifesting in front of Chris. Apparently Tim had a very important message for him. He wanted Chris to disclose who he truly was to others and finally come "out of the closet" so to speak.

For all of these years, Chris had hidden from the world that he was gay. Yet, here he was, in his mid 50's, being told by a ghost who was gay that died in his 50's, that it was important for him not to be afraid of his identity and to bring it out into the open. After much hesitation, Chris reassured Tim that he would.

Just like Carol, Chris also encouraged Tim to go to the light and once Chris disclosed to his family, friends and employer that he was gay, Tim the ghost disappeared and has not been seen or heard of since.

For Chris, he was relieved to finally have his secret out for the world to see and know. No longer did he have to hide who he was, and he had Tim, the gay ghost to thank for his encouragement, support and direction.

Carol, Anne, their neighbours and Chris took a long time to process what had transpired and why Tim was so insistent on hanging around his house. Although no one knows this for sure, it also appeared that this ghost finally went to the light once Chris came forward and acknowledged who he truly was inside.

Everyone surmised that Tim had served a very special purpose. Interestingly Carol and Anne were drawn to Tim's house, bought it and rented their basement apartment to a tenant who was also gay, but not open about his sexual identity. Although Tim only made his presence known a few times to Carol and Anne, he manifested a number of times in front of Chris to help him finally shed his fears and come out into the open. Everyone felt that Tim had found peace and could now move on as he knew his house was being taken care of the way that he wanted it to be and by people he felt akin to.

What is equally interesting is that Carol and Anne have since sold that home, but to this day, the house seems to draw other purchasers who are openly gay. Although Carol and Anne have not talked to those who currently live in the house, it would be interesting to know if Tim continues to make his presence known, or if he has indeed gone to the light and crossed over. It would also be interesting to know if Tim would manifest once again if his home was sold to someone who is not gay. That is something that we may never know.

This story has many interesting twists and turns: an earthbound ghost who watched over his house and made sure that those who purchased or lived in it were likeminded and led similar lifestyles. Tim also found a way to help those uncomfortable with disclosure of their gay lifestyle to accept who they are. All of these important life lessons were provided by Tim the "Gay Ghost."

Highway Motel

Insight:

The personality of a ghost often reflects their personality when they were alive and in human form ~ good or bad.

Caution—This story may upset and frighten some readers

Over the years, Hollywood has been successful in creating movies that impact on our minds and play havoc with our thoughts. "Psycho" was a 1960's horror movie by the famous Alfred Hitchcock. Although by today's standards "Psycho" is considered mild in comparison to what viewers watch and demand, at the time, few movies compared to this classic psychological and suspenseful thriller.

The primary set for this movie, the Bates Motel is still etched on the minds of terrified viewers who well remember some of the twisted acts carried out by Norman Bates (played by Anthony Perkins) at the site.

This story also takes place in a motel, a motel that seems to carry some violent memories of rape and other secrets. It is a motel that is situated alongside a long desolate stretch of highway in the north, in the middle of nowhere...not completely isolated but in a tiny town in between kilometres and kilometres of highway, crystal clear inland lakes, and large, mature forests that engulf the area. Pristine and beautiful to some but very remote to others.

Sarah and her teenage daughter Becky were travelling north to pick up Sarah's elderly mother who lived over 1,000 kilometres away and was no longer capable of looking after herself. Although not looking forward to the long trek there and back, Sarah and Becky enjoyed their time together. It also allowed for a bit of mother and daughter time, before Sarah's mother moved in.

Although accustomed to long drives for concerts and work, this time, the distance felt interminable and Sarah grew tired. After about seven or eight hours of driving, they decided to stop at a small town for the night. However, this town which had been a prosperous mining and lumber town many years ago, had become downsized with little work available.

Given the town's past prosperity, numerous motels had sprung up for family members who were visiting, as well as trade workers and company executives who were in town for business. So, there should have been some rooms available to stay for the night, however for some reason, on this day, there wasn't a room to be found. They were booked up for the night, so Sarah decided to continue on their way to the next hamlet up the highway.

Deciding she could no longer drive because of sheer fatigue and fear of falling asleep behind the wheel, Sarah found herself pulling into a tiny motel along the highway. She did not like these kinds of motels and this one definitely gave her an uncomfortable and uneasy feeling.

She drank a bit of her ginger ale as they pulled into the parking lot and despite her discomfort about the motel, fatigue had taken over. She spoke to the owners who were a pleasant young couple, but a bit of a throwback to the hippie era.

They had a room available, so Sarah and Becky gathered up what they needed for the night and went into their room. The room was quite cozy and it was clear that the owners had taken the time to add little extras to make it more comfortable. In addition to two beds and a bathroom (with puzzles of all things!) and other items, there was a small kitchen area where you could prepare a meal or heat up some water for coffee or tea in the morning.

Sarah, who, by now was exhausted, remembers lying in her bed, reading for a short while and then dozing off to sleep. Becky on the other hand, being a normal teenager, decided to leave the lights on and watch television into the early morning hours.

Sarah doesn't remember much after that, but what she does remember is looking over at Becky during the night and for whatever reason thought that she should check on her to make sure she was all right. From what Sarah can remember, Becky was lying down and still had the lights on. After assessing that everything seemed okay, Sarah turned off the lights and went back to sleep.

In the morning, Sarah looked at Becky and asked her how she had slept. Becky initially said, "Okay" but Sarah, knowing her daughter like most mothers do, knew that something wasn't right. At first, Sarah thought she may have somehow disturbed Becky through the night. She asked if she had kept her awake, but Becky said, "No" and they went about packing their belongings and getting ready to continue on their long journey to get Sarah's mother.

It wasn't until they were almost done, when Becky began to reluctantly recount a most frightening tale. Becky was uncomfortable telling her mom at first, as she thought her mom might think she was crazy, but as the story unfolded it was clear that Becky had experienced something significant during the night.

Becky was adamant that she was still awake and watching television with the lights on when she felt the presence of a male entity enter the room and sit down on her bed. He then aggressively moved towards her. He crawled over top of her with his knees on each side of her body while holding her down. At that moment, Becky said that he was so forceful in his actions, that she knew he was trying to rape her.

Becky tried to scream to wake her mother but he held his hand over her mouth so tightly that her screams were not heard. She struggled and broke free and tried to get away from this entity by crawling on the floor towards the bathroom. He then grabbed her, pulled her back and threw her onto the bed to finish what he had started. She even recalls the feeling of the carpet on her knees and that burning sensation of a rug burn as he tried to drag her towards him.

It was like a parallel event happening as Becky could still vividly see her mother sound asleep and that everything in the room was still where it was when they both went to bed. She even remembers looking over at her crystal earrings that were still on the counter where she had left them for the night. At that moment, she knew that whatever was happening to her was not real in the physical sense, but something beyond this world.

Suddenly, everything stopped. Becky crawled back into her bed, still shaking, frightened and not wanting to sleep. She decided to leave the lights on, and not wake her mother who was so exhausted and needed her rest. Becky also began to question herself asking whether or not what just happened was real or if it was a vivid lucid dream. However, as she sat there thinking about the frightening ordeal, she looked over her bed and distinctly saw the impressions on it—the indentation where someone sat on her bed. This was same spot the male ghost sat before he attacked her. The next thing Becky remembers is waking up. The lights were now out and she drifted back off to sleep.

As mentioned, at first Becky was quite reluctant to share her story with her mother. Sarah was horrified at her daughter's tale and asked why she did not wake her. Becky said she couldn't. The ghost had gagged her mouth so tightly that nothing could come out. She felt that her experience was real. There was a strong negative presence in the room, which Becky suspected may have attacked other women in a similar fashion. She believed that she may have been reliving or witnessing a previous event that is still imprinted on the room today.

Sarah quickly gathered their things, not wanting to stay a moment longer. They paid their bill, never asking the owners if something terrible had happened in that room in the past. They did not want to know and they did not want to stay.

As Sarah and Becky got into their car, Sarah took a drink of her now stale ginger ale and almost choked. By the time she realized what was happening, she had already swallowed a mouthful of what tasted like mould. She knew that the pop could not have become mouldy so quickly through the night and felt that somehow this was connected to the entity in the room.

By now they were both frightened and quickly drove off leaving that motel far behind on the road, but not in their thoughts.

While they never explored what happened that night any further, a lot of questions remain. Was it Becky's moment of recognition that the event was supernatural in nature that stopped the scene from playing out? Or was it the moment that her mother, during her sleep, was prompted to check on her daughter? Or did something else stop this negative and aggressive male entity from continuing?

What we have learned in writing these stories and sharing our own, is that some ghosts or spiritual entities are pleasant and benign and give off positive energy, and on the opposite end of the spectrum, others are negative, destructive and cold. We also know that energy doesn't die and sometimes, positive or negative energy and events can be imprinted in a house, a place or on something such as furniture and personal jewellery.

As mentioned in other stories, think of a time when you have walked into a party or into someone's home and felt a coldness or negativity in the air—it could be a negative energy in the house from a fight that just happened, a terrible event from the past that is still imprinted in the house, or it could be coming from someone in human or in spirit form that is present. In Becky's case it seems like she felt both the negative imprint of what had happened in the past, and had experienced the negative entity in the present.

Again, what is also believed is that what you were like on earth does not change once you die and enter the spiritual realm. In fact, many feel that the personality or the persona of the individual who dies, remains the same in spirit. We saw an example of this in Marion's story about the psychic medium named Betty. If you recall, the deceased father of a woman in her audience psychically attacked her during a meditation she was using at a spiritual conference. In that story, Betty, who was an accomplished psychic medium, began choking during a meditation that she was guiding her large audience through. This meditation was meant to help release ties with those who have caused great harm and pain in your current life. The entity tried to enter the psychic medium's body and attack her.

The story of Sarah and Becky illustrates how a ghost with wicked intent can in fact try to take over on the physical plane just like they did when they were alive and in human form. What we have also learned is that it is important to spiritually protect yourself or surround yourself with white light particularly when this type of presence is ever felt. Whether this would have helped Becky in her encounter with this male entity who had attempted to rape her is unknown. What we do know is that good or evil can transcend death and make their presence known by impacting us and our surroundings in visible and invisible ways.

Pet Spirits

Insight:

All matter is energy. Since energy never dies, the energy of all life, including animal life, must survive death in some manner. Spirit/soul energy survives physical death. Bodily energy is recycled on the earthly plane.

Over the last 10 to 15 years, we have witnessed an unprecedented level of attention to spiritual matters, at least in our lifetime. Some say it is related to a growing awareness of things happening in our universe. Others say it is because we live in a time when it is okay to talk about matters of spirit (and aren't burned at the stake). Another possibility is that our world is becoming more secular.

To support this premise, stories of ghosts, hauntings, communicating with the dead and other paranormal activities have also begun to flood network television, movies, books and the internet. While many focus on the negative, scarier side of spiritual activity, or hauntings where ghosts become earthbound and have not yet gone to the light (as we have seen in many of our stories), little has focused on pets that have died.

In my mind, the question is why? In writing this book, I have come across several people who have experienced some aspect of their beloved pets after they have died. It doesn't matter whether the pet was cremated, or buried with full body, or rather full shell intact, their spirit continues to live on, just like humans.

Before sharing two stories of people who I personally know have seen and sensed the presence of their pets, I would like to once again go back to the same psychic medium named Betty who is discussed in Marion's story "The Medium" and my story "Highway Motel."

As mentioned, Marion and I have attended several spiritual conferences. This particular one was held in a large Ontario city. Betty, who was an exuberant and enthusiastic psychic medium, took the stage. Her calling card was her ability to communicate with pets. At first glance it sounded a bit nonsensical and trivial to me, but after listening to her speak and communicate with pets of those in the audience, I had to step back and revisit what I have come to believe, and remember that energy never dies.

Betty's stories touched the heart of all pet lovers. One by one, she spoke to select audience members whose pets had come through. She provided specific details about their pet and their relationship with that pet. In some cases, their pets had an important message for them.

One story that stood out was about a pet rat. Of all of the animals that I would never be attached to, it is a rat and if I recall correctly, I think his name was Charlie. Charlie had died a few years earlier, and Betty was trying to find the animal's owner in the audience. Betty, in her very animated way, said that she could feel the rat snuggling on her neck and nipping at her ear.

It took a few minutes, but a young woman with a tall red Mohawk haircut stood up. Charlie was her pet rat that died about a year earlier. Charlie's owner confirmed that he loved to climb up on her shoulder, snuggle into her neck and nibble at her ear; in fact he liked to pull off her earrings.

Charlie had a message for his owner. He missed her a lot and he was not very happy with one of the two rats that this young woman had recently adopted; in fact it sounded like he was a bit jealous. As an audience, we chuckled, but as Betty and the young woman spoke, it was clear that there was a special bond between this unusual pet and her owner, and that they truly missed each other.

This is not the first story of spirit communication that has involved animals. Indigenous people have long believed in animal spirits and in fact named many of their clans after animals. Various spiritual writers have also talked about pets that have died and say that they continue to carry on a relationship with their living human friends or their spirits visit occasionally. Some have also said that when you die, all of your pets come to greet you, similar to other loved ones that have died.

In writing this story, a quick search on the internet indeed showed that many have talked about some sort of connection, communication or visitation by their beloved pet. I have also met two people who have firsthand experience with pets that have died and have come visiting. In fact, I have also felt the energy of one of these animals.

Ellie the Guide Dog

My first story is of a close friend of mine who is hearing impaired; in fact she has two stories. Her first story is of her long time friend and companion Ellie. Ellie was a border collie mix who had been trained as a puppy to assist those who are hearing impaired—to become the ears of those who could not hear.

Ellie was a delightful dog and was absolutely committed to my friend Karen. Everywhere Karen went, Ellie went. She guarded Karen by waking her when she needed to get up, nudging her when someone was at the door, walking beside her in traffic to protect her, and pushing at her when the baby was crying...she was a loyal, gentle and committed companion.

After more than a decade, as Ellie grew old, Karen needed to retire her as a working dog. This meant that Ellie no longer needed to wear the familiar orange jacket, and could now enjoy spending her time running around on the farm, and doing things that dogs do. It took Ellie a while to transition from being a working dog to a retired companion. Then, as every living thing grows old and breaks down, after a long life and several surgeries, Ellie's body could no longer hang on. She had distinctly developed signs of "doggie" dementia. When she was nearly 14 (in human years), Ellie needed to be euthanized.

Karen is a pragmatic woman and although she was sad for Ellie, she knew it was her time to go, but at the time of her death, Ellie wasn't quite ready to ascend to the spiritual world, at least not yet. For several weeks after Ellie had died, Karen (with the assistance of her fitted hearing aid), and her husband Shawn could hear the familiar sound of Ellie running in the house. It was the sound of her clicking nails as they hit the hardwood floor on the familiar route that she always took about the house. Karen just remembers smiling at Shawn when they would hear the sound as they knew it was Ellie still hanging around.

Over the next two weeks, Karen and Shawn continued to hear Ellie moving throughout the house and then one day the sound stopped. Karen and Shawn both believe that Ellie knew that Karen would be okay without her, and that she could now move on to the spiritual plane to join others.

"When you have had the privilege of owning such a gifted animal, you never forget the highlights and dedication that such an animal has on your life" said Karen. "I still feel like she drops in from time to time to watch over me."

Gidget, the Tortoiseshell Tabby

This story is another story about Karen. I think Karen must have a special affinity with animals. She has seen more than one of her beloved pets after they have died. This is a story about her special cat named Gidget.

What I found out in writing this story is that throughout Karen's life she has learned to deeply love animals. Gidget was one of her many special pets and she was close to 16 years of age (human years) before she needed to be euthanized.

As Gidget aged, she became quite ill and developed a cancer that spread underneath her right jawbone. It is horrible to imagine a person going through this and for many, it is equally difficult for a loved pet to go through this as well. It was the very first time that Karen had ever experienced such an awful disease in one of her pets.

Much like Karen, her husband Shawn is also a gentle soul. Late one sunny August day, he decided to take Gidget to the veterinarian to see if anything could be done to help their ailing pet. The news was not good. The vet said he was unable to do anything for the tortoiseshell tabby, so Shawn chose to bring her back home. He set her up comfortably in an oversized pen so that she could safely enjoy the warm summer breeze. He then called Karen to give her the bad news; that nothing more could be done for Gidget.

Upon her arrival home that day Karen decided that given Gidget's failing health, that she needed to take her back to the veterinarian and that it was best to have her euthanized. It was a very peaceful passing and although Karen, (as noted in the previous story about Ellie) dealt directly with life's challenges, she was sad and softly cried although she knew it was best.

One week had passed after Gidget's death, and Karen was at home alone. It was almost dark and as she looked out over their treed backyard, she captured a very clear image of Gidget on the back patio. Her beloved cat looked over at Karen, and then slowly turned and walked away into the dusky night. It was just for a moment, but it clearly was Gidget. Karen strongly felt that her cat had come to say goodbye and that she was going to be okay.

As mentioned earlier, Karen is hearing impaired and there are a lot of studies that have shown when one the five senses is affected, that others become stronger. Could this hold true for what we call our sixth sense where there is a stronger connection to matters of spirit and a greater ability to tune into other energy vibrations?...and in Karen's case with her longstanding and beloved pet companions? It would make perfect sense that Karen has a special gift that has allowed her to see, feel and recognize the warm and positive energy of two of her pets that played an important part in her life. After all, they too are living energy and energy never dies.

Kitty Love

The second story is of a cat named Pumpkin that died in her early 20s in human years. Pumpkin belonged to one of my sisters who had raised her since she was a kitten.

Over a ten year period, my sister and Pumpkin lived in several different households which had cats and dogs. Pumpkin generally got along with most other animals even though she was smaller than every other pet. She was a petite cat even when she was full-grown.

Pumpkin was a tabby, but had very distinctive markings like some cats do. Her most distinctive feature was a most unusual marking around her mouth which looked like painted on black lipstick, and as a result, was called Lipstick by my mom.

Pumpkin was a bit of a timid cat at times, but not with me. I recall that when I would visit, the moment that I sat on the couch, she would climb right up onto my chest and snuggle in under my chin. It was most peculiar, but she was very clear about whom she liked and did not like.

As mentioned, Pumpkin grew to be an older cat and died in her early 20s. My sister euthanized Pumpkin as she had become so ill from old age, but it was very hard on my sister, and her partner Tara.

Tara and my sister decided to cremate Pumpkin and her ashes were placed in a box that they now have in their home. However, even though Pumpkin died several years ago, the energy of her tiny little spirit is stronger than ever. I have since visited many times, and I always feel Pumpkin in the house. Often I look around as if she is there. I have even sat on that familiar couch that she used to come and snuggle on, and still feel like she is jumping up to tuck under my chin.

One day I mentioned this to my sister who was very surprised, however Tara also said that she feels and senses Pumpkin in the house. She too feels the familiar routine of Pumpkin, however her experiences are different.

When Pumpkin was alive, every morning she would lay on the bed in the master bedroom while my sister was getting ready for work. My sister worked out of the house, whereas Tara ran a business out of their home. The first thing that Tara did in the morning was turn on her computer to check her emails. The computer was set up on a desk located on the landing at the top of the stairs just outside the master bedroom. The area was made into a small makeshift office with filing cabinets, a shelf for binders and current working folders, and a computer desk with the monitor and the printer.

As soon as my sister left for work, Pumpkin would jump off the bed, walk over to where Tara was sitting, and jump onto her lap for a while. This was her morning routine.

When Pumpkin died, the routine did not stop. For some time after Pumpkin's death, every morning when Tara went to the computer, she could still hear Pumpkin jump off the bed, walk over to her and jump onto her lap. This would only happen during the daytime, and continued until recently.

Tara said that from time to time she still hears Pumpkin jump off the bed, however she no longer jumps onto her lap. Maybe Pumpkin is finally beginning to cross over and move to the spiritual world, and just like humans, found that since everything at home was okay that she could move on to where she is supposed to be.

Afterthought ~

For those of us who are pet lovers, and I include myself in this, it is very hard to own a pet who will inevitably grow old and die much sooner than us. The hardest part is knowing that their lifespan is much shorter and that they are only with us for a very short time compared to the lifespan of a human. Nevertheless, they become a significant part of our families and our lives; often loved and pampered by most members. In return, most pets provide unconditional love and provide comfort, love and companionship.

From the story of Ellie, the loyal companion dog of Karen and her cat Gidget, along with the story of Pumpkin the pampered and loved cat, animals tug at the very depth of our hearts. Just like humans, they too are living energy. Many believe that they move on into spirit when they die. Some people continue to feel their presence and communicate with them once they have died.

Some cultures and religions believe that human souls incarnate into animal souls and others believe that animal souls incarnate into human souls. So, is it possible that we have all been animals at one time or another in the past?...or that we may return as an animal in the future? While I am not sure how I feel about this, one thing is for sure: if you love animals, it is comforting to know that they do move on in spirit, and many psychics tell us that we will see them once again when we die.

Fleeting Moments

Insight:

While some people actually see spirits, many of us only sense their presence which can be distinct or subtle. Sometimes it is a fleeting moment, a shadowy figure or an apparition that actually manifests.

Brian and my daughter Jenny first connected on the university's social networking page powered by "Facebook" and within a few weeks of meeting each other, began to date. Brian was a soccer star and Jenny was an academic who in her spare time loved to ride horses.

Several years earlier, Jenny had been in a serious riding accident where a horse she was testing out, reared and began bucking. She decided to dismount but as she did so, the horse reared up and would have crushed her if she did not roll out of the way. Despite her quick actions, she severely injured her knee.

She had already been through various medical procedures prior to meeting Brian and was waiting for another one to repair a damaged ligament that tore during this time given the added stress on her leg. This surgery however, was to be a bit more complicated than others as surgeons needed to remove a piece of her hamstring, drill through the bone in her leg and then pull the hamstring through her knee to create a new ligament to help keep her knee in place.

According to the surgeons, Jenny had to wait for this procedure until her bones stopped growing. To do so earlier could impact on her growth. So, we waited until Jenny was a young adult, in her second year of university. Given the type of surgery that she needed, Jenny would be in a special brace for several months until all was healed.

Even though we lived in a mid-sized city, it was difficult for one of the local orthopaedic surgeons to perform the surgery given his significant caseload and the lack of operating space. As a result, he referred her to another surgeon out of town who specialized in sports medicine injuries. Conveniently, this surgeon was located in the same community where my mother lived which would provide a place for us to stay during the operation and the initial post surgery recovery period.

The surgery, while hard on Jenny, was necessary. Her damaged knee already compromised her ability to ride horses and do other activities, even simple activities such as walking, as her knee would pop out of place. This caused a great deal of pain and aggravated her injured knee even further.

The time had come for the surgery, so Jenny, Brian and I drove to my mom's house, then proceeded to the hospital. All went well with the surgery and while the initial hours after surgery were as uncomfortable as expected, we were able to bring Jenny to my mom's home late in the day where she could rest more comfortably. Everything was ready for her once we arrived. She stayed on a couch in the living room where she could watch television, and her boyfriend Brian slept in the downstairs recreation room on a pull-out couch. He tried to attend to her emotional and physical needs.

On the first morning after the surgery, while Jenny lay sleeping upstairs, Brian got up to see how she was doing and then went off to shower. With all of the activity in the house, once he was done, he went back downstairs to do some reading for his history course. He sat in one of the comfy chairs down in the recreation room, when suddenly he felt the presence of a male entity sitting in the chair next to him.

Brian wasn't overly frightened, but more startled at what he was feeling and sensing. The entity felt male and was strictly just "chilling" with him. He felt the ghost was in his 40's but couldn't quite make out who he was or why he was there, but he did not make him feel uncomfortable. The ghost stayed for a short while and then left.

Brian quietly went upstairs to tell Jenny as he couldn't believe what had just happened but he knew what he experienced was real. Jenny waited for her grandmother to be out of earshot and called me up into the living room where she lay, to talk about what Brian had just sensed. He described what had happened. I believe he was more surprised than frightened by what he saw.

I told Brian that for many years, at different times, several of my sisters slept downstairs on the pull-out couch as it was cozy especially when the fireplace was on. It also allowed for some private space away from the hustle and bustle of the rest of the house when everyone was visiting. However, over the last few years, one by one, each of them has moved upstairs to sleep while visiting as they had sensed "something" downstairs. One of my sisters even recalls sensing and then seeing a shadowy figure in the night. Since that time she has never slept down there again.

No one ever dared tell my mother as she lives alone. No one wanted to frighten her, but here was Jenny's boyfriend, who was generally not convinced about these kinds of things one way or another, seeing the shadowy figure of a male entity sitting right next to him while he was reading.

Jenny was uncomfortable with the story and did not want to stay. She is always spooked when it comes to matters of the paranormal, and asked if we could make the long trek home so she could stay in the comfort of her own house. We decided it was as good a time as any and packed up our things to head north. The timing was right as the weather was turning bad and we wanted to get home before the snow fell.

Brian and I packed up the car and made a special spot for Jenny in the back seat so that she could sleep on the demanding six-hour ride home. However, as Brian went out to the car, a completely different spirit revealed himself in the garage and Brian sensed he was looking directly at him. Brian dared not tell Jenny at first, but came to me and said, "I saw another one." I asked him what he meant by that and he said he saw another ghost, but it was not the same one he had seen earlier in the day downstairs when he was reading.

He described this one as an older male energy. He could not see his face, but he sensed that he had dark hair and was wearing a pair of coveralls. At first Brian thought it might have been be Jenny's grandfather in a younger form who died earlier that year, but the description just didn't seem right as Jenny's grandfather never wore coveralls. It did, however, sound like Jenny's uncle or Zio as described in the story "Bedside Visit" whom Brian had never met. If you recall in that story, Zio and his wife appeared in front of me when Jenny was in hospital and very ill, to assure me that she would be okay. They dearly loved Jenny and it would not have surprised me at all that he was dropping in to see how she was doing once again. Appearing in front of her would likely have frightened her too much, but manifesting in front of her boyfriend would mean Zio would get the attention that he wanted. It would also let Jenny know he was once again watching over her.

Like the entity in the basement, this one did not make Brian feel uncomfortable, it just startled him. Again, it was not something he was accustomed to seeing, and in Brian's case he not only saw one that day but two! And while both were different spirit energies, both were male and did not feel frightening to Brian at all.

To this day, we still don't know the identity of the spirit in the basement, and we are not even sure whether it's still there. In fact, we believe that he may have already left. Regardless, most of the family members who are now aware of the story will trek downstairs for various reasons, but keep looking about and wondering if they will see the spirit. One thing is for sure, to this day, none of us dares to sleep down there. Every time I go downstairs in my mom's house I say, "Okay, if you are here, I don't want to see you."

Again, this story is most intriguing. Everyone in the house has sensed the presence of this entity and Brian certainly was not previously aware of my siblings' concerns. Oddly, both spirits showed themselves to Brian at a time of heightened stress for Jenny.

Interestingly enough, several years later, Brian was doing some work for Jenny's dad on a boat trailer inside a large garage. He was sanding the frame and getting it ready to paint. As he bent over working, he suddenly felt the presence of someone watching him. At first he thought it was Jenny's dad but when he looked up, there was no one there. This happened several times and one time he saw a shadowy figure but every time he looked up, it was gone. He describes it like that feeling in the movie "Sixth Sense" with actor Bruce Willis (as noted earlier in Marion's story "The Smallest Seer"), just knowing something or someone is there.

The figure was male and had a similar energy to the one that he saw in the garage at my mother's house. This time the ghost was just hanging around and watching the work, but this time Brian was a bit more comfortable. In an inquisitive way, he asked the entity, by thinking to himself, "Why are you here?" and he felt the ghost say, "I'm just watching and by the way you missed a spot."

Brian chuckled as he recounted the story and once I heard what the entity said back, I knew it was Jenny's Zio as that would have been something he would have said when he was alive! He used to love just hanging around and watching Jenny's dad when he worked on mechanical things. He himself was very active in tinkering, repairing and fixing things in life and here he was in spirit doing something that he enjoyed most.

It was interesting for me to learn that Brian has had other psychic experiences as a child. He said that in one house that his family lived in for several years, he often told his mother that there was a man standing at the foot of his bed at night. Brian was about four or five years of age at the time and his mother wrote it off to the active imagination of a child, which most parents do. If you remember in many of our other stories, it is well acknowledged that young children see spirits much more easily than adults, up until about the age of ten.

During their time in that house however, Brian was often quite sick. The doctors would always say the same thing; that there is nothing wrong with him. Once they moved from this house, Brian's health significantly improved. His mother said that the ghost in the house must have been angry which would have been making Brian ill, although she did not acknowledge the presence of the ghost to Brian at the time. Given that Brian has had a history of ghostly experiences, even as a child, it should come as no surprise that he has seen several entities since.

While this story is about ghostly sightings, it shows us a number of things. Heightened stress can change the energy vibration in a house and in the people in that house which might make it easier for spirits to enter. Fortunately, all the entities that Brian has seen, (with the exception of the one he saw as a child) had a positive energy and were just around.

This story also shows us that once again, love has no boundaries. The spirit of Jenny's deceased uncle has come around several times, usually when Jenny has been in dire straits with medical issues, but in the last visit he just came to hang out and do the thing that he loved most—telling you what to do!

Even ghosts have a sense of humour.

Ghostly Snippets

Insight:

Ghosts, including the spirit of loved ones can come in many forms and at various times throughout our lives.

Throughout this book, we have told various stories about ghosts and other apparitions. This chapter is simply a collection of snippets told to me by people that I know, involving sightings of ghosts in familiar places. They serve as a constant reminder that any one of us can have a metaphysical experience in our lifetime, but many of us either refuse to acknowledge it, or choose to ignore it.

Home from Work

In my home community I heard the story of an older man, whom I'll call Ben. Ben died before he could retire, but continues his daily schedule and practices in spirit. When he was alive, his day, like most of us was based on familiar routines: up for work in the morning, gone all day, and home at night, wanting to relax before the next day.

For most of his adult life, Ben, like many in this community, worked for the large industrial company in town. He had originally immigrated from a small European country. He never married, and he owned his own little home which was well looked after.

When he died, his home was sold to a young couple. When they moved in however, they would hear the most peculiar sounds. Every night around 5:00 p.m., shortly after they arrived home from work and began preparations for dinner, they could hear the sound of someone opening the back door near the kitchen. They would then hear the sound of someone walking across the floor and the distinct sound of a metal lunch pail being placed on the counter. The footsteps would then continue down the hallway and slowly fade away.

Understandably, at first, the young couple was frightened and confused by what they were hearing every day. They decided to investigate the history of the home and its previous owners. They discovered and came to believe that it was likely Ben, simply reliving his daily routine; something he had done for the majority of his earthly life.

I never heard any more about this story, but from what I gather, it sounds like the spirit of Ben became earthbound as he, in all likelihood, had not yet acknowledged his death. In cases such as these, ghosts like Ben are generally not harmful, but it is always good to encourage such entities to go to the light, and hopefully one day Ben will—if he hasn't already.

Hospital Visitor

This is another story of an earthbound ghost, but in this case, it is a young teenage boy I will call Ricky. As the story goes, Ricky had lived a very tough life and was moved from foster home to foster home as a child. When he was eight years old, he was diagnosed with a terminal illness. He was in and out of hospital for a number of years, and finally hospitalized in a palliative care unit until he died in his mid teens.

The floor that Ricky died on is now reserved for adults who are dying. Apparently, however, on the palliative care floor of this hospital, it is not unusual to see Ricky playing and sometimes it is reported that he can be heard laughing in a childlike fashion. He does not mean any harm, and always brings great comfort and solace to those who are there. He is said to always appear when someone is close to death.

While no one knows for sure why he is still around, some say it is because he found the hospital to be one place that provided stability and where he was loved by all of the staff. In other words, it was the only home and family that he had known where everyone cared about him when he was alive.

Others say that he appears just before someone dies, to help the family cope with the impending death of a loved one, and to help the loved one who is dying, to cross over.

Whatever Ricky's story is, he has been seen by many individuals who work in the hospital and by countless others who are on the floor as patients or as visiting family members. He is not viewed as an omen of death, but rather someone who brings warmth, comfort and solace to those who are dying and to their family members.

While in most cases we would consider Ricky an earthbound spirit who has not yet moved on to the light, I would be hard pressed to say that his presence doesn't serve a far greater purpose beyond his own needs; and that is to remind families that the physical body of their loved one may have died, but that their spirit lives on. In my view, Ricky provides a message of hope. He provides a message that that there is more to life than what we see, and that one day we will be united with those we love.

Deadly Fire

In many households, the Christmas season is a joyous one—where family and friends gather, special food is prepared, and gifts are shared. Although not all families celebrate this holiday, Darren's family certainly did.

Darren and his family lived in a remote community where everyone knew each other. During the summer months, most families spent their time at their summer camp to enjoy the outdoors, the beautiful lakes, and the endless fishing—life was good. Their relaxed and leisurely lifestyle was the envy of most. Winter, however, was completely different with lots of snow and extremely cold temperatures. During the winter season, leisure activities included playing hockey, curling, ice-fishing and snowmobiling. Given the remoteness of the area, most of the children went to the same elementary school, and as teens, attended the same high school. As adults, if they remained in the area, many married their high school sweethearts.

At Christmastime, it was tradition for families to scour the nearby forest for their Christmas tree. During this particular year, Darren's family had already found and cut the perfect tree. Once they got it home, they adorned it with homemade decorations, that nestled amongst the store-bought kind.

Then disaster struck. Although I did not know Darren at the time, it is my understanding that one night, just before Christmas, the fully decorated tree in their house caught fire. Everyone escaped the burning house, but Darren's father went back into the house to try to retrieve some of the gifts under the tree. Tragically, he never made it out, and died.

I don't think anyone can imagine the pain that Darren, who was a teen at the time, and his family must have experienced at losing their father in that devastating fire.

It wasn't until many years later that I met Darren—he was in his mid-40s. He was somewhat aware of my interest in spiritual issues and approached me about something that had been happening to him.

Darren no longer lives in the community where his father died many years ago. However, when he drives up the road past the area where his childhood home once stood, he always feels the warm and strong presence of his father in the passenger seat. Several times, Darren felt that he has actually seen his father sitting there. For years he kept this to himself. He eventually tried speaking to others, including his wife (whom I also knew), but most family members and friends were not comfortable talking about matters of spirit even though they were religious in their beliefs. In fact, his family asked him not to talk about it again.

When Darren approached me he did so reluctantly. He described what was happening to him and wondered if he was going crazy. He didn't know what to believe or who to talk to as none of his family members wanted to discuss any matters related to ghosts. Of all people that I have known, Darren is certainly not crazy.

As I spoke to him, I realized that all he wanted was to be reassured that what he was seeing and feeling was indeed possible; that his father was visiting him each time he came through town and drove by the place where his family home once stood. I assured Darren that, from what I understood, it was indeed possible that his father was there, and that he should not be afraid. I told him that sometimes spirits remain earthbound, but spirits of loved often come around to visit when someone needs them most. We have seen evidence of this in many of the stories that are in this book.

In Darren's case, while I can't say why his father is still around (if he is earthbound or just visiting) I reassured him that it was quite all right to talk to his dad, to let him know that he loves him and that he (Darren) is okay. I also told Darren I would send him some books by spiritual authors who might help him to understand what has happened and why his father is around or coming to visit him at the lamentable site of his death.

Afterthought ~

Each of these stories provides a very small snapshot into the experiences of others who have heard, sensed or seen spirits. As we have witnessed in many of these ghostly encounters, most are benign and harmless. Some want to go about their business as if they aren't dead. Some might want attention or acknowledgement of some kind, and others may simply be bringing messages of hope and love.

Whispers

Insight:

Sometimes ghosts and other spirits will make their presence known to provide important insights or information.

Moving can be a daunting task. There is no way around it—packing your belongings and transporting them to a new location is a lot of work. This of course is followed by the tedious task of unpacking and finding a place for everything that is just right.

Although Jake had already moved several times in this large city, trying to find the right apartment was exceptionally difficult. He had already had his fill of noisy tenants, difficult landlords and excessive crime rates. Rents were at an all time high and space in a good area was at a premium.

Jake finally found an apartment that he and his two cats could settle into. It was affordable and was in a reasonably good area downtown. It had two bedrooms: one that he could use for his own bedroom and the other for an office–studio. Although it was on the main floor of the building, which increased the potential risk of break-ins, he was pleased to have a small deck and a backyard to enjoy the outdoors. The apartment also had an unusually large 4-person indoor jacuzzi. Apparently the previous tenant was a "lady of the night" and often entertained friends and guests in her apartment and, of course, her hot tub.

Surrounded by boxes and exhausted from moving, Jake slept very soundly on his first night in his new home. The two cats were also enjoying their new space and spent time searching about all of the nooks and crannies of their new abode.

On the first morning, Jake got up early, eager to begin the process of unpacking his belongings. He made a pot of coffee, and began to stroll through his new place with cup in hand. He went over to the patio doors that went out onto the back deck and opened them to enjoy some fresh air. Jake turned to go back into the apartment and began to walk though the living room, wondering where he was going to put everything.

Suddenly, out of nowhere, he heard a women's voice from behind him and off to his left. Her voice was firm and distinct but had a whispering sound. She said, "There is jewellery hidden in this house." He quickly turned thinking that someone had come in through the open patio doors, but was equally startled when he saw no one there.

He shook his head in disbelief. Throughout the course of Jake's lifetime, he has experienced several ghosts and while he is more intuitive than most, he wasn't sure if it was a ghost or just his imagination. The voice did not scare him but it certainly did startle him. If there was a spirit, she did not feel threatening in any way, although the firmness in her voice was apparent. She was intent on providing him with an important message.

Neither of the cats seemed to indicate that anything unusual had just happened and went about their usual business, playing with each other and snooping all around their new home. As mentioned in previous stories, animals are much more sensitive to other vibrations than humans, so if the spirit meant any harm or felt negative, Jake thought that the cats surely would have picked up on this right away.

Jake stood there for a few minutes and then thought; "I may as well take a good look around the apartment." He began to do a bit of searching and saw that the landlord had left some garbage in a few small bags in one of the rooms. Jake figured he would look through the garbage just in case something was inadvertently put into one of the bags.

Like a sleuth he began rummaging through the bags and much to his surprise he found a beautiful silver necklace with peachy pink onyx stones strung onto the chain. He thought—this must be what the female ghost wanted him to find. Smiling, he went back to work unpacking his belongings and didn't think much more of it.

The next morning, he arose and went over to the patio doors and once again, opened them to enjoy some fresh air. He could smell his coffee brewing and went over to pour himself a cup. Once again, he began to stroll through the apartment looking about. He was just taking a sip when he heard a female voice behind him say, "There is jewellery hidden in this house." He turned around quickly to see who it was, and again no one was there. It was the same voice that he had heard the morning before. This time he said out loud, "What—there's more?" but no one answered.

On the previous day, he had done a pretty thorough job of looking all over the apartment; behind doors, in cupboards and any place that he could think of. Although he had found a necklace the day before, he couldn't think of where else to look. The voice of the female entity was once again whispering but intent. Jake then thought, "I know where I haven't looked—out in the yard."

Off he went into the yard which was not very big, but a good size for an inner-city apartment. Beautiful linden and maple trees had been planted on each side of the yard which helped to provide some sense of privacy in this busy city. The soil was quite sandy and the entire yard needed a bit of landscaping. Jake walked around the yard, looking behind the trees and rocks when his eye caught a glint of something. Could there be more jewellery buried in the yard?

He proceeded to uncover a shiny object in the yard and as he dug it out, he found a peachy pink onyx Aztec amulet head that stood about four inches tall. He said out loud, "This must be it!" very proud of his new find. He dug a bit more of the soil in the area, just in case something else was buried there, but didn't find anything more.

Satisfied that he had found the treasure that the ghost had urged him to look for, he thought he was done. Jake still had a lot of work to do, so he went back into his apartment to continue to unpack for the remainder of the day. As anyone knows, unpacking can sometimes take weeks depending on how many belongings you have and how big your place is. By late evening he was once again tired and went off to bed.

The next morning, to Jake's surprise, the same thing happened again. He got up for coffee, opened the patio door, and did a bit of a walk about, when once again he heard a female voice behind him say, "There is jewellery hidden in this house." He was completely flabbergasted. "What, there's more—where?" he said to the ghost, but nothing, no answer just like every other morning.

This time, Jake decided, okay, I am going to look in every little potential hiding place in this apartment. He checked the ceiling fans, unscrewed vents, reached inside ducts, but nothing. He searched for hours.

Suddenly, he heard his two cats moving about on the inside wall of the hot tub. He wondered how on earth they got in there. He searched around for an opening and found a large cut-out inside one of the kitchen cabinets by the sink where the pump housing for the hot tub was located. Jake noticed that the screen that is usually screwed over the opening had somehow come loose, and of course his two snoopy cats found this secret spot and had to investigate.

He then thought, "I wonder if this is the spot where the jewellery is hidden?" He crawled into the small space that held the pump and felt all around, but nothing. He coaxed both of the cats out and decided he better close off the area so they could no longer get in.

As he went back under the sink with a screw driver, he noticed a large space between the bottom back wall of the kitchen and the bottom of the kitchen cabinets. He decided to take a closer look and much to his surprise he saw a small bag that had fallen in or had been put into that space. He had a hard time reaching for it but as he grabbed the bag, he could feel it brush up against something else. This time it was a long piece of velvet cloth with something wrapped inside and it too was nestled against a third item—another small bag!

By now, Jake was trembling. He placed everything on the floor and slowly began to open each piece, one by one.

In total, he found a dozen sets of earrings made of gold and other precious stones such as amethysts. He also found a number of gold rings with precious stones and about twenty gold chains amongst other items. One of the bags also held some small jewellery making equipment.

He couldn't believe what he had just found. Here, hidden away in his new apartment was a cache of handmade jewellery, and an insistent ghost was the one to tell him about it.

Given the age of the building and its location, the apartment had already been home to a number of people over the years. Jake asked various shop owners and others in the neighbourhood about previous owners or tenants, but was unable to find the owner or maker of the jewellery. As Jake had no need for this type of treasure, he decided to give it away to some of his close friends and family members that Christmas.

Like all of the stories about ghosts throughout this book, there are many reasons why they either stay earthbound or return to visit. We have found that some do not know they are dead and continue about their daily routine. Some become attached to people, places or things and in the case of the ghost in Jake's apartment, they have important information to share.

As Jake told me this story, he and I wondered how many people actually hear spirits and whether anyone else had ever heard the female ghost in his apartment. As mentioned, Jake has had several previous paranormal experiences, so his sensitivity to other energy vibrations may be a bit more heightened. He did not feel threatened by the ghost in any way, and nor did his cats. Jake recognized that she had an important message for him that she wanted to share. Whether or not the ghost was a previous tenant of the apartment or the owner of the building or the jewellery remains a mystery.

Incidentally, Jake lived in the apartment for a number of years, but never heard from the ghost again. She could now move on as someone had finally heard her intent whisper that, "There is jewellery hidden in this house."

Out of This World

While many of my stories have dealt with a variety of metaphysical phenomena, there is a category of paranormal events that warrants attention, and that is of UFOs and time warps. While I believe that most people have had a paranormal experience of some kind in their life, it is less clear how many people have had experiences related to UFOs and similar events.

For more than 50 years, television shows have been produced on UFOs and aliens, yet many, including governments, continue to publicly deny their existence. Interestingly, this book is being written at a time when the world famous Stephen Hawking (physicist and cosmologist) who, as it happens does not believe God's existence, publicly proclaimed his belief that extraterrestrial life in all likelihood does exist and if it finds its way to earth, it will not be friendly. That is not a reassuring thought. According to a documentary[20] released in 2010, Hawking likens aliens to humans and suggests that their goal may be to conquer and colonize planets such as earth.

Hovering

The first incident happened when I was about 12 or 13 years old. My parent's home was located in a subdivision out in the country, about five kilometres from a medium-sized city. Most of the people that lived in the area built their homes on oversized lots, so all of the houses were spaced well apart. This is unlike many major cities today where homes are so crunched together that you can see inside your neighbour's windows.

On this particular day, I was visiting a friend up the road, about a 15 minute walk away. My girlfriend and I were outside playing catch in her large backyard when we noticed a dull sliver shaped disc up in the sky. It wasn't lying flat but it was on its side on a slight angle and spinning rapidly. I have no idea how far up it was or how big it was, but it was fairly large and stayed hovering over the area my friend and I were playing. We didn't notice any lights on it, but the craft was clearly visible in the daylight, and for more than an hour it would move away for a few minutes, and then return to the area where we were.

At first we thought it would simply go away, but as time went on it did not leave. It began to make both of us very uncomfortable and with my girlfriend's parents not home, we became quite scared. It didn't come at us in any threatening way, but it just stayed, hovering over us and not leaving. We felt watched.

It started to move down a bit closer and we became frightened. My girlfriend got very scared and said, "We better get inside." She ran inside and rather than follow her, I decided to run home. Whatever it was, it decided to shadow me. I ran as quickly as I could, but it moved much faster than I did and would slow down and kept hovering near me off to my right.

Once I got home, I ran inside and waited, looking out of my bedroom window. Whatever it was it went back and forth moving about in front of my house. I can still see it like it was today. It continued to spin on its side and situated itself above my neighbour's house across the street and to the right. I did not know very much about UFOs at that time, but this thing really began to frighten me as it was not going away.

About 15 minutes passed and I thought I better tell my dad who was home at the time. I told him what was going on and the odd looking craft outside of the house. He quickly ran outside with me, but as soon I pointed it out, it immediately left—in the blink of an eye. I am not even sure if my dad actually ever saw it, but he told me to quickly get inside and stay there. He went around the house several times and stayed out in front for a long time, all the while checking up in the sky, but nothing, it was gone.

Again, I did not know much about UFOs at that time, but recently I watched a television program called "UFO Hunters" which is a series on OLN (originally the Outdoor Learning Network). In this particular episode, I saw it—I saw a UFO exactly like the one I saw as a child! I have since come to learn that many, many people have had sightings right across the world, right across cultures and all walks of life. It is the age old question of "Are we alone in our universe? And are we the only intelligent life that exists in the vastness of our universe?" I think not, and I believe Stephen Hawking would agree with this premise as well.

Time Out

Before having children, my former husband and I spent a lot of time at the family camp. We both enjoyed the outdoors a great deal and at that time I did a lot of hunting for partridge and larger game such as moose and deer. I no longer hunt, but we would spend every free moment, every weekend at camp.

The camp was located just over an hour from town and half of the journey was on a well-travelled highway and the other, a secondary road. The secondary road which I will call Melon's Road was about 100 kilometres in length and at the end of the road was a small town of about 300 people in the winter and over 1,000 in the summer. It was situated on a large lake, one of the Great Lakes, and during the summer months, the town was bursting at the seams with visitors by water, land and air from Canada and the United States.

All along Melon's Road, there were numerous dirt roads, some more travelled than others. Some were used by loggers in the area and some branched off to various small lakes that were surrounded by camps. Most of the camps were not winterized and did not have services such as hydro, running water or indoor plumbing. These camps were generally heated by wood stoves where the cooking was done and at that time, some people had propane to power a stove or refrigerator. No one had televisions, microwaves or computers like some camps now have. If you got lost wandering in the surrounding bush, you might not survive given the ruggedness of the terrain, and remoteness of the area.

The family camp that we stayed at was one of those places. It was nestled amongst beautiful tall pine trees and was situated on a medium-sized lake. It was a bit more rugged than some camps, but it was exactly what Anthony and I loved. We shared a love of the wilderness, the beautiful lakes, and the remoteness of the area and the fact that you seldom saw anyone while you were out there unless you chose to go visiting.

Most of Anthony's family were older (as mentioned in previous stories) and few used the family camp. They also did not want to take the trek out to the area as most did not like being in the wilderness without the amenities of home. Since we spent a lot of time there before our children were born, we looked after most of the work that comes with this kind of property—cutting the lawn, cleaning the beach area, chopping firewood, fixing the dock, maintaining the boat and motors, and doing whatever needed to be done.

We usually packed up everything the moment we got home from work on Friday, and stayed at the camp until we had to come home late on Sunday. It could be snowing, a terrible thunderstorm or gorgeous sunny weather, it did not matter—we always went out. We knew every little twist and turn in the road and even knew if we just passed a certain landmark such as an odd shaped outcrop of rocks, the railway tracks, the bridge, a swamp or another camp road, that the next landmark was so many minutes away. If our speed was consistent, we had it timed right down to the minute.

On this occasion, it was already fall. It was a beautiful sunny, yet brisk weekend and we were out hunting for partridge as the big game season had not yet opened. Once autumn hits, most of the camps were shut down for the winter as an early freeze could cause breaks in the waterlines that ran from the lake. As a result, by the Canadian Thanksgiving weekend, only hunters and those travelling to and from the small town at the end of the road were out there.

It was already getting late on a Sunday afternoon, so we decided to call it a day, pack up and head home. It would be dark around 6:30 p.m. One of the things about all of the fresh air, walking long distances in the forest and late night dinners and saunas, was that by the time the weekend was done, we were both pretty tired.

All packed, we began the trek up Melon's Road which led to the highway, then home. On Melon's Road our usual markers included several swamps, a few camp roads, the railway track, an old Bailey bridge, a long hydro line area that had been clear cut, a few more camps roads and the stop sign at the main highway where we needed to turn left. To get from the camp to the railway track was about 25 minutes and while there were other landmarks in between, the stop sign or rather the highway, was about another 15 minutes past the tracks.

We had just left the camp and like always, we checked our watches to see what time it was, just as we were about to turn left onto Melon's Road. It was 5:30 p.m. if memory serves me correctly.

We were both tired, and began the drive up Melon's Road when Anthony and I both looked at each other, as if we were coming out of a long sleep. All of a sudden, half-dazed, at the same time, we both said, "Where are we?" and realizing where we were, said, "How did we get here?" We had already gone over the bridge and were already at the railway tracks which were about 25 minutes up the road. I instinctively looked at my watch, but it was 5:25 p.m., 5 minutes BEFORE we turned onto Melon's Road!

We looked at each other, stunned. Anthony, who was driving at the time, pulled over onto the side of the road, just past the tracks. We were both shaking.

He said, "What just happened?" I firmly said, "I don't know!" He said, "Are you sure we left at 5:30 p.m.?" but he already knew the answer. We had both checked our watches at that time as we made a bit of a game about the time while travelling back and forth to camp, especially on our way home, and especially when we were both tired. Both of our watches couldn't run backwards.

Here we were, sitting in our truck just past the bridge and the railway tracks and there was no mistake about it; we both believe we actually went backwards in time and gained 30 minutes. We didn't talk much the rest of the way home, but still mystified by what had happened, kept asking each other, "How is it possible?" We even half joked about being abducted by aliens and returned to earth, but really we had no way of explaining what had just taken place.

Once we got home, we unpacked, and each of us had a shower. Although I can laugh about it now, both of us also checked to be sure we didn't have any unusual puncture marks on our bodies, the kinds that we had heard about from people who claim to have been abducted by aliens. Nope, we both checked out clear.

We talked about it on and off for several years, trying to make sense of what had happened. To this day I don't really know. More and more I have heard of people who have been affected by changed time.

At one spiritual conference that Marion and I went to, we heard one speaker talk about a similar situation. A number of years earlier, he left late for a meeting, knowing full well that he would be several hours late, but decided to go anyway, just in case they would wait. Much to his surprise, he recalls some sort of snowstorm that he travelled in and out of, but he actually arrived early... a physical impossibility for the distance he drove.

There are also numerous other stories and the most famous ones come from the Bermuda Triangle[21] which has many unusual occurrences, some of which include time warps—time loss or gain.

Planes and ships have been lost in fog in the Bermuda Triangle and come out in locations which they could not have physically reached in the time that had elapsed. Several pilots who are still living today, have told the story of being overtaken by an unusual electric-filled fog or cloud which renders their compasses completely dysfunctional. Many have died in the Bermuda Triangle. In most cases, bodies of those who have perished and any evidence of vessels that have gone missing, have never been found. For those few who have survived, their tale is an extraordinary one.

What is the explanation? Einstein's theories show that time and space are on a continuum and that it may be possible to bend or fold this continuum.

Carrying this a step further, this would mean that time and space can also bend, fold or be altered. Is it possible that Anthony and I caught a blip on this continuum and at that very moment, or split second in time, we were in a physical place where time bent and pushed us backwards?

To this day, I still don't know what the answer is, but I have come to believe that time is relative and subjective. That the past, present and future all melt into each other along a continuum we call time. What physics or quantum physics is behind all of this, I certainly don't know, but what I do know is that on that warm fall evening on Melon's Road, time moved backwards.

Making Sense of It All

Insight:

Once you begin to understand some of the basic principles of energy, you will see that our world really is a metaphysical world.

Throughout the stories that I have written, I have attempted to open your mind to the possibility that there is much more than what we see in our physical world. That there are scientific, cosmic and spiritual factors that are at play here that influence how we interact with our world, why things happen to us and to others, and why bad things happen to good people and vice versa. These factors also influence why our lives follow certain paths and why the same patterns tend to repeat themselves until they are properly addressed.

I have come to believe that it is part of a destiny that we have carved out for ourselves in the space between lives and with the help of those on the other side. This destiny is actually a contract or a blueprint that we develop and agree to before we incarnate into each new life here on earth. In other words, it is the life that you have chosen for this incarnation. Some of it is etched in stone. There are pre-planned, key events that you will go through in this lifetime regardless of what happens. Some parts however are left to your individual free will, and other parts are based on karma that is carried over—lessons that will continue until they are fully experienced and the learning has been achieved. You may also choose to incarnate into another life to help someone else achieve their lessons.

For me, spiritual growth and openness came about as a result of a number of synchronistic events in my life; and believe me, none of these were expected. My questioning of prevailing religious ideologies and practices, coupled with my chosen career, the life-altering changes in my marriage, and the inexplicable connection with the man I spoke about in "Spiritual Mentor," all led me right to the place that I am in this very moment writing my stories for this book.

My continuous hunger to learn has not stopped and the more I have learned, the more questions that I have. I have read numerous books by world-renowned mystics, psychics and healers; have attended spiritual conferences and energy workshops; have had hundreds of conversations with my co-author and likeminded individuals; and have tried readings by various psychics.

My initial experiences with psychics were not overly positive. I have come to learn that if information is presented in a negative way, you should question its authenticity. Nothing however, is more powerful than someone who is able to provide an accurate reading and share the information, even if it is difficult, in a positive and caring way. I have found someone from the west coast of Canada who does exceptional channelled readings. She has confirmed for me that indeed your spirit guides are able to access information about you from the blueprint of your life. They can tell you about key events that are about to unfold in the near future. It continues to amaze me how accurate and helpful these readings are. They peel back the outward layers that you convey to the world, to touch the very core of who you are—the part that often remains hidden to others, and is often ignored by you.

The life experiences of my co-author and I have been completely different, yet somehow our worlds met. Both of us feel that the friendship that we have developed was not by chance. We both came to the same place in our thinking at different times and because of extraordinarily different life circumstances. We have come to believe that nothing is by chance and that we are all connected to each other, to our world, to our universe and beyond. We also believe that the energy of the spiritual world and the world of science don't just intersect on occasion, but rather are a convergence of all that is. Once you cross this river of understanding, it is not possible to go back—to look at life any other way.

Marion is an experienced energy worker and I am still a novice. Her thoughts are more developed around energy than mine but we both agree that energy holds the key to understanding who we are and how we influence our world and the world around us. It is a scientific fact that energy never dies. Bodily energy is recycled but the animating force or soul energy survives. The physical shell will die but the spirit or the energy will not.

Our energy however is unique to our life experiences, to our history, the history of our families and our past lives. No one is the same, but the core fundamental of who we are, in fact everything that we see and don't see including ghosts, angels and spirit guides is the same—all is energy; energy that vibrates at different levels.

As discussed in many of our stories, energy exists on a continuum; where some are at the most negative end of the continuum (lower vibration) and some are at the higher most positive end and carry a corresponding higher energy vibration.

Some energy workers and healers rebalance energy vibrations to create a positive impact on the health, and emotional and spiritual well-being of others. Science now suggests that love for our world and those in it can actually enhance energy vibrations and change the magnetic field that surrounds and protects the earth *(see quote, page 191)*. As farfetched as that may sound, just think for a moment of a time when you may have fallen in love. Think back to that time and you will see how love is magnetic and actually creates a shift in the energy between two people. Unconditional love really is the impetus to enhancing energy flow.

God, or whatever you choose to call God is the highest vibrating source energy of pure unconditional love that encompasses all. Every religion and every faith has a name, but ultimately it is the Source, the All or the Universal Consciousness of everything that was, is and/or will be. It is however indescribable by us.

My hope is that from these stories, you will take away many things. On their own, each story, as a single account might not sound significant, earth-shattering, or even profound. In some cases you may even toss them aside as a coincidence or something weird that just happened. However, when you string them together, you will see that each and every one of us has had a metaphysical experience of one kind or another, even though we may choose not to acknowledge it. For me, and I believe for Marion, we are only on the tiniest tip of grasping who we are, why we are here and understanding the intricate and connected part that every one of us plays in the universe.

Part Three
By
Marion K. Williams
&
Elena J. Michaels

Postscript ~ Convergence

Insights:
We are only at the threshold of understanding.
We know what we know but we don't know much.

In the midst of writing our stories, we decided to try out a new energy healing discipline, and this one was beyond anything we had ever experienced. It taught us how little we actually know. Each of our stories has given us another piece of the puzzle, but this discipline sent us scrambling for answers.

With a light touch from the practitioner and one simple question, we found ourselves pinned to a wall. The question itself was innocuous; the response was profound. It went like this, "How would it feel if you were not affected by "x"-situation?" Then the practitioner touched an area of our bodies and we found ourselves propelled backwards and onto a wall behind us. Neither of us felt we could move until the issue resolved and released. We were pinned at the shoulder or by some other bodily part. The therapist continued to ask questions until there were no corresponding physical reactions in our bodies. Through it all, we felt like rag-dolls. We were lucky to be appended to a wall—it could have been the ceiling! We had no control.

What stunned us most was the fact that one touch and one question could so move and disable us. We were not in a trance and did not anticipate this result. As observers and participants, we were both fully conscious during the whole process. What does this say about the power of words and the power of touch? When we began to write our stories we thought we understood some aspects of directed energy. We now know that we did not fully comprehend this underlying power, which can literally kill or cure.

For years we have all watched televised church services where people are "touched" and collapse on the floor and viewers are meant to assume that the individuals involved are either saved or cured. It always appeared so staged and so hokey that it never occurred to either of us that some of these scenes could be genuine. After our experience, nothing is so certain any more.

The power of touch has been understood in the East for thousands of years. Ayurvedic practices include knowledge of the marma[22] points. Today these are used in healing practices but originally, they had a much wider application. They are powerful portals in the body. In the hands of a master, these therapies are astounding. Acupuncture also recognizes meridian lines and treatment points on the body, and today many energy disciplines work with energy and touch.

Both Eastern and Western Societies are familiar with the power of words. We know about prayer and chanting, and conversely, cursing. Cursing has a long tradition of use. Australian Aborigines allegedly "point the bone"[23] to will death. Anecdotal stories talk of gypsy curses which allegedly wreak havoc on people's lives, as do voodoo curses. For years actors have commented on the "accidents" associated with Shakespeare's[24] "Macbeth." There is a suspicion that the witches' curses in the play are not mumble-jumble but rather an age-old incantation. Are the actors' stories mere coincidence or the power of suggestion? We will probably never know.

On the upside, we heard a fascinating story about a hospice worker who was persuaded to conduct a burial for a resident's cat. The worker read a religious text at the graveside. When she looked up, she saw thousands of ghostly figures who joined her at the reading. They appeared to her to be good souls, but she didn't know why they were there. What drew them? She consulted a local minister. He informed her that very old prayers carry with them the energy of all who have ever prayed them. There is a collective energy that goes into the words, and this build-up is compounded with use, over time. The worker was a psychic seer and so she saw the effect of the prayer; most people would not. Nonetheless, she was not expecting this result and especially for a cat!

Consider the word "om" which is often used in meditation, and which in Hinduism "represents both the unmanifest (*nirguna*) and manifest (*saguna*) aspects of God."[25] Anyone who has participated in an om-chant will immediately recognise the power of the word. It has centuries of history, and is used by religious and secular people the world over.

Chanting has a long history and wide application. It is fundamental to Eastern Religions, and used to be a more significant part of Western ones. Today, Gregorian chant survives in Catholic rites.

There are also sites across the world that absorb the imprint of prayer—the Wailing Wall in Jerusalem[26] is one such place—but each tradition has its own sites and its own prayers.

There is one further application of the power of words which Marion, in particular, referred to in her stories—blessed energy. We see this in Holy Water. There is a very particular reason why Holy Water is used to clear bad energy. This water has the power of prayer directed into it. Once the vibration of the water is raised, it improves the vibration of whatever it comes into contact with. It is not mere superstition to throw Holy Water about. It is a powerful act. Likewise, other religious objects carry the power of directed energy. However, things need not be religious to raise energy levels. For example, love has the power to raise energy levels between people, and may imprint surroundings (homes), and items such as rings.

It seems that wherever people have a heartfelt connection there is a corresponding result. Heartfelt connections can be accessed in many ways: through love and words of love, and through both prayer and meditation. These all attract transmitted and received energy. It is a two-way process.

Prayer and meditation are in many ways the reverse of one another. Prayer is an outward appeal to God/Creator/Source, and meditation is an inward journey of self.[27] The heart connection seems to be the catalyst for change, but any change must be aligned with our soul purpose. There is a master plan, and what we think we want is not always what we have contracted for—in other words, we don't always get what we think we need.

It has become clear to us that we are only at the threshold of understanding the world of energy and all of its applications in daily lives. Energy takes many forms and encompasses so much more than we know or can imagine. Our experiences tell us that we can direct energy with our minds, our thoughts, our words and our actions. We impact everyone and everything, and vice versa. These energy transactions can be positive or negative and are not confined to one plane of existence. Understanding this, it becomes critical that we conduct ourselves in a mindful way in all we think, say and do. We are powerful beings who have learned to use a mere portion of our abilities.

Neither of us is a scientist, and these stories, while extraordinary, occur in everyday lives. We were not aware of the broad scope of possibility until we started to put this collection together and began to appreciate that metaphysical phenomena may happen to any one of us. Each story has either reconfirmed our views or challenged our thoughts and underlying beliefs.

We have come to see that energy really is the foundational principle for so much. It really is the secret of the universe and we believe, the convergence of all that is.

Glossary of Terms

as Defined by the Authors

Alternative Medicine comprises all non-western medical practices.

Auras are full body halos of energy. All matter, living and non-living, has an aura. Auras may be seen and felt, and photographed through Kirlian photography.

Chakras are the energy centres in the body. Eastern wisdom dictates that there are seven major chakras (see illustration at the end of Part 1) and many minor ones, which are found, for example, on the palms of the hands and soles of the feet. Chakras are sometimes explained as being wheels or vortices of energy. They moderate the vibrational flow of energy into and out of the body.

Complementary Medicine includes those alternative practices which have been recognized and approved for use in conjunction with western medical practice.

Energy fields extend out from the chakra centres in the body. The authors believe that energy fields are in repeating series of seven. Each series is a holographic version of the one preceding it, but in a finer vibration. The energy fields comprise the more visible aura, and all the finer vibrational fields beyond. Alternative energy practitioners believe that the energy around a body may be manipulated for wellness purposes and to bring the body back to a state of balance or harmony.

Kirlian photography is a process by which the chakra and aura systems may be captured on film.

Notes

Flying High

1. Marion has studied energy healing over the past 17 or so years with several different disciplines—Reiki, Therapeutic Touch,™ Reflexology, Tai Chi and Qigong, and her Yoga practices go back to her schooldays. Nowadays she is a registered practitioner of three disciplines and teaches one.

   There are a great many clinical trials and medical studies which show that if the energy field around a body is restored to a state of balance—that is, without energy blockages, overloads or deficits—then the body will move itself towards a state of well-being. Our bodies often only need a nudge in the right direction as they have an intrinsic sense of order, which comes about with balance. Clinical trials show that energy work relaxes the body, and changes the perception of pain, amongst other things. Energy work cannot replace medical science, but it can work very well in tandem with it.

   Energy fields can be seen, felt, photographed, and visualized from a distance. We are energy beings and our energy extends many feet beyond our skin borders and unites us with our world. In creation there are worlds within worlds, and we are quite literally at one with our universe.

The Death Mask

2. Holy Water has the power of prayer directed into it. Once the vibration of the water is raised, it improves the vibration of whatever it comes into contact with. Thus, it is not mere superstition to throw Holy Water about; it is a powerful act.

Afterwards

3. From the song "Turn, Turn, Turn" by the Byrds. See excerpt from Wikipedia: "'Turn! Turn! Turn! (to Everything There Is a Season)", often abbreviated to "Turn! Turn! Turn!", is a song adapted entirely from the Book of Ecclesiastes in the Bible (with the exception of the last line) and put to music by Pete Seeger in 1959. ... The song became an international hit in late 1965, when it was covered by The Byrds.'

    See: http://*en*.wikipedia.org/wiki/Turn!_Turn!_Turn! (accessed December 2010).

The Bridge

4. "Tramping, known elsewhere as hiking or bushwalking, is a popular activity in New Zealand. Tramping is defined as a recreational activity involving walking over rough country carrying all the required food and equipment.[1] The term is used for trips that are of at least one overnight stay in the backcountry."

    See: http://en.wikipedia.org/wiki/Tramping_in_New_Zealand (accessed February 2011).

    Although this story was related to Marion by a stranger, it is included in the collection as both Marion and her husband found the stranger credible.

Martha's Jump

5. Soul body—As opposed to the physical self, the soul body is the spiritual and eternal aspect of self.

6. Eldon Taylor – See: http://www.eldontaylor.com/

7. Taylor, Eldon, "What Does That Mean? Exploring Mind, Meaning and Mysteries." Hay House.

Cassie's Family

8. "'Don't Worry, Be Happy" is the title and principal lyric of a song by musician Bobby McFerrin. Released in September 1988, it became the first a cappella song to reach number one on the Billboard Hot 100 chart, a position it held for two weeks.'

    See: http://en.wikipedia.org/wiki/Don't_Worry,_Be_Happy (accessed February 2011).

Taking Ways

9. The former Colonel William progressed from breaking and entering to steal underwear from young girls and women, to stalking, rape and murder. He was charged and found guilty.

The Smallest Seer

10. "*The Sixth Sense* is a 1999 American psychological thriller written and directed by M. Night Shyamalan. The film tells the story of Cole Sear (Haley Joel Osment), a troubled, isolated boy who is able to see and talk to the dead, and an equally troubled child psychologist (Bruce Willis) who tries to help him. The film established Shyamalan as a writer and director, and introduced the cinema public to his signatures, most notably his affinity for twist endings. The film was nominated for six Academy Awards, including Best Picture."
See: http://en.wikipedia.org/wiki/The_Sixth_Sense (accessed February 2011).

The Psychic

11. Excerpt from Wikipedia: "**Kirlian photography** refers to a form of photogram made with voltage. It is named after Semyon Kirlian, who in 1939 accidentally discovered that if an object on a photographic plate is connected to a source of voltage an image is produced on the photographic plate.[1]
Kirlian's work, from 1939 onward, involved an independent rediscovery of a phenomenon and technique variously called "electrography", "electrophotography" and "corona discharge photography." The Kirlian technique is contact photography, in which the subject is in direct contact with a film placed upon a charged metal plate."
See: http://en.wikipedia.org/wiki/Kirlian_photography (accessed February 2011).

Electrical Interference

12. Excerpt from Wikipedia: "... **Murphy's law** is an adage or epigram that is typically stated as: "Anything that can go wrong, will go

wrong...." See http://en.wikipedia.org/wiki/Murphy's_Law_
(disambiguation) (accessed March 25, 2011).

Judith's Ring

13. Cold water has the reputation of dispelling negative energy.
14. Natural fibres will hold positive or negative energy for lengthy periods.

Time-Tracks

15. "Regression through the Mirrors of Time, Featuring a Meditation to Inner Peace, Love and Joy," by Brian L. Weiss, M.D.

So, What Now?

16. Excerpt from Wikipedia: "Padre Pio (1887-1968), Catholic saint, who had stigmata, is said to have been able to levitate, as well as being able to bilocate."
    See: http://en.wikipedia.org/wiki/Levitation_(paranormal) (accessed October 26, 2010).

Evidence from the Past ~ Historic Trauma

17. "Spontaneous Evolution – Our Positive Future (and a way to get there from here)" by Bruce Lipton, Ph.D. and Steve Bhaerman, 30.
18. BBC. *The Ghost in Your Genes.* See: http://www.bbc.co.uk/sn/ tvradio/programmes/horizon/ghostgenes.shtml.

Uncovering Past Lives ~ Reincarnation

19. For more information, see: Weiss, Brian L., M.D. *Many Masters, Many Lives.* New York: Simon and Schuster, 1988.

Out of This World

20. Stephen Hawking, world renowned British physicist in his new documentary "Into the Universe with Stephen Hawking" featured on the Discovery Channel 2010 shares his views of alien life in our universe and the potential impact on planets such as earth.
21. "The "Bermuda or Devil's Triangle" is an imaginary area located off the southeastern Atlantic coast of the United States, which is noted for a high incidence of unexplained losses of ships, small

boats, and aircraft." See: http://www.byerly.org/bt.htm (accessed February 2011).

Postscript ~ Convergence

22. Marma points on the body see: http://bing.search.sympatico. ca/?q=Google&mkt=en-ca&setLang=en-CA (accessed November 2010).

23. Pointing the bone—Australian Aborigine curses, see: http:// en.wikipedia.org/wiki/Kurdaitcha (accessed December 2010).

24. William Shakespeare.

25. Om or Aum see: http://hinduism.about.com/od/omaum/a/ meaningofom.htm
   and http://en.wikipedia.org/wiki/Aum (accessed January 2011).

26. "The **Western Wall** (Hebrew: הַכּוֹתֶל הַמַּעֲרָבִי, translit.: *HaKotel HaMa'aravi*), **Wailing Wall** or **Kotel** (lit. Wall; Ashkenazic pronunciation: *Kosel*); (Arabic: حائط البراق, translit.: "Ḥā'iṭ Al-Bur q", translat.: "The Buraq Wall") is located in the Old City of Jerusalem at the foot of the western side of the Temple Mount. It is a remnant of the ancient wall that surrounded the Jewish Temple's courtyard and is one of the most sacred sites in Judaism…"
   See: http://en.wikipedia.org/wiki/Western_Wall (accessed March 2011).

27. There is a body of thought that believes that the seat of all human consciousness (and indeed all life consciousness) lies outside the body, and is accessed via receptors within the body.
   The authors believe that universal consciousness is available, with limitations, to all life forms on all planes, and that access is dictated by the nature of the various and distinct receptors.
   During meditation, the body's receptors are able to tune in to receive information from this universal source—similar to dialling into a particular radio station on a specific band width frequency.

Bibliography

BBC. *The Ghost in Your Genes.* See: http://www.bbc.co.uk/sn/tvradio/programmes/horizon/ghostgenes.shtml.

Braden, Gregg. *Fractal Time, The Secret of 2012 and a New World Age.* California: Hay House Inc., 2009. 253.

Braden, Gregg. *The Spontaneous Healing of Belief, Shattering the Paradigm of False Limits.* 2008. 5th ed. California: Hay House Inc., 2009. 217.

Browne, Sylvia with Lindsay Harrison. *A Psychic's Guide to Our World and Beyond – The Other Side and Back.* New York: Signet—New American Library, a division of Penguin Putnam Inc., 2000.

Dyer, Wayne. *The Power of Intention—Learning to Co-create Your World Your Way.* Carlsband, California: Hay House Inc., 2004.

Lipton, Bruce and Steve Bhaerman. *Spontaneous Evolution—Our Positive Future (and a way to get there from here).* Hay House Inc., 2009.

MSNBC Com staff and news report. Hawking: Aliens may pose risks to Earth Astrophysicist says extraterrestrials likely exist but could be dangerous. http://www.msnbc.msn.com/id/36769422/ns/technology_and_science-space/ April 2010. (accessed on January 20, 2010).

Stern, Jess. *Edgar Cayce—The Sleeping Prophet.* New York: Doubleday & Co. Inc., Laffont Special Edition, 1966-67. 280.

Therapeutic Touch™ Network of Ontario, see: http://therapeutictouchontario.org/index.php/

Weiss, Brian L., M.D. *Many Masters, Many Lives.* New York: Simon and Schuster, 1988.

Weiss, Brian L., M.D., *Regression through the Mirrors of Time,* 1994. Hay House, Inc., 2008. Audio.